Modernist Fiction and News

MODERNIST FICTION AND NEWS

REPRESENTING EXPERIENCE IN THE EARLY TWENTIETH CENTURY

David Rando

MODERNIST FICTION AND NEWS
Copyright © David Rando, 2011.

First published in 2011 by
PALGRAVE MACMILLAN®
in the United States—a division of St. Martin's Press LLC,
175 Fifth Avenue, New York, NY 10010.

Where this book is distributed in the UK, Europe and the rest of the World,
this is by Palgrave Macmillan, a division of Macmillan Publishers Limited,
registered in England, company number 785998, of Houndmills,
Basingstoke, Hampshire RG21 6XS.

Palgrave Macmillan is the global academic imprint of the above
companies and has companies and representatives throughout the world.

Palgrave® and Macmillan® are registered trademarks in the United
States, the United Kingdom, Europe and other countries.

ISBN: 978–0–230–11451–7

Library of Congress Cataloging-in-Publication Data

Rando, David.
  Modernist fiction and news : representing experience in the early
  twentieth century / David Rando.
    p.   cm.
  ISBN 978–0–230–11451–7 (hardback)
  1. Fiction—20th century—History and criticism.
  2. Modernism (Literature)   3. Press and journalism in
  literature.   4. Experience in literature.   5. Literature and
  society—History—20th century.   I. Title.
  PN56.M54.R36 2011
  809.3′041—dc22   2011000539

A catalogue record of the book is available from the British Library

Design by Integra Software Services

First edition: July 2011

10 9 8 7 6 5 4 3 2 1

Printed in the United States of America.

For Shannon

CONTENTS

ACKNOWLEDGMENTS

I am happy to thank the many people who helped me to conceive and complete *Modernist Fiction and News*. Molly Hite, Laura Brown, and Jonathan Culler oversaw this project at its earliest stages at Cornell University, and I am deeply indebted to them for their care and guidance. Paul Sawyer and Douglas Mao were early readers who offered critical feedback. I am also grateful for Susan Buck-Morss's Modern Social Theory seminar, which came at an important time in my thinking about this book. Cornell University supported this project with a Sage Fellowship.

More recently, Sean Latham became an indispensable reader of *Modernist Fiction and News*. Sean saw the better book within my book, and more than anybody else he helped me to draw it to the surface.

At Trinity University, I thank Victoria Aarons and Judith Fisher for their support as chairs of the English Department. I am grateful to all of my colleagues at Trinity in the English Department and beyond. Trinity University supported this project in the form of two Summer Stipend Fellowships. I am especially grateful for the friendship and support of Claudia Stokes, Betsy Winakur Tontiplaphol, and Thomas Jenkins.

Brigitte Shull has been an ideal editor at Palgrave Macmillan. Joanna Roberts has been a most patient and helpful editorial assistant.

I would like to acknowledge a wider group of people who have encouraged and sustained me on the path that led to this book. Richard Sha and Jonathan Loesberg inspired and encouraged me to pursue this career. Charles Rossman and Alan Friedman welcomed me warmly to the world of Joyce studies. Several *Finnegans Wake* reading groups have kept me in weekly touch with Joyce for the last decade. I am grateful to all my friends in these groups, especially Jim LeBlanc, Samuel Frederick, Ana Rojas, Patrick Foran, Ari Lieberman, Christina Dahl, Joshua Corey, Bill Sullivan, Barbara Sullivan, Paul Myers, Jeffrey Rufo, and Shannon Mariotti.

My life would be much poorer without the friendship of Sam Frederick, Maryam Murday Frederick, and Henry Maurice Frederick.

Thank you to my family, and, above all, to my beloved wife and partner, Shannon Mariotti.

INTRODUCTION: MODERNISM, NEWS, AND THE REPRESENTATION OF EXPERIENCE

EVERY INSTANT BRINGS US NEWS FROM ACROSS THE GLOBE, yet we are poor in noteworthy stories. The previous sentence is adapted from Walter Benjamin's statement in his 1936 essay, "The Storyteller"; I have substituted "instant" for "morning" and perhaps that is modification enough to make Benjamin's idea absolutely contemporary.[1] In the twenty-first century, the stream of information that for Benjamin threatened to overwhelm our ability to communicate meaningful experiences has only intensified. Today it is difficult to know exactly where in the information matrix to locate the exchange of communicable experiences, or noteworthy stories, that Benjamin valued for their ability to help us overcome the "increasing atrophy of experience"[2] that results from the constant streams and shocks of modernity's data to the senses. As John McCole explains, Benjamin "began to work with a distinction between two fundamentally different kinds of experience—*Erlebnis*, 'immediate,' 'living' experience, and *Erfahrung*, an accumulating stock of integrated, 'lived' experience. The atrophy of modern experience could then be characterized as a shift from *Erfahrung* to *Erlebnis* and diagnosed in terms of an increasing dissociation of memory."[3] The early twentieth century was the first period to face the impossibility of adequately storing, remembering, and prioritizing the avalanche of information that new recording technologies and mass communication networks pressed upon consciousness, thereby altering not only human experience but also reality itself. In modernism's attempt to articulate human experience in a time of rapidly changing media, we begin to understand the transfigurations and dislocations of experience that have only intensified in our era.

When news baron Alfred Harmsworth, Lord Northcliffe, summarized the immense changes in mass media that his newspapers helped to inaugurate or intensify in the early years of the twentieth century, he declared with satisfaction, "What we did was to extend its purview to life as a whole."[4] However, this "Northcliffe Revolution" or the New Journalism,[5] Raymond Williams argues, was produced in the first instance not by a primary desire to widen the range of what could be considered reportable, but rather by changes in the economic base of the industry: newspapers came to rely upon circulation numbers and advertising revenue, thereby making news content newly and principally responsive to the market.[6] The adoption of capitalist models of organization and finance released newspapers from the constraints of political patronage, and the battle for circulation pushed newspaper content farther than ever out into new branches of "life as a whole" in order to discover what would resonate with a popular audience. Now that the market was master, newspapers emphasized features and entertainment content and streamlined the news itself for a new popular audience, especially to demographic categories such as women and the lower middle class. In doing so, news began to overlap with the wide array of life that literary representation traditionally assumed as its province, perhaps to an extent unrivalled since the sixteenth century when "novels" and "newes" had once been indistinguishable.[7]

The novel had long enjoyed the privilege of representing life as a whole, of both entertaining and informing its readers with a comprehensive vision of reality that was free to seize any dimension of human experience as its object. This was precisely the representational territory that the news quickly colonized and transformed during the late nineteenth and early twentieth centuries.[8] Nor was it the first time that a traditional privilege of literature had been challenged. Early in the nineteenth century, for instance, literature had been put on the defensive by other incursions from without, as when Percy Bysshe Shelley felt forced to defend poetry against the new sciences and technologies that threatened to undermine literary cultural influence and prestige. Famously, he concluded, "Poets are the unacknowledged legislators of the World."[9] It is useful to keep this Romantic defense or defensiveness in mind when more than 200 years later William Carlos Williams cautioned readers about where and where not to locate the news:

My heart rouses
      thinking to bring you news
         of something
that concerns you
      and concerns many men. Look at
        what passes for the new.

You will not find it there but in
        despised poems.
                It is difficult
to get the news from poems
                yet men die miserably every day
                        for lack
of what is found there.[10]

In the late nineteenth century, when mass newspapers began to revolu-
tionize journalism into "a living thing, palpitating with actuality, in touch
with life at all points,"[11] news had pretensions of covering the world as
only literature had been accustomed to do. But by the 1950s, a modernist
poet whose life had spanned these changes had to argue for poetry's
own relevancy by claiming the cultural power of the reporter: poets, says
William Carlos Williams, are the unacknowledged news writers of the
world.

We must ask what was at stake in Williams's claim that the news
really issued (though with difficulty) from despised poetry, or, for that
matter, in Ezra Pound's assertion that "Literature is news that STAYS
news."[12] Recently, critics such as Keith Williams, Mark Morrisson, and
Patrick Collier have questioned the purely oppositional posture of such
modernist formulations in order to stress instead the inevitable and complex relationships between modernism and news media that are also
crystallized in such pronouncements.[13] Many recent studies of modernism
and mass media argue that the health of public sphere democracy is at
stake in these relationships.[14] Other critics are concerned with the possibilities for a much more radical or revolutionary intervention in modern
bourgeois life. In *After the Great Divide,* Andreas Huyssen sees the avant-
garde commitment[15] to the shock and disruption of mass-mediated life
as "a prerequisite for any revolutionary reorganization of everyday life."[16]
In the relationship between modernist and news articulations of experience, we may thus find matters of both democratic and revolutionary
potential at stake. However, it is not only our understanding of the past,
literary history, or media history that exploring this relationship would
help to clarify; it should also clarify our understanding of the present
in relation to the past and the present conditions of both news and
experience.

Raymond Williams persuasively argues that accounts of modernism
"must start from the fact that the late nineteenth century was the occasion
of the greatest changes ever seen in the media of cultural production."[17]
Similarly, Michael North maintains that modernism "can be largely
defined . . . by the influence of mechanical mediation on the old media."[18]

The field of modernist studies is still learning to come to terms with the effects of new recording and mass communication technologies on literary modernism, but the critical effects of this project have already been transformational.[19] For instance, Friedrich Kittler has argued that phonography and cinematography effectively ended writing's monopoly on information storage.[20] Writing once had the sole privilege of recording some forms of experience, and whatever could not be fitted to an alphabet or an ideogram simply passed out of historical memory.[21] Thus, in 1829, Goethe could quite accurately define literature as "a fragment of fragments; only the smallest proportion of what took place and what was said was written down, while only the smallest proportion of what was written down has survived."[22] How much things would change in a century, to say nothing of two centuries! With new storage technologies, Kittler claims, "The dream of a real visible or audible world arising from words has come to an end. The historical synchronicity of cinema, phonography, and typewriting separated optical, acoustic, and written data flows, thereby rendering them autonomous."[23] The effects of the new autonomy of these data flows on literature cannot be underestimated. "As long as the book was responsible for all serial data flows," Kittler writes, "words quivered with sensuality and memory. It was the passion of all reading to hallucinate meaning between lines and letters."[24] This change suggests that literature would either cease to quiver with experience altogether or adapt to its lost monopoly. In any event, it implies that experience that had once been concentrated in words was now being dispersed along a growing continuum of new media. This set the stage for a fundamental crisis in the novelistic representation of experience.

MODERNIST FICTION AS ARCHIVE

This book thus defines the modernist novel and narrative prose as that set of writings that first responded to the technological possibility of total information storage. Utopian visions of total information storage had long tantalized the literary imagination, as in William Blake's great city of Golgonooza in *Jerusalem*, which contains "all that has existed in the space of six thousand years:/Permanent, & not lost not lost nor vanishd, & every little act,/Word, work, & wish, that has existed, all remaining still...."[25] In the early nineteenth century this vision of a total record of everything was the stuff of Romantic imagination. Later in that century, when Gerard Manley Hopkins contemplated aging and the fading of beauty, it was still only God who could conserve and store everything, even in the photographic age: "See; not a hair is, not an eyelash, not the least lash lost;

every hair/Is, hair of the head, numbered."[26] But by 1922, when Stephen Dedalus envisioned "Akasic records of all that ever anywhere whenever was," the technology existed to at least begin such a record for the future, if not to retrieve lost time.[27]

Similarly, when Proust contemplated lost time in the same era of technological possibility, he exposed as an increasingly poor assumption the idea that more elements of ourselves will be forgotten than remembered:

> ... we imagine that all the peripheral aspects of our speech and gestures make little imprint in the consciousness of the people we talk to, let alone stay in their memory. . . . However, it is quite possible that, even in relation to the immemorial march of humanity, the newspaper columnist's philosophy that everything passes away into oblivion may be less reliable than the opposite prediction, that all things will last. [. . . *qu'une philosophie contraire qui prédirait la conservation de toutes choses.*][28]

The Moncrieff translation renders the last phrase in terms that even more strongly emphasize recording and storage: "a contrary philosophy which would predict *the conservation of everything.*"[29] Proust is, of course, remarking on the extraordinary recording capabilities of human memory in spite of what we imagine will be the inevitable erasures of passing time, which he associates here with newspaper columnists. However, technological aids to memory and storage had by Proust's time created a challenge for modernist novelists that involved not merely salvaging memory but, indeed, shaping and sorting the almost infinite amount of information that technologies of memory now collected or promised to capture. A problem that thus defines the modernist novel is how to select, prioritize, and shape the totality of recordable information that early twentieth-century storage and disseminating technologies increasingly conserved, recirculated, or enabled.

Modernism is inseparable from the historical moment in which it is not only imaginable but actually theoretically possible to record, starting from a given moment, every potential sound, movement, or instant of human existence. If that is the condition of the modernist novel, it follows that it must also be defined as an art of relative and strategic selection. Because modernist fiction faces the necessity of selecting and prioritizing a new theoretical infinity of information, Jacques Derrida's discussion of the concept of the archive may provide a useful model for thinking about modernist texts as kinds of archives.[30] After all, what else are James Joyce's *Ulysses*, T. S. Eliot's *The Waste Land*, Ezra Pound's *Cantos*, Gertrude Stein's *Tender Buttons*, or Marianne Moore's "imaginary gardens with real toads in them"[31] than, as Derrida describes the archive, sites of commencement (privileged places), commandment (shaped by the law of an archon[32] through a kind of self-founding violence that is at once revolutionary and conservative), and consignation (constituting an ideal gathering of signs)?[33]

It is familiar to think about modernist texts as privileged spaces presided over by authoritative (or even authoritarian) artificers wherein an ideal configuration of signifiers is arranged and set off from all other signifiers as a monument held up for the future.[34] But by understanding such texts as information era archives, they can also be understood as motivated in a fundamental way by an "archive drive," or a "conservation drive,"[35] which we could then read in relation to the conservation and recording technologies that surround and compete with modernist archives. Derrida argues that the ability to imagine an archive is contingent upon Freud's model of the psyche, an archive that houses but also represses memory in the unconscious. Like the psyche, the archive has an archive drive, a drive to remember, to collect, and to conserve. But, also like the psyche, the archive has an "archive fever" or a "death drive" that is intent upon forgetting, effacing, erasing its own traces, and destroying the archive.[36] In these terms, modernism is that set of texts that are compelled to conserve experience at the moment when all experience suddenly seems recordable. Yet every attempt to carve a space of consignation is simultaneously an act of repressing, forgetting, or erasing of something else.[37]

Modernism's loss of memory is crucial to its definition as archive, not only because of its significant repressions, but also because repression in Derrida's model of the archive can be understood as a kind of archiving by other means, or as a special form of archiving "otherwise."[38] Repression is thus a special form of remembering. To see an example of this, one need only think of the great feminist revisions of modernism generated through the last decades of the twentieth century.[39] Hugh Kenner's *Pound Era* opened literally and symptomatically by forgetting a conversation between two women, Dorothy Shakespear and Henry James's niece, while remembering at least a scrap of the simultaneous conversation between Pound and James that occurred one evening during the twilight of the nineteenth century, a scrap that Kenner interprets as a passing of the literary torch from one master to the next.[40] Shari Benstock takes this moment as one of her epigraphs for *Women of the Left Bank*, a book whose reconfiguration of modernism belies the finality of forgetting and attests to the power of repression as a means of later remembering.[41] Modernist texts can similarly be understood as highly selective archives culled from the possibilities of total information storage, but at the same time they somehow remember exactly what they set out to forget.

Derrida's model of the archive has more possibilities for modernism than can be explored here.[42] For now, let us only consider the role Derrida gives to technology for shaping the archive. On the one hand, Derrida seems to acknowledge that technology determines the shape and character of the archive: "the technical structure of the *archiving* archive also determines the structure of the *archivable* content even in its very coming into existence and in its relationship to the future."[43] The simple example Derrida gives is how different the Freud archive, indeed psychoanalysis itself, would be had Freud used e-mail. The archive or conservation drive is inseparable from recording technology that not only stores it, but also determines the very scope of what is archivable. Moreover, the technology available to the archive determines our very sense of what a recordable *event* is.[44] Given the effects of technology on the archive, an archival model of modernist texts would make it possible to see every act of consignation as a selection from the new infinity of the recordable that also determines the extent and range of what may be selected or identified as content.

On the other hand, Derrida is judiciously skeptical of claims that new information technologies result in radical changes to the archive. For Derrida, all such technologies (Freud's mystic pad, typewriter, telephone, answering machine, portable tape recorder, computer, printer, fax, and e-mail)[45] are merely new kinds of writing machines, and writing is itself a machine to the extent that it acts as a prosthesis for memory. For him, it is the prosthesis or supplement to memory that creates the psyche, whose very existence is predicated on the threat of forgetting: "There would indeed be no archive desire without the radical finitude, without the possibility of a forgetfulness which does not limit itself to repression."[46] This explains why the archive or conservation drive and the archive fever are effectively two sides of the same coin, both in Derrida's model and, as I propose, in modernist texts.

We must then ask this overwhelming question: what in modernism's historical moment constitutes the greatest perceived threat to memory that animates its conservation drive? The answer seems paradoxical: it is the new potential impossibility of forgetting (enabled by the new technologies of remembering) that constitutes the greatest challenge to modernist memory. This represents the special historical condition of modernist texts that marks them as peculiarly archival in orientation. As we have seen, modernists were aware that the possibilities of forgetfulness were smaller than in any previous time in recorded and recordable history, and in this sense, modernism is like a technology that has outlasted its historical moment. Although it boasted its own newness, in truth it was already too old. Words had lost, as Kittler would say, the cultural monopoly on quivering with sensuality and memory.

In the grip of this powerful cultural and technological shift, modernist fiction must inescapably select and record its content with full consciousness of the powerful new recording technologies and a mass media—cinema, broadcasting, mass press, and more—that at the same historical moment challenged literature's traditional privilege of recording, representing, and shaping the broadest range of experience. Raymond Williams recognizes that these changes in media produce, "at the first historical level," the movements of modernism: "Photography, cinema, radio, television, reproduction and recording all make their decisive advances during the period identified as Modernist, and it is in response to these that there arise what in the first instance were formed as defensive cultural groupings, rapidly if partially becoming competitively self-promoting."[47] Helping to establish a critical language that enables us to discuss and understand modernism's defensive response, Mark Wollaeger suggests that modernism and contemporaneous media are profitably understood as part of a single "media ecology," that is, as "proximate information practices operating within a system of interrelated practices."[48] Within this model, Wollaeger makes a claim that I believe is crucial for comprehending a responsive and defensive modernism within this media ecology: "In some fundamental sense much of modernism can be read as *an attempt to clear a space* within the pseudo-environment *for more authentic modes of communication*."[49] We have already encountered Benjamin's claim that the world is "not richer but poorer in communicable experience when every day brings news from across the world."[50] The principles of clearing space and communicating authentically within this context are essential to the modernist imagination. Wollaeger's formulation enables us to see modernism as the attempt to transmit communicable experience (Benjamin's *Erfahrung*) by clearing a space in the media ecology (for Benjamin a major factor in the modern dominance of *Erlebnis*) within which modernism comes into being and advances itself.[51]

Before we turn to the modernist practice of clearing space in the media ecology for communicable experience, consider an example from contemporary literature that not only makes explicit this clearing, but also suggests that this crucial imaginative habit of modernism persists. After Toni Morrison had left her job as a book editor in order to work full time as a writer, she struggled to develop a story that would allow her to explore "what 'free' could possibly mean to women."[52] One day, her mind fastened upon a newspaper clipping from *The Black Book,* which she had edited in her former profession, a clipping that contained the outline of an experience that might be explored in terms of her theme. However, the terms that Morrison uses to describe her process of transforming the news story about Margaret Garner into *Beloved* are telling: "The historical Margaret Garner is fascinating, but, to a novelist, confining. *Too little imaginative space there* for my purposes. So I would invent her thoughts, plumb them for a subtext that was historically true in essence, but not strictly factual in order to relate her history to contemporary issues about freedom, responsibility, and women's 'place.' "[53] Morrison says that there is too little imaginative space in the historical Margaret Garner, which is of course different from saying that there is too little space in the news clipping. Yet Morrison's emphasis on the constraints of the strictly factual helps to indicate that the space of the news story itself is also at issue. Thus, it was that out of this short and largely instrumental news clipping (instrumental, because the story of Margaret Garner was reported in the abolitionist *American Baptist* for the obvious purpose of condemning slavery, and not of exploring Margaret Garner's terrible choice beyond its fact),[54] Toni Morrison crafted a novel of as much nearness of experience as has perhaps ever been written. Indeed, I am not aware of any literary instance that more powerfully reconfigures news reportage into a representation of experience than *Beloved* does. Morrison takes a story that has been instrumentalized to represent the evils of slavery and rewrites it through the experiential channel of love, showing what the insolubly vexed experience of a former slave might be when freedom is the ability to love, but love is bound to possession, and possession is the central dimension of the slavery she herself endured. Of course, there is seldom such a concrete relationship between an individual news story and a particular literary text, but *Modernist Fiction and News* suggests that there is a distinctive and defining relationship between modernism and certain conceptual configurations or styles of news stories for articulating experience.

THE MODERNIST NOVEL AND THE NEWS

Although modernist poetry and drama can also be broadly defined as texts that respond to new recording technologies within a reconfigured media ecology, *Modernist Fiction and News* is principally concerned with the modernist novel and prose narrative. Long considered the quintessential expression of frustration with existing narrative norms, the modernist novel is usually defined in terms of its rejection of traditional forms of storytelling as inadequate to the expression of real life and experience.[55] To limit our understanding of modernist frustration with storytelling conventions to traditional realism, however, is to isolate modernism in a formal sphere rather than to see it in relation to the much more determining cultural and technological environment of the larger media ecology. It is in the novel and narrative prose that the technological imprint and the tensions within the media ecology are most developed and vividly on display. As *Modernist Fiction and News* will show, the new predominance of news stories mobilized modernist fiction's experimental energies in the service of making the news new.

Modernist Fiction and News thus aims to develop a theory of the modernist novel as a development in the old relationship between novels and news. Critics as diverse as Mikhail Bakhtin, Georg Lukács, Benedict Anderson, David Lodge, and Lennard Davis have forwarded different models of this relationship, but all have recognized that historically novels and news are mutually constitutive and mutually constructing, their stories constantly intertwined as each evolves in relation to the other. In Bakhtin's formulation, novels are heteroglossic forms that draw upon, reproduce, and put into dialogue various social discourses, among them "forms used by reporters in newspaper articles."[56] Lennard Davis's inquiry into the sixteenth-century origins of the English novel finds an "undifferentiated matrix out of which journalism and history will be distinguished from novels—that is factual narratives will be clearly differentiated from fictional ones," although at first this distinction was not made.[57] The rise of the realistic fiction in the eighteenth century brought the novel and news into a new configuration. Lodge defines realism as *"the representation of experience in a manner which approximates closely to descriptions of similar experience in nonliterary texts of the same culture,"* including newspapers.[58] For Benedict Anderson, news and novels are related discourses that make possible the conception of homogeneous, empty time, the crucial precondition of the modern nation as an imagined community.[59] Finally, for Lukács, journalism and modernist fiction are related symptoms of modern capitalism. According to Lukács, art must above all provide terms for examining characters in relation to their social conditions, a responsibility for which, in his estimation, realism excels. Modernism and journalism, on the other hand, forfeit this responsibility by presenting chaotic and autonomous fields of description and information without an overarching perspective,[60] or, in other words, they ideologically reproduce, rather than diagnose, the conditions and symptoms of modern alienation.[61] What these disparate models demonstrate is that the special mutual orientation between news and novels is, at the very least, overdetermined. Their close, mutually constitutive relationship made it inevitable that emerging recording technologies would make a strong simultaneous imprint upon the capitalized news industry and the modernist novel.

By focusing on the relationship between mass news and modernist fiction as overlapping spaces in the new media ecology, *Modernist Fiction and News* argues that modernist novelists perceive news not only as a challenge to the novel's privilege of narrating a broad swath of reality, but also as an instrumental, distancing, and inauthentic mode for representing human experience. Moreover, experience itself is increasingly seen as the victim of the numbing media assault, as meaningful experience *(Erfahrung)* is displaced by the fleeting sensations of immediate experience *(Erlebnis)*. The information age not only threatens the traditional means of communicating meaningful experience, but also, according to Benjamin's formulation, diminishes one's capacity to even *have* real experiences. Experience itself becomes impoverished and atrophied by the negative shocks of modernity, exemplified in many ways by the stream of news. In response to this, Benjamin imagines a revolutionary language that would provide a counter-shock, thus reawakening experience *(Erfahrung)*.[62] This is precisely what I argue the modernist novel attempts to do through revolutionary uses of language in relation to news discourse, centered on the contested area of experience. I focus on the variegated range of ways that modernist prose narratives attempt to archive experience by literary strategies of commencement, commandment, and consignment, carving privileged spaces of experience out of the media ecology, while also indirectly responding to, contesting, and productively engaging it. But even so, it is necessary to maintain the understanding that modernist novels and mass media are not stable binary terms in any practical sense.[63] Even in a theoretical sense, news and modernist fiction are apt to collapse into one another, for both fundamentally seek to create, shape, store, and prioritize information and both selectively forget, repress, or erase much in the process.

Because news and modernist novels both respond to these archiving and repressing imperatives, they must thus be seen as merely different forms of response to the same transformed media ecology that Kittler theorizes. Each basically functions as a "news recording machine," as Harmsworth characterized the newspaper.[64] That is, news and modernist novels both take as their starting point and foundation the newly expanded recording technologies that opened a theoretically infinite horizon for what might be archived or reported. Both are impelled by imperatives and problems that issue from the massive volume of information that recording technologies enabled for the first time in human history. These technologies simultaneously press urgent questions about how and why one thing might be archived, reported, or valued over another. Further, these technologies demand principles and strategies of selection and presentation or storage that shape the respective directions of both news and modernism.

Thus, a particular moment of technological potentiality throws the long mutual history of news and the novel into a new configuration that then takes on a particular urgency because of the embattled state of modern experience. How does the modernist novel intervene at this moment of their entwined story? To what extent does it wish, on the one hand, to reignite or, on the other, to definitively break from their mutual origin and history? Close attention to the modernist novel reveals that it contains dialectical impulses in two directions, tensely seeking at once to reignite and to break the relationship with news discourse, with which it is now forced into newly intensified contact. While the modernist novel wishes to wrest certain modes and privileges of representing experience back from the incursive news media, in other ways it also embraces the blurred boundaries between the two, exploiting opportunities that the renewed contact between news and the novel makes possible.[65] It is important to recognize that as much as it demonstrates antagonism toward certain elements of the press, the modernist novel also stands to gain by sharing in the sensational stories and popular content that sent daily newspaper circulation soaring. The popularity and ubiquity of news stories meant that the newspaper's content took on tremendous cultural power, and the modernist novel was happy to share some of this power by overlapping in content.

But if the enabling conditions for news and modernism are the same, then how do we account for their evident differences in selection and strategy or their different orientations toward *Erfahrung* and *Erlebnis?* One way to examine the differences between the respective orientations of news and modernist fiction might be to point to differences in form and content. It is tempting to hypothesize that recording technologies of total information storage promoted forms that were streamlined for quick consumption and featured terse, fast-paced, and arbitrarily juxtaposed information such as those developed in newspapers. Though it always emphasized difficulty rather than streamlined consumption, the modernist novel shares some of the formal attributes that could be understood as technologically determined. One could then argue that whereas news embraces its technologically determined form and capitulates to the kind of content and storytelling encouraged by it *(Erlebnis)*, modernism creates a tension with the determined form it shares with news by resisting it on the level of content. Modernist fiction would thus appeal in its storytelling to the older, embattled form of experience *(Erfahrung)* rather than embracing *Erlebnis* as news does. The modernist novel could then be seen as a kind of atavistic response at the level of content to the recording technologies that news embraces at the level of form. However, there are reasons why I am skeptical of this form/content hypothesis. First, I am less of a technological determinist than Kittler. Recording technologies create the conditions and the range of possibility (the range, as Derrida says, of what can be identified as archivable), but they cannot fully determine the response even on the level of form. There are simply too many other influences upon form to see recording technologies as more than the conditioning of archival possibility. After all, both newspapers and modernist novels were capable of great formal innovation, which might be better attributed, respectively, to the necessity of advertising and the demands of circulation and to the desire for literary distinction and prestige, than to recording technology. Nor can historical differentiation of the novel and news be discounted, for novels and news had been accustomed to certain forms and functions long before new recording technology reconfigured the archivable.

But even more importantly, modernism is less an atavistic response to new technological and media conditions than it is a creative opening up of unexpected possibilities from these conditions. After all, responses to new technologies are not limited only to deterministic capitulation or reactionary resistance. In fact, responses to new technologies often result in startlingly new possibilities, outcomes, or wishes. For instance, according to Benjamin, emerging technologies can cultivate new collective utopian possibilities at the same time that the capitalist order struggles to assimilate them into the status quo.[66] To the extent that new technologies emerge with possibilities that point toward either *Erfahrung* or *Erlebnis,* modernism is less the expression of an atavistic desire to roll back technological changes than it is an opportune attempt to embrace certain potentialities in recording technology that opened in its moment of emergence. This initiates the historical moment in which news media are busy adopting and tailoring recording technologies to the market by employing capitalist production techniques, a process that culminates in the instrumentalizing and alienating effects that Benjamin associates with *Erlebnis.* At the same time, modernists are also seizing upon these new technological possibilities in order to break with the immediate past (to "make it new") and to direct this technology toward the very ends and effects that are most threatened by modernity's trends: the representation and production of experience *(Erfahrung).*

Such an understanding of the dialectical tension within the attitudes of the modernist novel toward news helps to uncover some of the differences that align news with *Erlebnis* and the modernist novel with the intention to break free of *Erlebnis* and to imagine more intimate states of experience and existence. In fact, just as critics have derived multiple and often contradictory models of the affinities between news and modernist novels, here too their differences from one another seem overdetermined by multiple factors. Within the shared space of their media ecology, modernist novels and news discourse diverge in as many ways as they can be said to converge, yet without ever quite ceasing to function as mirrors of one another.

If in both the historical and theoretical sense, then, modernist novels and news can be seen as peculiarly different versions of one another, they remain most distinguished in the arena of experience. By establishing experimental spaces in which to potentially represent experience with greater immediacy, less instrumentalization, and more faithfulness to reality, modernist novels work to archive specific forms of experience that were misrepresented in the news. At stake for modernists was the future of experience itself.

Let us consider an example from Gertrude Stein. In a lecture given in the United States during her 1934–1935 tour, Stein addresses news narration and attempts to distinguish between newspapers, novels, detective stories, biographies, autobiographies, histories, and conversations. As Richard Bridgman notes of this lecture, "Gertrude Stein was drawing together evidence for her contention that the modern reader desired immediacy in his literature, a need that newspapers could not meet."[67] Only a short passage need concern us here:

> I love my love with a b because she is peculiar. One can say this. That has nothing to do with what a newspaper does and that is the reason why that is the reason that newspapers and with it history as it mostly exists has nothing to do with anything that is living.[68]

There is, one admits, an initial opacity, though nobody ever said it was easy to get the news from Gertrude Stein. We could begin by noting how "I love my love with a b because she is peculiar" evokes the children's alphabet game in which each player produces an adjective for each letter of the alphabet. We might then note how Stein contrasts this language of the nursery, and by implication the time of childhood (which is decidedly prior to the adult world of the newspaper), with newspapers and history. Moreover, newspapers and history do not have anything to do with what is living, while childhood playfulness and the nursery language do. In fact, these living qualities are related to transgression, for Stein characteristically breaks the rules of the game: the "b" word produces a "p" word: "peculiar." Thus, we can tell that whatever Stein claims in "I love my love with a b because she is peculiar," she believes it is living, playful, rule breaking, and elusive of news and history.

What is it then that the newspaper or history cannot say *if* it cannot say, "I love my love with a b because she is peculiar?" The repetition of and thus emphasis on "love" hints that news or history cannot speak of an experience of love, for instance, of Stein's love for Alice B. Tolkas, whose middle initial Stein delighted in playing on. Perhaps, Stein loves this love with a "b" in her name because this lover is peculiar, or, according to the *OED*, "distinguished in nature, character, or attributes from others; unlike others." But perhaps Stein also loves her peculiar love with a "b" in part because her lover is a woman, and Stein and Toklas mirror each other as a "b" mirrors a "p." In the language of her day, let us not forget, sexologists would have called Stein and Toklas "inverts."[69] But etymologizing can perhaps take us still further.[70] "Peculiar" comes from the Latin word for private property, *peculium,* which in turn stems from *pecu,* the word for cattle. Perhaps then Stein figures Alice as her private property. The meanings multiply: I love Alice B. Toklas because she is unlike others, because she mirrors me (is a woman), and because she is mine—and all these meanings are reserved and withheld from both news and history. Finally, initiates of Stein's lexicon know that a "cow" (cattle) can mean both female genitals and orgasm.[71] Thus, to love one's love with the letter "b" might be to both physically make love to Alice B. Toklas and figuratively make love to her with an alphabet, a technique in which Gertrude Stein excelled.[72]

These love experiences are deliberately set in contrast to the newspaper, but it is important to consider how both relate to archivization and storage. Stein has archived a form of experience that the newspaper cannot, but unlike the newspaper that does everything to facilitate the ease and speed of consumption, Stein's experience is carefully recorded to resist consumption and can only be understood with great patience. In fact, so wholly does Stein record her experience in ways that directly contrast the ease and speed of the newspaper that she risks repressing this experience altogether.[73] Her sedimentary technique threatens to erase or forget experience even as it attempts to differentiate and withhold experience from news narration. It is so protective of the experience of love, so elusive of reportage, that it risks being lost. Thus, the conservation drive and archive fever exist simultaneously in the exact same space in Stein's writing. To say that this passage evokes all of the problems associated with modernist "difficulty" is merely to say that when experiences are selected for recording in direct contrast with the techniques of the news, it is difficult to get the news. But neither should it surprise us when, with critical effort, we uncover other news and experiences. In Stein we find experience valued enough that it was lovingly archived and erased so that it resists consumption as news, yet, as William Carlos Williams would have it, gives us the "news/of something/that concerns you/and concerns many men."

Another way of looking at this textual process is as the particular kind of archiving that Benjamin calls collecting.[74] For Benjamin, to collect something is above all to remove it, to liberate it, from circulation, instrumentalization, and consumption: "What is decisive about collection is that the object is detached from all its original functions in order to enter into the closest conceivable relation to things of the same kind. This relation is the diametric opposite of any utility, and falls into the peculiar category of completeness."[75] Collected objects are liberated from endless circulation in the market where they had formerly been reduced to exchange values. By analogy, if news uses or instrumentalizes experience as exchange value in the newspaper market, then modernism would collect experience in order to remove it from circulation or to rob it of exchange value,[76] as Stein carefully removes the experience of loving Alice B. Toklas from circulation. The shape of Stein's modernism is often of intimate experience liberated and protected from usefulness. Benjamin adds, "It is the deepest enchantment of the collector to enclose the particular item within a magic circle, where, as a last shudder runs through it (the shudder of being acquired), it turns to stone."[77] Again, part of Gertrude Stein's compositional process lies in conflating the shudder of archiving experience with the shudder of sexual pleasure. The writing is a kind of pleasure of collecting loving experiences that is inseparable from the pleasure of loving Alice Toklas. This represents Stein's way of permanently marrying herself to Toklas and archiving their experiences in writing, a writing that both crystallizes and reserves experience in direct contrast to what the newspaper cannot say.[78]

TEXTS AND METHOD

This reading is characteristic of the general methodology of this project. While I situate the modernist writers whom I treat within a broad historical, institutional, and technological framework, I do not offer substantial revisions of social, cultural, or institutional histories. Pertinent histories of this kind have been written, as I have detailed in previous sections. Though cultural and institutional histories of modernism have positively transformed the field of modernist studies in the last decade or two, these histories have sometimes come at the expense of attention to modernist texts themselves.[79] *Modernist Fiction and News* differs in approach from other studies of modernism and mass media by focusing less on revising modernist history or writing "a sociology of modernism"[80] and more on exploring modernism's implicit challenge and response to contemporary ideologies and practices of technology.

The textual emphasis in *Modernist Fiction and News* may be attributed to the centrality it grants to the archival and experiential character of texts. Critics have obviously addressed themselves to these texts for many years. It may eventually come to seem as though they no longer respond to one's inquiries. Why should we keep interrogating the same texts over and over? But, as Derrida notes about archives, it is an illusion to think that they have *ever* responded to us. The archive is "a bit like the answering machine whose voice outlives its moment of recording: you call, the other person is dead, now, whether you know it or not, and the voice responds to you, in a very precise fashion, sometimes cheerfully, it instructs you, it can even give you instructions, make declarations to you, address your requests, prayers, promises, injunctions."[81] In other words, though it does not respond, or can only give a spectral response, "the phantom continues to speak."[82] I approach modernist texts as answering machine recordings, peculiar and characteristic recordings that pick up when we call in order to tell us that experience is not where we thought it would be found, but rather out, away, indisposed at the moment, but assuredly somewhere else, perhaps even dead. We listen to the recording and leave a message after the tone. The entire telephone exchange between recorded voice and caller is thus a momentary encounter in which past and present temporarily constellate together.

In constelling the particular set of "answering machines" addressed in *Modernist Fiction and News,* I have sought to explore some crucial categories that the modernist novel negotiates with news discourse: nearness, scandal, character, identity, and war. The choice of these particular themes requires some preliminary discussion and justification. Why these themes, for instance, but not celebrity, privacy,[83] immediacy, or even narrative simultaneity? The answer is that this grouping of themes, while not exhaustive, seemed to strike an efficacious balance between, on the one hand, the most important changes in newspaper content and recording technologies during the period and, on the other, the changes that modernists themselves were most likely to seize upon, as well as the modes with which they contested these changes.

Press historian Jean Chalaby provides evidence of the New Journalism's sensationalism and scope by surveying a mere two pages of Northcliffe's *Daily Mirror* for October 13, 1908:

> Readers were entertained with the divorce of the Earl of Yarmouth; the opening of a school of orators by an anti-socialist union; the charge of cruelty to a cat brought against a lieutenant-colonel by the Humanitarian League; the story of a woman killed to save her dog from a motor-car; a romance between an Italian duke and an American lady; the death

of Ireland's allegedly oldest inhabitant; a taxicab dispute; a balloon race accident; the journey of the King to Newmarket; and a British warship's movements off the coast of Spain.[84]

This characteristically diverse catalog hints at every theme highlighted in *Modernist Fiction and News,* but the overriding preoccupation in a constellation of headlines such as this is the promise of nearness.

The newspaper promises to bring geographically and thematically diverse material right to one's breakfast table, to make the distant close, the concealed accessible, the military civilian, and the private public. From military maneuvers, accidents, and romances to divorces, royal visits, and animal stories, the New Journalism sought to deliver the news of the wide world in narrow columns. That, at least, is the promise. As Benjamin observed, the incredible amount and range of information that the newspaper collects does not necessarily bring what is reported from a distance any nearer to a reader in a meaningful manner. In fact, the sheer volume of information (to say nothing, for now, of narrative form or the influences of material production) threatens to undermine both the experiences reported and the experience of reading about the experiences of others. Nearness thus represents the matter that modernist novelists identified at the heart of other, more particular and thematic changes in newspaper content. It is through the theme of nearness that modernists responded in the deepest fashion to the contested narrative terrain within the media ecology. Most important of all, modernists perceived a growing distance between news reporting and lived experience, and they developed and honed narrative techniques and an experimental resolve that made nearness and experience defining values. Improving on what the newspaper promised but failed to do, modernist novelists hoped not just to "make it new," but also to "make it near."

A glance back to the examples we have seen makes this ambition of nearness clear. Toni Morrison begins with the Margaret Garner of the *American Baptist*—an emblematic "slave mother" who "caught a shovel and struck two of her children on the head, and then took a knife and cut the throat of the third"[85]—and revises this newspaper character into the intimately known Sethe Garner and her children: "Two were lying open-eyed in sawdust; a third pumped blood down the dress of the main one—the woman schoolteacher bragged about, the one he said made fine ink, damn good soup, pressed his collars the way he liked besides having at least ten breeding years left."[86] The anemic empirical report of the newspaper is reimagined with full-pumping blood: information becomes experience brought shockingly near. Similarly, when Gertrude Stein sediments multiple layers and meaning of loving Alice Toklas in "I love my love with a b because she is peculiar," she confronts the newspaper with the difficult nearness and intimacy from which it is most remote.

The other major themes of this book can also be traced in Chalaby's catalog of two *Daily Mirror* pages. Scandal is a well-documented facet of the New Journalism, as in the divorce of the Earl of Yarmouth and perhaps the romance between an Italian duke and an American lady. As *Daily Mirror* and *Daily Mail* owner Alfred Harmsworth boasted, "Most of the things that interest [the new sort of newspaper reader] are things which the pre-*Mail* newspapers never used to mention. The reason why the *Mail* caused such a sensation was that it dealt with these things, played them up, increased the interest in them a hundred-fold."[87] Chief among those things that formerly were never mentioned were stories about divorce and sex scandals. The newspaper made greater and more sensational incursions into intimate life and experience than ever before. Again, there is a strong resemblance to the newspaper in the impulses behind the modernist novel, for there too was the private life and intimate experience explored with a depth and candor seldom attempted by earlier novelists. The newspaper and the novel during this period both claimed the previously undisclosed and unspoken in intimate life as their territory. However, modernist novelists were troubled by the way in which newspapers handled scandal, especially the newspaper's assumption that scandalous experiences can be objectively and unproblematically reported. At the same time that it shares in the newspaper's incursion into private life, modernist fiction complicates the report of scandal with epistemological questions, and even at times questions the very ontological reportability or recordability of scandalous experiences.

All of the stories in Chalaby's sampling also suggest certain ways of conceiving character and identity. These two well-established categories of modernist experimentation are central to both the modernist novel and the news: how can character be represented? What comprises identity, and how shall it be represented? The newspaper's publicity and celebrity machinery, its incursions into private lives, and the formal stamp that it could put on any representation of individuals led inevitably to crises in the closely related categories of character and identity for modernist writers. In "Modern Fiction," Virginia Woolf argues that these questions must be answered in new and revolutionary ways. She makes this revolution in the representation of character and identity the guiding imperative for modernist innovation. Modernist novelists necessarily wrote and innovated with character in relation to the aggregate effect of character creation within a rapidly emerging and changing media ecology. Here again, the examples of *Beloved* and Stein's "Narration" lecture are apposite, both positioned in direct relation to what the other major character-creating machines in the shared media ecology have done and can or cannot do. A major premise of *Modernist Fiction and News* is thus that each novelist necessarily (even if implicitly) negotiates with the character and identity machines of news discourse in his or her representation of individual experience. One may love one's love with a b because she is peculiar, but to say so is explicitly or implicitly to challenge the vision of identity and character that dominates representation in a market-driven media environment.

Finally, the warship story in Chalaby's catalog shows just a trace of the major expansion and innovation of war reporting, a category of journalism that became distinctive of early twentieth-century news discourse. War reporting became a crucial cultural function of newspapers, and nothing did more to increase newspaper circulation than wars. The Boer War pushed the *Daily Mail*'s circulation over one million for the first time.[88] World War I more than doubled daily newspaper circulation in England, and the daily newspaper achieved something like ubiquity during World War II.[89] It may have been in the arena of war reporting that newspapers were most successfully able to bring the distant near. Although censorship and propaganda play major roles in war reporting of the period, over the course of the first half of the twentieth century, war reporting nonetheless focused increasingly upon the stories of individual soldiers and their experiences in ways that are recognizably literary. The vivid body of World War II reportage evidences how skillfully and vividly correspondents were able to cover the war, borrowing techniques from novelistic representation to powerful effect. However, even here modernists perceived damaging constraints on the newspaper's ability to render the experiences of war in formally significant ways. Just as the concern for nearness and the struggles over the representation of scandal, character, and identity animate the modernist engagement with news, here modernist fiction turns to innovations in form that expose limitations of war reportage's vivid content.

Nearness, scandal, character, identity, and war thus constitute the vital shared and contested territory upon which the modernist novel and the newspaper negotiate the shape of twentieth-century experience. My approach necessitates close attention to the ways in which these dimensions of experience are minutely and patiently made to converse in literary texts with the new representations of news media, and as a result I focus these categories through a limited set of literary texts and writers: Virginia Woolf's stories "Sympathy" and "The Mark on the Wall"; James Joyce's *Ulysses,* but more prominently *Finnegans Wake;* John Dos Passos's *U.S.A.*; and Gertrude Stein's autobiographies, primarily *Everybody's Autobiography* and *Wars I Have Seen.* If this is a peculiar selection, it may demonstrate the variety of modernist texts that can be (in some cases unexpectedly) defined by their relationship to news discourse and experience. In this sense, these texts can be understood as representative of what may be found in many other modernist texts. In another sense, these are the texts that finally seemed to me to engage news discourse and experience in the richest and most startling ways around the categories that emerged as central to modernism's project with respect to news. As such chapters are organized around these categories of nearness, scandal, character, identity, and war, and the texts can be seen as explorations of each category as well as tests for the claims about modernist fiction that this book makes.

It is no accident that most of these signal texts were published in the 1930s. In "The Storyteller," Benjamin looks back at the peculiar absence of communicable experience observable among returning World War I soldiers, but he does so from the vantage of 1936. Similarly, the revolutions in the news industry and the technological shifts that Kittler locates in the late nineteenth and early twentieth centuries are felt most powerfully in the literary works of the 1930s. There are several reasons for this apparent lag between the start of the changes and their literary expression. First, changes in news and technology that began full steam in the 1900s and 1910s took time to finally mature and come to fruition. What Kittler argues about the technological ability to record any and everything becomes full fledged only in the 1930s. Second, it took time for the effects of these changes to come into focus for modernist writers. It took time to recognize the gradual impoverishment of experience in day-to-day discourse that began early in the century and constantly intensified. Experience drains out of the public sphere slowly, until one day, like realizing that one has not heard any birds singing in a while, one feels its absence. It also took time for modernists to develop their most mature and meaningful responses to these changes. Modernist texts from the 1910s and 1920s have not, for the most part, assimilated the changed position of experience in public discourse, nor have they yet developed the consistent strategies of intimacy and difficult nearness that emerged as their mature response. For reasons such as these, as I will now detail, *Modernist Fiction and News* focuses only briefly on Woolf's story stories from the late 1910s or Joyce's *Ulysses* from 1922, and dwells considerably longer on *Finnegans Wake, U.S.A.*, and Stein's autobiographical excursions of the 1930s.

Specifically, Chapter 1 examines experience in the form of "Nearness," signaling the centrality of nearness to the understanding of experience in *Modernist Fiction and News*. It begins with a discussion of nearness as a crucial component of Walter Benjamin's vision of modernity and modernism. For Benjamin, the growth and expansion of news floods the world with information that positions experience at a remove from readers and impoverishes their ability to even have meaningful experiences. Benjamin values forms of narrative such as the anecdote that bring experience into the intimate space of readers in unmediated and often shocking forms. The chapter then moves on to examine important transitional stories in the development of Virginia Woolf's modernist vision, stories that open experimental spaces for the nearness of experience in direct and deliberate relation to news discourse and newspaper readers in the first decades of the twentieth century.

Chapter 2, "Scandal," begins by examining the ways in which *Ulysses* promotes its own fiction in direct contrast and as mimetically superior to the newspaper. However, this chapter understands not *Ulysses,* but *Finnegans Wake* as the culmination of Joyce's career-long interest in news scandals and scandalous experiences. In *Finnegans Wake,* Joyce finally undermines the assumptions about reportable experience that seem shared in common by both the newspaper and *Ulysses. Finnegans Wake* positions itself as a report on a variety of sexually scandalous behaviors, but one that is so resistant to explanation that it challenges the common assumption of news as well as of modernist novels such as *Ulysses* that such experiences can be reported or comprehended on a literal level at all. In contrast, the painstaking scrutiny that *Finnegans Wake* requires from readers enables unmediated, or at least boundless, scandalous experiences to emerge with difficult and shocking nearness.

Chapter 3, "Character," views the category of character as a major contested space between the modernist novel and news discourse. Dos Passos experiments by articulating character across his lengthy trilogy in ways associated with news reports. However, by retaining shards of experience that readers have come to associate with novels rather than newspapers, Dos Passos creates deeply unsettling effects and also exposes the ways in which damaging assumptions about the supposed distinction between novels and news in effect marginalize experience in the public sphere. By upsetting the false dichotomy between novels and news, *U.S.A.* demonstrates that modernists struggle with news and other powerful institutions over a single and irreducible language. This linguistic struggle mirrors the class struggle in America to control the understanding and practice of the single, but unstable, language of American freedom and democracy.

Chapter 4, "Identity," begins with Stein's assertion that newspapers create falsely stable conceptualizations of identity by suppressing temporal differences between the day of an event and the day of its reportage. As when Joyce looks back at the news-like assumptions that underpin *Ulysses* from the perspective of *Finnegans Wake,* Stein comes to view her own previous representations of identity in *The Autobiography of Alice B. Toklas* as participating in a similar pattern of suppression and repression. In Joyce and Stein, we find examples of the slowly emerging modernist recognition and response to the changed representation of experience in the public sphere. Stein and Joyce look back to their earlier work and, finally judging it as complicit with news discourse, construct their later work in clear contrast to both news and their own former representational practices. Stein in particular begins to feel that modern identity itself has come to be structured like news discourse. Thus, in *Everybody's Autobiography*, Stein experimentally intervenes in both news and autobiographical identity formation to craft a new autobiographical form of process, particularity, and discovery from which a strong personality can break forth without suppressing temporal difference or hypostatizing false identities.

Chapter 5, "War," compares Stein's *Wars I Have Seen* with the vivid World War II correspondence of Ernie Pyle. With so many techniques and intentions in common, it is almost impossible to maintain a convincing distinction between Stein's autobiography and war correspondence. However, Stein observes that the representation of meaningful experience hinges upon the ability to bring formal closure to texts. For Stein this is a capability that newspapers lack, however vivid the correspondence they contain, because the news itself cannot end and thus cannot arrest the flow of events or content in a meaningful form. In contrast, Stein's technique in *Wars I Have Seen* is to write the experience of war as inflected through endings of all kinds: of stories, lives, the war, and finally of *Wars I Have Seen* itself. This final chapter thus returns to the questions with which I began this introduction, locating experience in significant formal configurations that temporarily arrest the flood of information.

Modernist Fiction and News concludes with a coda, "Make It Now," which reframes the project in terms of our own contemporary media ecology, as well as current critical methodologies of modernism. Modernist novelists are seen as the first tentative denizens of the information age who responded creatively, and thus, for us, importantly, to a media environment and public orientation toward experience that has by now become quite naturalized. In addition, the coda calls for a reorientation of modernist criticism toward the present moment, emphasizing the important experience of reading modernist fiction in and with an eye on the present.

Because *Modernist Fiction and News* prioritizes the key themes of nearness, scandal, character, identity, and war, the literary texts that it examines are not presented chronologically. Chapters move from *Finnegans Wake* (1939) back to *U.S.A.* (1930–1936) and then on to *The Autobiography of Alice B. Toklas* (1933), *Everybody's Autobiography* (1937), and *Wars I Have Seen* (1945). At the expense of chronology, then, a certain thematic logic has been foregrounded. Nearness and intimacy are the signal themes of this book, and in an important sense everything that follows partakes in the broad conflict between *Erfahrung* and *Erlebnis* in which Benjamin and the modernists were invested. The themes of scandal and character are logically presented next because they grow directly out of this conflict over whose experiences are represented, and in what way. Scandal and character in turn give rise to urgent questions about identity, and I thus finally turn to Stein's autobiographies to examine this issue. The book concludes with Stein's exploration of identity and her related engagement with the major news innovations in war reporting. Moreover, it is in war reporting that nearness and experience are evoked with deepest urgency. If nearness is a signal theme of *Modernist Fiction and News,* then war is its limit case; these two crucial themes should echo back and forth to one another across the other chapters.

One final word on the place of history in this book: *Modernist Fiction and News* is historicist in only the most general sense. In fact, it grows out of a specific critique of historicism that might itself be seen as modernist: Walter Benjamin's model of materialist historiography.[90] For Benjamin, there was little value in a historicism that saw the past as a vast desert (which he termed "homogeneous, empty time") that could be irrigated by a mass of factual data, if we could only collect enough of it. He contrasts this to his own peculiar materialist historiography, which is an attempt to arrest the present in a tense but productive constellation with the past.[91] Michael Jennings underscores the crucial element in Benjamin's literary critical methodology that "claims for the work of art a power to provide us with the *experience* of truth otherwise inaccessible to us. This same claim remains valid throughout Benjamin's career, as he finds in surrealist poetry, Soviet film and finally Baudelaire's lyrics a revolutionary and thus potentially redemptive form of true experience."[92] Using elements of Benjamin's method for prioritizing historical experience in conjunction with close attention to language,[93] this book attempts to uncover the way historical experience, what, as we shall see, Benjamin calls the "pathos of nearness,"[94] is always at stake in these texts, precisely because of and in relation to the rise of mass media. Above all, it endeavors to reveal these texts' preoccupation with historical experience, as it was mediated through and influenced by their engagement with news discourse.

In this sense, *Modernist Fiction and News* can also be seen as another attempt to explore the possibilities of Walter Benjamin's diverse philosophical and historical thought for literary criticism,[95] but especially for Anglo-American literary modernism. However, in order to think about this branch of modernism and Benjamin together, it is necessary to blast both out of the historical continuum, not least because their critical histories have tended to mutually exclude one another.[96] These histories have had more extensive effects than we might realize.[97] Even after many critical revisions, it is usually only Benjamin's work of art essay that is brought to bear on Anglo-American modernists,[98] an essay whose particular composition history and place within Benjamin's work makes it somewhat less than representative.[99] *Modernist Fiction and News* thus attempts to explore some possibilities of Benjamin's late materialist historiography for literary modernism.

This would also entail doing something quite different from many prevailing histories, sociologies, or revisions of modernism in new modernist studies, because for Benjamin value lies not in studying the past or artworks only in their own contexts or on their own terms, but rather in the image that results when the past and the present momentarily flash together: "It's not that what is past casts its light on what is present, or what is present its light on what is past; rather, [the] image is that wherein what has been comes together in a flash with the now to form a constellation. In other words, dialectics at a standstill."[100] As David Ferris notes, "It goes without saying (or at least it should) that historical understanding in Benjamin has little to do with the recovery of the historical context or conditions of an event or even an artwork. Such a view would see history as a fixed source of meaning, as if the moment in which an event or events took place had already an unchanging meaning that later generations only had to uncover."[101] Thus, as Benjamin's materialist historiography values the apprehension of the past in such a way that it productively and shockingly forms an image with the present, so the premise and motivation for *Modernist Fiction and News* is in a particular form of apprehending modernism, news, and the fate of experience in constellation with the present. This is the belief that if we are to come to terms with the present and future problems of the information age[102] and the continual impoverishment of experience that we have inherited from the early twentieth century, we must arrest modernism in a relationship with our moment[103] and read the resultant image not as a continuum of history, but as a form of potential awakening.

CHAPTER 1

NEARNESS

FOR WALTER BENJAMIN, MODERNITY COULD BE UNDERSTOOD as a crisis in human experience and communication, both of which were under assault from multiple sources that ranged from economic inflation to contemporary forms of warfare. However, Benjamin granted a major role in this crisis to the newspaper, central as it is to the representation and reproduction of human affairs. Thus, as we have seen, Benjamin could assert what at first seems paradoxical: "Every morning brings us news from across the globe, yet we are poor in noteworthy stories."[1] There is no paradox, however, if the newsworthy can be distinguished from the noteworthy, a point of distinction that for Benjamin also divides explanation from experience, empathy from pathos, and distance from nearness. Indeed, these distinctions together inform Benjamin's basic view of communicable experience in the mass-mediated age in which the very language of experience *(Erfahrung)* is so scarce that it becomes saturated with revolutionary potential. For Benjamin, this potential is above all located in intimate or anecdotal forms that can communicate unmediated experience, prompting a flash of awakened consciousness that he terms the "pathos of nearness" *(Pathos der Nähe).*[2] This kind of awakening and nearness forms the basis not only for Benjamin's theory of experience, but also for his radical materialist historiography of awakening, which he contrasts against the static and conservative vision of historicism: "Historicism presents the eternal image of the past, whereas historical materialism presents a given experience with the past—an experience that is unique."[3]

In the following, I show how Benjamin aligns the newspaper with the static temporal cognition of historicism, both of which are rooted in the concept of homogenous, empty time. Further, I argue that the pathos of nearness that underscores Benjamin's materialist historiography as well as his theory of experience may also be seen to animate the modernist engagement with mass media concerning the problem of representing experience. Turning to two of Virginia Woolf's early short stories, "Sympathy" and "The Mark on the Wall," I suggest that modernist fiction attempts to represent experience with immediacy precisely in relation to news discourse, using similar strategies of nearness, intimacy, and shock that animate Benjamin's own interventions. Moreover, modernism's attempt to archive or articulate experience is always calculated to fold out into a second experience, that of reading. Given the innovative and often challenging forms to be found in writers like Woolf, to consume such stories is necessarily to receive them into one's space and to struggle with them there, on an intimate scale, and to meet their represented experiences with a concomitant experience of being struck or arrested. However, as we shall see, Woolf's story also exposes the modernist archive drive as marked by characteristic suppressions and repressions that polarize the modernist project as at once experimental and conservative, archival and archive destroying ("anarchival"), one that establishes intimate spaces for experience through a process of conservation and destruction.

WALTER BENJAMIN READS THE NEWSPAPER

Benjamin's theory of language is rooted in his theory of experience. As Beatrice Hanssen writes, "what distinguishes all of his language work is that, from its inception, it was guided by a large-scale theory about the changed structure of experience *(Erfahrung)* and perception."[4] For Benjamin, the negative shock experiences of modernity—for instance, from mass media, commodity fetishism, and modern warfare—have eroded the basis for meaningful forms of experience. This must be understood within Benjamin's larger vision of capitalism as a giant dream or phantasmagoria that enchanted Europe during the nineteenth century.[5] As Susan Buck-Morss notes, Benjamin's theory of modernity is in direct contrast with that of a thinker such as Max Weber. Weber sees modernity under capitalism as a process of "demythification and disenchantment of the social world. In contrast, and in keeping with the Surrealist vision, Benjamin's central argument in the *Passagen-Werk* was that under the conditions of capitalism, industrialization had brought about a *re*enchantment of the social world," or what Buck-Morss calls a "dream world of mass culture."[6]

In "On Some Motifs in Baudelaire," Benjamin relates the increasing atrophy of experience under the phantasmagoria of capitalism to the newspaper in particular:

> Newspapers constitute one of the many indications of such a decrease
> [of the likelihood that one's external concerns will be assimilated to one's

experience]. If it were the intention of the press to have the reader assimilate the information it supplies as part of his own experience, it would not achieve its purpose. But its intention is just the opposite, and it is achieved: to isolate events from the realm in which they could affect the experience of the reader. The principles of journalistic information (newness, brevity, clarity, and, above all, lack of connection between the individual news items) contribute as much to this as the layout of the pages and the style of writing.[7]

Part of what troubles Benjamin about the newspaper is the way it instrumentalizes experience as something to be almost arbitrarily collected, printed or archived, and then summarily dispensed with. No point exists within the process of news consumption in which the events explained and reported can be meaningfully assimilated with the reader's own experience. This is similar to the claim we have already seen from Benjamin's "The Storyteller" essay, in which he goes on to claim, "nowadays no event comes to us without already being shot through with explanations."[8] Indeed, according to Benjamin, everything in the intention that stands behind newspaper production conspires against communicable experience, from the formal layout and the writing style to the journalistic values of newness, brevity, and clarity.[9]

Above all, however, Benjamin diagnoses in the newspaper the significant "lack of connection between the individual news items." This raises what are for Benjamin two important and related problems. The first has to do with the relatively arbitrary relationship between the parts and the whole of the newspaper. Drawing upon Benjamin's terms of historical analysis, Benedict Anderson illustrates this situation elegantly: "If we were to look at a sample front page of, say, *The New York Times*, we might find there stories about Soviet dissidents, famine in Mali, a gruesome murder, a coup in Iraq, the discovery of a rare fossil in Zimbabwe, and a speech by Mitterand. Why are these events so juxtaposed? What connects them to each other?"[10] For Anderson there are two important reasons that the newspaper's events are so juxtaposed. The first is "simply calendrical coincidence. The date at the top of the newspaper, the single most important emblem on it, provides the essential connection—the steady onward clocking of homogeneous, empty time."[11]

This calendrical coincidence is quite obvious, of course, but Anderson's insight that this coincidence merely clocks the progression of homogenous, empty time helps to underscore part of what Benjamin finds so problematic in the newspaper from a historical materialist's standpoint. As we have seen, Benjamin associates the concept of history as homogenous, empty time with the negative values of universal history and historicism. To view time as a continuum is to set the conceptual stage for false narratives of historical progress. Werner Hamacher explains that for Benjamin, such a concept of empty time represents a "danger that threatens historical cognition": "At the base of the social and political conformism that threatens historical cognition, and thus history itself, lies the transcendental conformism of the perception of 'time,' through which time is represented as the homogeneous continuum of punctual events."[12] The empty columns of the newspaper are like empty time itself, merely waiting for the punctual arrival of events to fill them and create the illusion of historical continuity and historical progression.

For Anderson, the other thing that links the events of the daily newspaper is the relationship between the newspaper itself and the market. The juxtaposition of events in the newspaper is determined not only by calendrical coincidence, but also by the demands of production and consumption. The newspaper packages its news as planned obsolescence for rapid, wide-scale, and simultaneous mass consumption: "the newspaper is merely an 'extreme form' of the book, a book sold on a colossal scale, but of ephemeral popularity. Might we say: one-day best-sellers?"[13] It should be clear how this second link also cuts to the heart of capitalist phantasmagoria for Benjamin. Capitalism forestalls the recognition that it is in reality the time of repetition, or Hell, only by constantly offering the illusion of real change and progress in the merely new and novel. Max Pensky explains how Benjamin sought to reveal modernity "as a Hell of unfulfillment; the promise of eternal newness and unlimited progress encoded in the imperatives of technological change and the cycles of consumption now appear as their opposite, as primal history, the mythic compulsion toward endless repetition."[14] This is similar to Benjamin's reading of fashion as repetition masquerading as the new and progressive. Of fashion Benjamin devilishly observes, "A definitive perspective on fashion follows solely from the consideration that to each generation the one immediately preceding it seems the most radical anti-aphrodisiac imaginable."[15] Shall we add to this the slight repulsion one feels toward yesterday's newspaper, left, perhaps, on a park bench? Thus, news goes hand in glove with the market need to generate the appearance of the new by filling the daily volume of homogeneous, empty time.

The second problem that emerges from Benjamin's observation that news stories lack connection with one another cuts to the quick of his theory of language and experience. For Benjamin, the question of the newspaper's ephemerality and the nearly arbitrary relationship between its component parts is crucially tied to experience and literary form. Because Benjamin links the atrophy of modern experience in part with the demise of storytelling, we can understand the demise of communicable experience as inseparable from a crisis of narrative form. Consider only the formal property of the ending. As John McCole explains, for Benjamin, "Whether or not stories may be said to have a single, unified meaning, the very issue of authoritative meanings can be raised only once the end of the story is known."[16] Narratives that end, such as literary texts,[17] will consequently have radically different relationships to communicable experience than those that cannot end, such as the newspaper, which must replenish its empty columns anew with news everyday.[18] But it is not just that endings help readers to evaluate stories in full retrospect and in relation to their own experiences. More than that, endings are meaningful because they formalize death itself, the ending that finally gives experience any meaning it has.[19]

Moreover, endings scale stories in meaningful ways to a human size, which for Benjamin is the only way the experiences of others can strike or become present to one, and thus hope to be redeemed. If historical experience is to be redeemed, it must be through the revolutionary potentialities that exist in the formal manipulation of language that would represent experience. Above all, what is crucial for Benjamin is language that can convey experience as a pathos of nearness. In a provocative passage in the "First Sketches" for the unfinished *Arcades Project,* Benjamin develops the idea of the pathos of nearness in relation to anecdotal (in contrast to empathetic) narrative forms.[20] Let us take the second part of this lengthy kernel first:

> Let us imagine that a man dies on the very day he turns fifty, which is the day on which his son is born, to whom the same thing happens, and so on. The result would be: since the birth of Christ, not forty men have lived. Purpose of this fiction: to apply a standard to historical times that would be adequate and comprehensible to human life. This pathos of nearness [*Pathos der Nähe*], the hatred of the abstract configuration of human life in epochs, has animated the great skeptics.[21]

For Benjamin, the human scale and size of a story is more important than its factual content. This recalls Toni Morrison's anecdotal perspective on Margaret Garner that was "historically true in essence, but not strictly factual."[22] Indeed, as in Benjamin's example, the anecdote could be sheer invention and still be capable of expressing historical truth. His anecdote of 40 men takes the otherwise imponderable stretch of historical time from Christ's birth to the present and rescues that time from abstraction by scaling it to a succession of human-sized experiences. In other words, Benjamin's small fiction applies to this time span (which would otherwise quickly become abstracted as homogenous, empty time) the largest measure of time that we can experience concretely: a lifetime. But, as we have already observed, for Benjamin the guarantor of experience is the finality of death, which obviously plays the crucial role in his small fiction.

NEWS OR ANECDOTE, EMPATHY OR PATHOS

Let us now proceed to an earlier passage in this rich cluster of ideas in the "First Sketches" in order to see how Benjamin defines anecdotal narrative forms, such as the Christ anecdote, against "empathetic" forms that he associates with the newspaper:

> The constructions of history are comparable to instructions that commandeer the true life and confine it to barracks. On the other hand: the street insurgence of the anecdote. The anecdote brings things near to us spatially, lets them enter our life. It represents the strict antithesis to the sort of history which demands "empathy," which makes everything abstract. *"Empathy": this is what newspaper reading terminates in.* The true method of making things present is: to represent them in our space (not to represent ourselves in their space). Only anecdotes can do this for us. Thus represented, the things allow no mediating construction from out of "large contexts."[23]

The forms of history that Benjamin opposes are those that end in empathy. Although it may seem counter to conventional positive connotations of the word "empathy," for Benjamin empathy is a negative imaginative process that he associates with historicist perception.[24] As Irving Wohlfarth writes, "While the materialist historian *constructs* a particular past according to the dictates of the hour, the historicist painstakingly *re*constructs some by-gone era out of a tell-tale need to *forget* the present. Part tourist, part archaeologist, he seeks to 'relive' the past through an idle act of empathy."[25] By extension then, newspaper readers may be seen as archaeologists of the present, but even better, as tourists of the present, an image that points toward crucial spatial dislocations.

The spatial arrangement of the newspaper, reader, and reported event prevents experience from emerging out of the constructions and abstractions of the narrative of historical continuity. Empathy leads us "to represent ourselves in [the objects'] space" rather than "to represent them in our space." The newspaper embodies this distance and produces empathy by representing a world "out there" that we must move out toward imaginatively, without having to accept its events as presences in our own physical, imaginative, or experiential space. As we have seen, at stake for Benjamin in newspaper reading as well as historiography is the relative likelihood that "one's external concerns will be assimilated to one's experience."[26] The imaginative distance we traverse in the empathetic process ensures that the distant and recent past remain temporally disconnected from the present and spatially dislocated from where we feel ourselves to be positioned. We cannot receive the distant or recent past into our experience, so we relinquish any claims that past and present are connected. Benjamin identifies this tendency as the fundamental flaw in historicism, which attempts to establish an empathetic relation to a past reconstructed in its own terms: a place for every event and every event in its place. It is this disconnection from and mediation of history, this movement outward from oneself toward some abstracted object, that Benjamin equates with newspaper reading.

These ideas seem distinctively Benjaminian, yet we can observe the empathetic dislocations of the news in other places in this period. For instance, Virginia Woolf's short story "Sympathy," called in its shorter form, "A Death in the Newspaper," dramatizes the peculiar way in which one may be said to wander at a distance from oneself while reading the newspaper. While we might finally want to insist upon a distinction between empathy and sympathy, the sympathetic imagination in Woolf's story is more or less indistinguishable from Benjamin's concept of empathy. In the story, told as interior monologue, the narrator reads of the death of an acquaintance. The narrative charts the speaker's sympathetic response to this death notice, but it is striking how thoroughly the speaker's response is defined by a spatial movement outward and away from the place where she reads the newspaper in the present moment. For instance, the narrator imagines following the deceased man's widow through the Manor just before she discovers her husband's body: "I follow her to his door; I see her turn the handle; then comes the blind moment, and when my fancy opens its eyes again I find her equipped for the world—a widow."[27] There are two important features here that we can read by Benjamin's analysis of the empathy in which newspaper reading culminates. The first is the imaginative distance that the narrator has traveled from her location to the house of the dead man and his new widow. In an instance of extreme spatial and experiential dislocation, the narrator imagines herself as a ghostly presence eavesdropping upon the widow.

The second feature to note is the failure of the crucial experience that happens in that house to materialize for the narrator: the "blind moment." The narrator admits a blindness or a blank when she fails to imagine the moment when Celia discovers her dead husband, Humphry Hammond. When the narrator's vision resumes, Celia has already assumed the subject position of widow. The actual transformational instant of discovery, that awful and powerful human moment when one is no longer a wife but not yet a widow, is precisely what the fantasy fails to communicate, the crucial moment of blindness. But of course, this experience of Celia's is the very heart of the matter. To transmit that experience to another would be to communicate the kind of meaningful experience that Benjamin sees as so threatened in the modern age. Later, the narrator imaginatively follows Celia out into the woods in another exercise of sympathetic imaginative movement. But she is soon forced to reflect on the artificiality and ineffectuality of this exercise, finally conceding, "But it's all fancy. I'm not in the room with her, nor out in the wood. I'm here in London, standing by the window, holding *The Times*" (109).

What the newspaper does transmit to the narrator, however, is a peculiar vision of death. We have seen in Benjamin how the finality of death, its concreteness, gives meaning to experience. However, death plays a far different role for the newspaper reader in Woolf's story, acting not as the concrete finality that ensures the meaningfulness of the particular, but rather as a universalized abstraction that emerges almost to haunt the sympathetic narrator. Instead of receiving the news of death as a shock of the particular and concrete (precisely that "blind moment" which the narrator could not see), this news pushes the narrator into an oddly detached, pseudo-philosophical reverie about a nearly anthropomorphized death: "Death has done it" (110). She has a vision of the universality of death, which waits for everybody she knows: "Freely in this fine air my friends pass dark across the horizon, all of them desiring goodness only, tenderly putting me by, and stepping off the rim of the world into the ship which waits to take them into storm or serenity" (110). However, this abstraction moves Humphry Hammond ever more distant, ever less near, generating ever more sympathetic abstraction, and ever less pathos. For there is no pathos in a death in the newspaper: "when I think of him I see nothing at all. And yet he died; the utmost he could do gives me now scarcely any sensation at all. Terrible! Terrible! to be so callous!" (111).

But the true failure of sympathy only makes itself felt in the final moments of the story when the narrator receives an invitation to dine at the Hammond's house. It is only then that the narrator realizes that the Humphry Hammond whose death was reported in the newspaper merely bore the same name as her still living acquaintance. The full exposure of the sympathetic gesture is disclosed in the shocking disappointment of the narrator: "O don't tell me he lives still! O why did you deceive me?" (111). Here Humphry Hammond's failure to die deprives the narrator of the pseudo-profundity of her abstract vision of death. The pathos of "Sympathy" thus derives from the terrible lack of pathos in the newspaper reader's response. The nearness of Woolf's story comes precisely from the reader's recognition of the callousness of the newspaper reader, and thus of one's own, perhaps inevitable, callousness when one takes on, as most of us daily do, that position.

A different, but related spatial and experiential dislocation may also be grasped through the visual idiom of Surrealism that influenced Benjamin so greatly. René Magritte's 1928 painting *Man with a Newspaper (L'Homme au journal)* may be said to represent visually the homogenous, empty time of the newspaper as homogeneous, empty space on a canvas. It represents newspaper reading as time spent outside of oneself, and perhaps as absent to oneself, as well as to one's immediate environment. The painting is divided into four quadrants, each depicting the same mundane bourgeois interior.[28] There is a round, clothed breakfast table and two stools, a draped window with a bouquet of flowers on the sill, a decorative wall hanging, and a framed painted landscape, partially obscured by a pipe running to the ceiling from the dark, cylindrical fuel stove fixed to the floor. In the upper left quadrant, a man sits at the table reading the newspaper. He does not appear in the other three quadrants, or, more precisely, the viewer recognizes that he is absent from the others. Seeing him once, especially in the upper left corner (the location where one might begin reading a newspaper or even a comic strip), the viewer becomes aware that the man has disappeared from the other three scenes. A.M. Hammacher interprets this disappearance as a mere emblem of the banality of quotidian life: "the man reading his newspaper did apparently represent something human. Yet the nonexistence of the existent newspaper reader evokes the idea of living in a rut. Magritte has rendered the awfulness of the banal and the vacuous in visible terms."[29] But the disappearance of the man may instead be read as signifying that while he reads the newspaper he is "with" the newspaper and ceases in important ways to exist. Perhaps Magritte's newspaper reader disappears from his home when he reads because he has imaginatively traveled so far away from himself in order to meet the distant events of the day. Newspaper reading, in many ways the quintessential modern experience, is then an experience that erases experience. If news in some way cancels out experiences by placing them at empathetic distance from readers, then there is a total nullification of experience when the news is read by a reader whose own experience is nullified in the reading process. The panels may be read sequentially as the spatial depiction of homogenous, empty time and its conceptual erasure of the experiences both of event and reader.

But, comparable to the placement of readers of Woolf's "Sympathy," viewers of Magritte's painting are put in a position quite different from that of the disappearing man. The viewer actively scrutinizes the other three quadrants, perhaps becoming suspicious, attentive to minutiae, searching not necessarily for the man, but for any tiny difference between the remaining objects and furniture, for any exception to the stark reproduction of the bare interior scene, or for some wrinkle that might account for the man's unexplained disappearance. Thus the mundane interior comes alive for the viewer, newly attuned and sensitized to its familiar setting, in a process akin to what the Russian formalists called *ostranenie,* or defamiliarization, or Brecht's *Verfremdungseffekt,* or alienation effect. It is possible under these circumstances that the reproduction of this setting comes to seem increasingly monstrous, to the point that the ideology that reproduces the bourgeois interior begins to seem monstrous as well. In contrast, and whatever their failures or difficulties, works of modernism require a reading or viewing experience to meet a represented experience. Because modernist texts are not streamlined for accessibility and consumption, and cannot be read from left column to right unproblematically, consumers of modernism hardly ever face the danger of empathy in the way Benjamin uses the term; just the opposite may be true: to access the experiential content of modernism requires a kind of exhaustive, active reading and self-consciousness, conditions that may themselves constitute a receptiveness to the experiences of others. These are the only reading conditions, for instance, that could hope to unearth experience from Stein's enigmatic "I love my love with a b because she is peculiar."

In opposition to the newspaper form, Benjamin locates the anecdote as a narrative unit that may indeed render experience on a human scale. The anecdote is a narrative method of admitting into one's space what might otherwise seem abstractly historical or far too large to comprehend with pathos. Empathy is replaced by the pathos of nearness: one is asked to receive the thing into one's own space, on one's own scale, and without mediation from large contexts or abstraction. Empathy is a feeling of identification, while pathos is the evocation of pity or sadness, from the Greek word for suffering and grief. In empathy, feeling moves outward, as it might in a news account of a death, a local disaster, or an international catastrophe, but in pathos one allows the anecdote to direct feelings of suffering and grief inward.

Benjamin introduces his discussion of the anecdote by asserting, "There has never been an epoch that did not feel itself to be 'modern' in the sense of most eccentric, and suppose itself to be standing directly before an abyss."[30] The alternative to this cognitive mistake is precisely the "revolution in historical perception" that Benjamin develops in the early stages of *The Arcades Project* as a "Copernican revolution" in which the present becomes the ground for historical awakening.[31] The Copernican revolution would break the false continuity of historicism[32] by "discovering that constellation of historical origins which has the power to explode history's 'continuum,'" as Buck-Morss describes it.[33] Benjamin's formulation employs the vocabulary of dream that we have already seen, and it is the task of materialist historiography to provide the conditions for awakening to the facts of history.[34] It also draws upon Marcel Proust's concept of *mémoire involontaire,* a form of "profane illumination" that Benjamin also drew from Surrealism and associated with his theory of dialectical images.[35]

In the same first sketch that we have been considering, Benjamin gives an architectural example of awakening, another form of what might be called anecdotal perception, which I shall argue is characteristic of modernism vis-à-vis mass media. Benjamin's architectural example contrasts empathetic and anecdotal forms of response and perception when one visits historical monuments, specifically a cathedral or temple. One visits, Benjamin writes, the cathedral of Chartres or the temple of Paestum "to receive them into our space (not to feel empathy with their builders or their priests). We don't displace our being into theirs; they step into our life."[36] Benjamin differentiates between the types of response one might have before the cathedral in such a way that underscores the empathetic distance of historicism and contrasts it with the anecdotal nearness of materialist historiography. One might see the cathedral and imagine what an impressive feat it was to build it or what it must have been like to worship within it. One might become curious about the lives of the individuals who laid the stones or of the priests who led the worship, but for Benjamin, by doing so one has already committed oneself to the crucial spatial and conceptual dislocation that he also identifies in newspaper reading. Just as the newspaper reader empathizes at a disconnected distance through news events and as Woolf's speaker in "Sympathy" becomes a hovering presence over the widow's shoulder, so does the empathetic gesture before the temple or cathedral dislocate the visitor from the experience of the edifice as a moment of present awakening. Crucially, in the terms of Benjamin's Copernican historical revolution or reversal, the visitor must receive the historical edifice in his or her own space, be struck by its existence for the first time.[37] This is an experience in which the object from the past shocks and arrests the visitor in the present. Historical continuity of the kind imagined in historicism is broken. In its place is an awakened consciousness of past and present in tense constellation.

Benjamin thus lends some of the magnitude of the Chartres cathedral to the tiny, seldom-esteemed form of the anecdote.[38] The language of being "struck," of revolution and awakening, evokes the language of insurgence and uprising that Benjamin associates with the anecdote. These terms resonate on at least two levels: the first, as we have seen, is as a counter to the barracks formed by the construction of history. The military figure is unavoidable, as is the element of liberation in its violent reversal, its "street insurgency." The second level is of a striking or awakening of consciousness itself. It is not enough that the anecdote represent things in one's space. It is the experience of the anecdotal form itself that jolts one awake, like standing before the cathedral. Benjamin's anecdote is inseparable from its pathos of nearness. The constructions of history provoke empathy, a projection of feeling onto the object, while the anecdote elicits pathos, awakening memory and consciousness within one.

Benjamin may have imagined the anecdote as a replacement of the story form, which had lost its aura in the age of art's technological reproducibility. As Harry Harootunian argues, for Benjamin, "Storytelling and its production of aura had long since passed into the past with the coming of disenchantment *(Entzauberung)*. Historical materialism must reject the form of the story because it can no longer adequately contain the content of the present. In place of the story, Benjamin proposed installing the anecdote because it represented the concrete crystal (as against the abstracting propensities of the narrative form), the kernel that was capable of being 'exhibited,' displayed."[39] One need only match the language Harootunian uses to describe Benjamin's anecdote to see its affinities with the literary modernism of, for instance, Ezra Pound's image or vortex or Joyce's epiphany, both of which share with Benjamin's anecdote a hatred of abstraction and therefore emphasize illumination through the concrete, crystal, and kernel. One could also point to the anecdotal and episodic forms of modernist fiction, which we will see later in this chapter and in the chapters to come, as suggesting an anecdotal perspective that predominates in fragmented modernist forms.

For Benjamin mass culture is importantly both source and potential cure of the phantasmagoria of modernity. As Susan Buck-Morss argues, Benjamin's theory, "takes mass culture seriously not merely as the source of the phantasmagoria of false consciousness, but as the source of collective energy to overcome it."[40] My claim here is that modernist fiction can be defined by its particular relationship to this collective energy within the mass media, making a space within the media ecology that desires to redeem the very experience that it compromises. What follows is an example of how this might be seen to work in Virginia Woolf's exemplary early short story "The Mark on the Wall," a narrative in which psychological experience is defined by, delays, and is finally restricted by mass media, all at the slow, but inexorable, pace of a snail. All the same, it is clear that modernist fiction is not finally separable from the news, merely that it struggles (hopelessly) for differentiation, and in the course of struggle may clear a space for fleeting moments of shocking nearness of experience.

VIRGINIA WOOLF READS THE NEWSPAPER

"The Mark on the Wall" is often acknowledged as a moment of discovery in Virginia Woolf's development of a literary voice, the experimental hinge that connects the early novels *The Voyage Out* and *Night and Day* with the more modernist *Jacob's Room, Mrs. Dalloway*, and *To the Lighthouse*. It was, as Julia Briggs observes, a wall that became a door: "Writing 'The Mark on the Wall' so quickly and easily had opened a door for Virginia, and in the wake of its publication, she was ready to walk through it."[41] Woolf herself acknowledged the important role that "The Mark on the Wall," along with "Kew Gardens" and "An Unwritten Novel," played in the development of her new conception of literary form: "conceive mark on the wall, K[ew].G[ardens]. & unwritten novel taking hands & dancing in unity. What the unity shall be I have yet to discover: the theme is a blank to me; but I see immense possibilities in the form I hit upon more or less by chance 2 weeks ago."[42] This transitional story therefore offers a privileged moment for understanding the imaginative and material conditions from which Woolf's mature modernism emerges. We can imagine Virginia Woolf writing this story during World War I with her entire career as a modernist before her. We may ask: how does it happen? What space does this story hit upon? Out of what medium (or media) does it carve this new space, the form that will become the stage for Woolf's decisive lark and plunge into modernist stylistics? What are the material and technological conditions that make this plunge possible, even necessary?[43]

"The Mark on the Wall" begins with the solitary speaker sitting across from a mystery mark. In the first paragraph of the story, the speaker establishes a sense of the interior setting through details such as the "three chrysanthemums in the round glass bowl of the mantelpiece."[44] We can connect the interior of the story with the bourgeois interior of Magritte's *Man with a Newspaper*,[45] and we can also compare how the relative absence or presence of the newspaper in both the story and painting modulates the scene. As we have seen in the painting, the absence of the man and his newspaper heightens the viewer's critical attentiveness and invites close scrutiny of what might otherwise seem unremarkable or even invisible elements of the interior. The canvas lures the viewer into an experience of close space. In a comparable manner, in "The Mark" the initial absence of the second speaker and his or her[46] discourse about the newspaper and the war enables the speaker to concentrate her attention upon her surroundings, so much so that she can be attentive even to a mark on the wall. In this sense, "The Mark" and *Man with a Newspaper* are mirrors of one another: in the first, the newspaper is absent and later arrives, while in the second the newspaper is present and later disappears. In both works, the presence of the newspaper carries attention away from the immediate spatial surroundings (empathy) and toward abstraction, while its absence or removal begins to create a space for intimate experience and, finally, perhaps, pathos.

"Perhaps it was the middle of January in the present year that I first looked up and saw the mark on the wall. In order to fix a date it is necessary to remember what one saw" (83). These first sentences of the story establish two hermeneutical enigmas,[47] which the story's formal and, indeed, experimental goal it is to avoid or at least defer answering. These enigmas are "what is the mark on the wall?" and "on what date did the narrator first notice it?" From the beginning we notice something unexpected or unusual about the relative priority given to these questions. The story's title tells us that we should concentrate on the mark as the central axis of the narrative. The first sentence reinforces this supposition, dramatizing the act of looking up and discovering the enigmatic mark. With the second sentence, however, the mark seems to become the mere necessary pretext for "fixing the date." The narrator immediately displaces our interest from the mark and begins to draw attention to the interior world of thought, thought that circles but avoids alighting upon the mark itself. It is thus symptomatic of this movement that even the prioritized enigma, fixing a date, seems casually brushed aside, also displaced. By the end of the passage the initial specificity of "January" spreads into an amorphous and blurry "winter time" (83).[48]

To "fix the date" in the manner of the newspaper, as we have seen, is to use the date as an emblem of the calendrical coincidence that clocks the daily passing of homogenous, empty time. The speaker's reluctance to clock time this way, indeed her determined resistance to doing so, is precisely what opens a space for alternative experiences and conceptualizations of time. Rather than to mentally flip back, as though in a newspaper archive, to a certain date in January, Woolf's speaker is more concerned to reclaim an experience *in* time and an experience *of* time. This reclamation or even redemption of historical experience will form the antithesis to the newspaper's homogenous, empty time, which is held off until the very end of the story. Benjamin might see this alternative as the speaker's attempt to redeem historical time in a kind of Copernican revolution that he called for. In order to fix (to redeem, to establish, to put to rights, to give form and stability to) historical time, one must return to one's own experiences, to what was actually seen and felt. It is not to remember what was clocked in the newspaper's factual procedure, but rather to return to the human-scaled, intimate experience of time, which is precisely what the story goes on to record in an intimate space.

Woolf attempts to archive a selective experience of consciousness, one unfettered by the facts and generalizations that are associated with the newspaper buyer at story's end. This thought-experience centers around creative speculations about the mystery mark on the wall, which Laura Marcus notes, "both incites thoughts and acts as a full stop to disagreeable ones."[49] Rebecca Walkowitz sees the narrator's thought-experiment as a kind of productive evasiveness that shields experience from euphemism: "Woolf demonstrates in 'The Mark,' as she will elsewhere, that to critique euphemism, which translates intense experiences into language that is habitual and therefore invisible, one must also critique literalism, which proposes that there is only one objective experience to present."[50] Against this processing of intense experience into literal or euphemistic formulae, the narrator intends to bracket or omit the world of facts of the very kind that would report on the war or identify the mark. The story can thus be read as an attempt to preside over a certain selective archive of experience against the overwhelming and constantly impinging world of fact and generalization, to return to Derrida's terms. Indeed, the narrator commands, commences, and consigns intimate experience within a space carved out from the media space that must itself be implicitly or explicitly engaged, mediated, or negotiated. It is my argument that there is no move more characteristic of modernist fiction than the demarcation of interiority and subjectivity from the competing attentions and challenges of the media ecology.

Like "Nature's game" as the narrator imagines it—"her prompting to take action as a way of ending any thought that threatens to excite or to pain" (88)—the narrator represses or actively suppresses unwanted factual determinations that would imperil the fragile thought-experiment.[51] However, the narrator's experiment in archiving experience and anarchiving[52] facts and objective reportage is interrupted when the repressed inevitably returns in the form of the second speaker. This speaker intends to purchase a newspaper to read the latest war reports. In the course of this intrusion, the second speaker also casually and emblematically identifies the mark on the wall that the narrator had fought so determinedly to leave indeterminate: a snail. This return of the hitherto carefully repressed not only destroys the fragile archive of the thought-experiment, but ends the story itself as well.

Before it ends, however, interspersed with irresistible guesses about the mark's identity ("How readily our thoughts swarm upon a new object" (84)), we find an experience of thinking, an exploration of depths rather than of surfaces. The speaker tells, among other things, of a cavalcade of red knights, about the former owners of her house, of lost things, of what it feels like to experience modern life (like "being blown through the Tube at fifty miles an hour" (84)), about the afterlife, Shakespeare, fantasies of veiled vanity and of the delicacy of our self-images, of Whitaker's Table of Precedency, of antiquaries, of utopian worlds without professors or specialists, of Nature's antipathy to painful or exciting thoughts, and of the growth of trees. In the very space that opens between the mark and its deferred identification, Woolf places a series of loosely connected anecdotal forms, each contributing to a vivid representation of an interior experience of the time to be archived. Each of these meditations brings a potential abstraction or generalization nearer to the reader, functioning much in the same manner as Benjamin's anecdote about the 40 tidy lifetimes since the birth of Christ.

The speaker's imperative to archive an intimate experience rather than an objective account of the date must be understood in the context of various kinds of archive fever that threaten this imperative, the threats to memory from various forms of destruction that in the story always seem to coincide with the space of remembering. These absences and erasures also leave their traces. For one thing, some experiences are now entirely lost to the speaker's knowledge or memory. Of the former owners of the speaker's house the speaker says: "I think of them so often, in such queer places, because one will never see them again, never know what happened next" (83). The former owners' subsequent experience is simply unavailable to the speaker; she can never bring this lost experience nearer, and this is emblematized spatially by the former owners' literal departure from her space.

But there are even more powerful archive-destroying (anarchiving) forces at work that the speaker is at once intensely aware of and also, as we shall see, tries to forget or erase. Modern life itself is a process of "perpetual waste and repair" (84). Even the ego is constantly threatened with destruction: "Suppose the looking-glass smashes, the image disappears" (85). The great emblem of destruction, dust, stretches from the speaker's mantelpiece all the way back to the ruins of Troy: "look at the dust on the mantelpiece... the dust which, so they say, buried Troy three times over, only fragments of pots utterly refusing annihilation" (84). Troy acts here as a displaced figure for the ruins of World War I, but this ruinous war is addressed directly when the narrator observes how even "the masculine point of view which governs our lives" has become "since the war half a phantom" and will soon "be laughed into the dustbin where the phantoms go" (86). Dust, fragments, and phantoms are the anarchival context for the narrator's reclamation of experience. Characteristically, the modernist conservation drive seems inseparable from certain symptomatic suppressions, repressions, and acts of destruction that at once make it a reactionary, troubling, but potentially ameliorative project on the level of representing experience.

The deferral or suppression of the mark seems a small triumph against the overwhelming compulsion to establish and fix facts: "I must jump up and see for myself what the mark on the wall really is—a nail, a roseleaf, a crack in the wood?" (88). The drama of the story relies upon the tension between the seemingly insoluble bond between facts and knowledge on the one hand, and on the other the impulse toward the "illegitimate freedom" of believing that supposedly real things "were indeed half phantoms" (86). The narrator says, "I want to sink deeper and deeper, away from the surface, with its hard separate facts" (85). At the origin of this stream of consciousness we might identify a sustained fantasy that explanations and facts can be indefinitely suspended, that one might dwell in illegitimate freedom, be released from the illusion that knowledge must be cobbled together from facts, and be exempted from the compulsion to live in the world clocked and charted by homogenous, empty time. This fantasy is offered as a programmatic imperative for (modernist) novelists:

> And the novelists in the future will realise more and more the importance of these reflections, for of course there is not one reflection but an almost infinite number; those are the depths they will explore, those the phantoms they will pursue, leaving the description of reality more and more out of their stories, taking a knowledge of it for granted, as the Greeks did and Shakespeare perhaps—but these generalisations are very worthless. The military sound of the word is enough. (85–86)

But even this programmatic fantasy is registered as a misstep. Just when the speaker seems able to identify the depths of experience worth writing about she finds that the very act of naming a program returns one to the level of "generalization" that one had set out to escape. "Generalisation" seems a particularly expressive name for the paradoxical moment when fresh depths of experience are drawn quickly to the surface and put into an abstract form. The "military sound" of "generalisation" expresses the violence of abstraction in which the heavy weight of the surface flattens depths and dimensions. The "military sound" also alludes to the historical moment of the narrative, World War I, although in another displaced form. Generalizations create their own kind of archive: they "bring back somehow Sunday in London, Sunday afternoon walks, Sunday luncheons, and also ways of speaking of the dead, clothes, and habits" (86). In other words, generalizations archive the day of greatest law and proscription, as well as exterior experiences, and social convention and constraints. In the terms we have been using, such an archive is governed by an empathetic imagination that envisions iterative and generalized routines set in temporal and spatial abstraction.

As Vincent Sherry notes, "By the spring of 1917, [Woolf] is writing short fiction, responding concurrently with the first efforts of other

London modernists. The resumption of her diary report, moreover, shows an alertness to the verbal culture of the war, whose literary potential may be taken to focus her engagement."[53] Thus, if "The Mark on the Wall" has a genre, perhaps it is a war story.[54] However, it is probably even more accurate, given Woolf's attention to "the verbal culture of the war," to call it a newspaper war story.[55] Sherry also observes how the war setting is inseparable from the journalism that reported on it: "A culture of journalism, which this second personage represents as a medium equally unreliable and irresistible, impinges vividly—not to say profanely—on the main speaker."[56] Indeed, even before its final "impingement," the war itself is cleverly and multiply present and displaced throughout the story. For instance, the mark reminds the narrator of the barrows on the South Downs of England, which historians feel could have been either camps or tombs. She seems to luxuriate in and to partially identify with the fantasy of a slightly ridiculous antiquary, a retired colonel, who would study such a question intently and yet suspend any decision about which it might have been. This fantasy touches lightly on the theme of war but carefully misses the "mark" by falling somewhere before it or after it. The antique barrows are piled full of the bones of the dead, a mass grave, but a grave hundreds of years covered over. It is another archive of destruction, but the colonel is retired and the wars are behind him. He is free to research and philosophize, even to keep "that great question of the camp or the tomb in perpetual suspension" (87), just as the narrator prefers to hold the mark. They both spend their time "accumulating evidence of both sides of the question" (87).

The fantasy of the antiquary ends, when he dies, with the question undecided still. Compared to the narrator's experience, however, this is perhaps an enviable death because at least it preserves the mystery that keeps inquiry alive and facts suspended. In contrast, the speaker will not enjoy this luxury for much longer. At the same moment that the speaker's project fails, the newspaper enters the story and the mark becomes merely a snail:

> Everything's moving, falling, slipping, vanishing.... There is a vast upheaval of matter. Someone is standing over me and saying—
> "I'm going out to buy a newspaper."
> "Yes?"
> "Though it's no good buying newspapers.... Nothing ever happens. Curse this war; God damn this war!... All the same, I don't see why we should have a snail on our wall."
> Ah, the mark on the wall! It was a snail. (89)

Anticipated in the first paragraph of the story as the other half of "we," the second speaker finally arrives and announces his or her errand, and

thereby recalls the narrator to the supposedly objective surface from her
vertiginous and intimate depths. The mental house of cards the narrator has been building now collapses. The news of the war again gives a
distinct shape to daily time just as the second speaker's offhand identification of the snail fixes the mark and neutralizes the possibilities that the
narrator sought to hold open. Paradoxically, the narrator's rapid interior
experience of the world is slowed to a stop by the exterior report of the
rapid war, though according to the newspaper buyer the reports of the
war make it seem to move as slowly as the snail. The newspaper attempts
to represent the war as directly as possible, but even the eager news consumer in the story acknowledges that nothing "happens" in any sense that
the newspaper can report.

As we have seen, the narrator deliberately tries to elude the war, the
mark, and the world of facts; she would live in a world of pure thought,
so pure that it would have no "mediating" contexts or abstractions in it at
all. In these terms, her final fantasy before the intrusion deserves special
attention. The speaker's fantasy about the solitary tree exemplifies this
desire to see the world without any media at all:

> I like to think of the tree itself: first the close dry sensation of being wood;
> then the grinding of the storm; then the slow, delicious ooze of sap. I like
> to think of it, too, on winter's nights standing in the empty field with all
> leaves close-furled, nothing tender exposed to the iron bullets of the moon,
> a naked mast upon an earth that goes tumbling, tumbling all night long.
> (88–89)

Perhaps of all things in the story, the tree is described as most vigorously
alive: it grows, it oozes sap, it stands in an empty field, it furls its leaves,
it tumbles in the wind all night long; when the storm comes, its fibers
snap, its branches drive deep in the ground. Even when the remains of the
tree are made into domestic furniture or wall panels, the narrator keeps
asserting its liveliness: "Even so, life isn't done with; there are a million
patient, watchful lives still for a tree, all over the world, in bedrooms, in
ships, on the pavement, lining rooms, where men and women sit after
tea, smoking cigarettes" (89). The tree is such a vivid presence near the
end of the story that it is easy to forget its initial understated appearance in the story: "The tree outside the window taps very gently on the
pane" (84). This was a very unassuming introduction, not at all like the
brash entrance of the newspaper buyer, but I think we are meant to notice
the difference. The tree taps gently at the window, while the newspaper
buyer seems to materialize suddenly, "standing over" the narrator. These
are significantly different bids for attention and significantly different
negotiations of personal space. Remembering that one afterlife in the

"million patient, watchful lives still for a tree" is as a newspaper, perhaps the newspaper buyer's intrusion is a fitting and resonant end for at once a thought-experiment, a story, and a tree.

Finally, there is an important social dimension introduced at the story's end. The addition of the second speaker changes the register of the story's discourse in revealing ways. This change is not only expressed in the appearance of quotation marks signaling speech, but in the relative poverty or banality of the words themselves. Where would the language of experience from the remainder of the story fit within this new, clipped, and practical discourse? There is space in the story's final social setting for little more than frustrated exclamation, the expression of consumerist intentions, and offhand comments that strangle interior thought. The speaker makes a studied effort to delay fixing the mark with an identity that would encircle it in a concept. However, in a characteristic mode of modernist engagement with the news, this delay opens a temporary space where it seems momentarily possible to access a more experiential order of reality. Some form of experience has been brought quite close to the reader, only to be realized at the moment it is snatched away and resituated in the language of the facts. How can this intimacy be shared with others as the field of information (exemplified by the newspaper) that surrounds us grows thicker and thicker? This is the crucial question of communication and meaningful experience that preoccupied Benjamin as well as modernist novelists. At the same time, although modernist fiction struggles to differentiate itself from the news in the media ecology, it neither finally separates itself nor avoids its own acts of suppression and destruction in the act of creating experimental spaces for experience.

CHAPTER 2

SCANDAL

"THE MARK ON THE WALL" ENDS WHEN A SECOND SPEAKER punctures the narrator's cultivated bubble of intimate experience by reintroducing information and facts from the newspaper world. Woolf thus brings meaningful experience to the edge of the individual, but it falters when pushed out into a social setting. Within a world where facts and information usually set the context for social interaction, we are left to wonder how personal experience can be communicated to another person, an exchange that conspicuously fails to materialize within the story. Yet it is possible to say that the communication of meaningful experience that falters in the story may in fact occur between story and reader. Indeed, again and again, we find this mechanism in modernist fiction: experiences represented but unshared within the fiction itself are made to fold out of the narrative into a reading experience characterized by difficulty and nearness.

However, the picture is still far from complete. Most importantly, intimate experience is not simply atrophied by mass media, but represented there as well. In the early twentieth century, Benjamin's *Erfahrung* is not only threatened by the *Erlebnis* associated with the media ecology, but also increasingly becomes the newspaper's own most desirable subject, under the guise of scandal. As we have seen, and as Joel Wiener succinctly summarizes, the New Journalism saw "a shift away from Parliamentary and political news to sport, gossip, crime, and sex."[1] Critics have begun to explore the historical relationship between the scandal culture of the New Journalism and the constitution and strategies of modernist texts. Sean Latham, for instance, has shown how libel laws exerted a far-reaching influence on tabloids and the modernist forms such as the roman à clef alike.[2] The affinities between the scandal culture of the New Journalism and modernism may be observed on a structural level as well. If, as James

Lull and Stephen Hinerman argue, "A media scandal occurs when private acts that disgrace or offend the idealized, dominant morality of a social community are made public and narrativized by the media, producing a range of effects from ideological and cultural retrenchment to disruption and change,"[3] then scandal would seem to intersect with modernism in a number of complex ways.

On the one hand, modernist texts participate in the economy of scandalous disclosure by offering their own narratives of exposure, often on a more intimate level than a newspaper could possibly access. In this sense, it is possible to say that modernism sinks its hooks deeper into the human subject than the scandal sheets can. From this perspective, modernism may be seen to intensify the culture of scandalous disclosure associated with the New Journalism, even though the former might disavow its relationship to fact while the latter might disavow its relationship to fiction. On the other hand, one might qualify this view by observing that modernist fiction simultaneously resists disclosure by making readers more aware that experience itself is a difficult thing to represent, and thus for readers to name or even access. It does so in large measure by foregrounding language itself as an obstacle to quick consumption and understanding, whereas newspapers obviously court readability and thus imply that the sphere of experience where scandal arises can be accessed and articulated through facts and plain print. Modernism does much to forestall such conclusions, and while modernist novels and news scandals are oriented toward the publication of ever more intimate experience, modernism tends to fold this impulse back upon itself into a different arrangement: as a dialectic of revealing and concealing. At its most extreme limits of experimentation, such modernist texts simultaneously archive and erase experience in a way that intervenes in and disrupts the assumptions of the prevailing culture of scandal and disclosure in which both modernism and news discourse participate. In addition, because modernist fiction can foreground epistemological problems, it seems to offer a space in which to complicate or contest the supposedly objective narrative of facts and events that scandal stories are typically built upon and verified by; indeed, these texts may do much to challenge objectivity itself. In the face of facts and events, modernist texts can offer wrinkles of circumstance, parallactic perspective, and depths of experience built upon even more depths of experience, built upon voids of uncertainty. This chapter thus focuses on a text that can be defined by its paradoxically intense extremes of scandalous disclosure and concealment. The scandals and experiences both published and withheld in James Joyce's *Finnegans Wake* suggest that Joyce strategically intervenes in both the news culture of scandal and in the modernist tendency to mirror the newspaper's preoccupation with and publication of intimate experience and sexual crime.

Through self-reflexive gestures as well as by its constant glints and hints of sexual intrigue and transgression, *Finnegans Wake* tells readers that it should be read as a peculiarly scandalous "allnights newseryreel,"[4] brimming with every variety of sexually scandalous disclosure. To do so, and yet to resist consumption or summary at such length and so stubbornly, is to reimagine what it means to archive or erase experience in the first instance. Indeed, *Finnegans Wake* discovers a point in the processes of archivization and erasure in which reporting and concealing, or the archive drive and archive fever, ceases to be opposed, but rather *converges* at a point of extremity. Because of this unusual and extreme polarity, *Finnegans Wake* positions itself to accomplish two very different operations at once whose effect relies upon the simultaneous presence of the other. It makes the literal explanation of experiences represented in the book look impoverished, embarrassing, or even ridiculous, overturning contemporary assumptions about what kinds and depths of experience are in any sense reportable. Simultaneously, because it pushes the extremes of intimate and scandalous publication but requires the closest attention and engagement from readers in order to be detected, intense and intimate experience can often emerge with unexpected or even shocking nearness. As we shall see, *Finnegans Wake* draws scandalous experience out of the empathetic and abstract sphere of the news and resituates it within the "in our space" of Benjamin's anecdote.

A REMARKABLE ROMANCE

In order to suggest a context for Joyce's later revision of reportage and experience in *Finnegans Wake,* it will be useful to begin with a scrap of newspaper that predates the publication of *Finnegans Wake* by 30 years. A yellowed news clipping entitled "Remarkable Romance" can be found among the papers of the James Joyce archive of Cornell University's Division of Rare and Manuscript Collections:[5]

> "I'm off for Venice, mother—goodbye!" Thus ran the message which a well-known and highly respected Galway woman received from her daughter almost two years ago. The latter had gone to a situation in Dublin and there made the acquaintance of a young man of good family and high educational attainments. They got married after a short courtship, and the scene was soon changed to classic, far-off Venice, to which the young man's occupation called him. In their happiness the young couple [was] never struck by the thought that in the lady's family circle in Galway there was uneasiness and worry, and finally consternation when they could find

no trace of her for some months. At the end of that period, however, a communication was received from the young lady that she was well and happy—and married. Her husband is just now on a visit to Galway and he has with him one of the handsomest little boys one could wish to see.

Although the clipping heralds its own remarkableness, it looks so penurious that it is easily passed over in preference for the other riches of Joyce's archive. George Healey, the collection's first curator, catalogs the clipping by writing, "Naming no names, but obviously the story of James and Nora and their flight to the Continent." Perhaps Joyce clipped the article himself while visiting Galway with his son Giorgio in 1909, or maybe it was forwarded to him by Nora's relatives sometime later. In whatever way Joyce came to possess it, the fact that the clipping survived any number of changes of address and spring cleanings seems itself remarkable.

Given the trends in New Journalism at the time, what may be finally most remarkable is that the clipping indeed "names no names." While anybody familiar with the outlines of Joyce's biography can detect in the clipping a narrative about Joyce's scandalous elopement with Nora, it is only through a journalistic screen, conspicuous by its very finessing of scandal and its implication that potential scandal had been averted. The "uneasy period" during which the unnamed woman did not communicate with her family is evoked only to be safely resolved by the end of the same sentence. A number of factual errors further conceal identities and scandal. For instance, Joyce and Nora left Ireland five years previously, not two. The handsome little boy with him had turned four years old just days before he and his father arrived in Ireland. The Galway woman and her young man left Dublin for Pola, Trieste, and Rome, but not for Venice. There is a final infelicity of fact, of course: by 1909, the two were still unmarried and would remain so until July 4, 1931. By then, Joyce's primary concern was that his marriage be made official without "a score of journalists with pencils in their hands intruding where they are not wanted."[6] This comment is consistent with Patrick Collier's argument that Joyce "would ultimately depict sensational journalism as a deeply oppressive invasion of privacy."[7]

But a greater issue than even factuality and privacy that "Remarkable Romance" raises is one of reportage and experience. The clipping reports on an elopement that was, as experienced, as emotionally removed from "happiness" as it was proximately distant from "classic, far-off Venice." While the clipping represents the upheaval of the elopement and relationship as happily settled, Joyce's own letters at the time find him accusing Nora of infidelity with his friend and questioning whether he was really the father of their son.[8] This notorious sequence of letters all belie how much reality and lived experience the news report fails to register or, perhaps, how little equipped it is to register these experiences at all. These seem like simple observations, but they contain the germ of ideas of intimacy, scandal, and experience that *Finnegans Wake* would later treat with great sophistication and complexity.

An intermediary step in this process consists of Joyce's contrasting treatment of fictional and journalistic worlds in *Ulysses*. "Aeolus," of course, represents the news culture of Dublin at length, but it is not until later in the novel that Joyce registers the troubling (and amusing) discrepancies between what took place on his fictional June 16, 1904, and how it is otherwise reported in the evening newspaper. In "Eumaeus," as Stephen and Bloom recuperate from their adventures in Bella Cohen's brothel, Bloom sees the *Telegraph* and begins by looking at the advertisements: "his eyes went aimlessly over the respective captions which came under his special province the allembracing give us this day our daily press."[9] The religious overtones, combining "daily press" and "daily bread," associate the evening news with something like a nightly prayer or devotion. The passage goes on to function as a kind of news coda for *Ulysses* itself, as we recognize how Dignam's funeral, Deasy's letter, the archbishop's letter, and the triumphant outsider associated all day long with Leopold Bloom—Throwaway—have all been inscribed in a news form that parallels the events in the novel. This of course helps to strengthen the mimetic or reality effect of *Ulysses* by borrowing from the same assumptions about journalism with which realism has long associated itself.

At the same time, Joyce calls attention to his fictional newspaper's departures from *Ulysses'* fictional reality. When Bloom points out that Stephen was erroneously listed among those at Dignam's funeral, Stephen recommends, "Text: open thy mouth and put thy foot in it" (16.1269), playing perhaps upon Deasy's letter about Foot and Mouth disease, which constitutes Stephen's other obscure contribution to the paper. Bloom notices additional factual errors and fantastical inventions in the account of Dignam's funeral: his own name is given as "L. Boom"; McCoy, like Stephen, is listed as attending, though he had only asked Bloom earlier in the day to put his name on the rolls. Bloom is "tickled" that he has managed to alter reality and history with this little wrinkle. In addition, the newspaper shows a line of "bitched" type that Bloom himself might have caused "where he called Monks the dayfather about Keyes's ad." These errors amount to "the usual crop of nonsensical howlers of misprints" that Bloom expects to find in the newspaper (16.1262–1267). Readers might remark on how many of the evening newspaper's distortions of reality are attributable to that most realistic of fictional characters, Bloom himself. Bloom also has a hand in what is perhaps the most interesting distortion in the newspaper: the invention of a man named "M'Intosh" among the list of mourners, a result of Hynes's misunderstanding of Bloom's gesture to an unknown man's jacket. With this error, the newspaper crosses definitively into the province of fiction by asserting the reality of a proper name, and thereby a person, who does not exist.

Of course, as an advertising agent, Bloom must often be tickled by the effects of his efforts upon the "daily organ" of reality. In fact, as much as Joyce borrows a reality effect from the newspaper, the occupation he chose for his hero seems calculated at least in part to challenge the reality effect of the newspaper, from the inside out. *Ulysses* asserts its own fiction's fidelity to experience by aligning itself with "reality" above and beyond the newspaper. While the newspaper is represented as an unstable, unreliable, and partly fictional province, *Ulysses* is asserted as reality itself, the illusion it works so hard to maintain, even through paradoxically fantastic episodes and experimental feats of modernist narration. The newspaper seems to mirror the people and events of *Ulysses,* but it does so poorly.

However, at the same time that *Ulysses* asserts its own reality by demonstrating the newspaper's fictiveness in relation to itself, it also discloses more of the private life than a newspaper could possibly make public. As Leo Bersani asks when he discusses *Ulysses* as a novel about Bloom's character, "Has any fictional character ever been so completely known?"[10] Joyce's project of verisimilitude and his desire to represent a "complete man"[11] in Leopold Bloom in distinction to more traditional literary representations of character can be said to have effects on privacy comparable to the New Journalism in relation to traditional journalism. If the New Journalism included deeper incursions into the lives of celebrities, public figures, and subjects of scandal in the sphere of news, then *Ulysses* can be seen as its complementary development in the sphere of fiction. Poor Bloom has few secrets from the discerning reader. Without engaging in contemporary debates about whether privacy is as outdated a concept as the Enlightenment subject upon which it is premised, it is still possible to show that both New Journalism and *Ulysses* dramatically intervene in the territory of privacy as it had been hitherto mapped, both pushing further from the shores into the unrepresented country of intimate experience. As Mark Wollaeger writes in a different context, "*Ulysses* extends technologies of surveillance to an unprecedented extent by recording in the public space of the page what had previously been shielded in the domain of the private."[12] But if *Ulysses* positions its own fiction as a sharper and deeper image than the one newspapers offer, his subsequent project seems to undermine the assumptions about recording experience that *Ulysses* shared with the news in spite of their competition. In contrast, *Finnegans Wake* may be read as a kind of revision of the evening paper that was found in "Eumaeus," a newspaper of the night in which "the night express sings his story"[13] (although whose and what story is far from clear). As we shall see, *Finnegans Wake* delivers the old "moaning pipers" (23.31) with a difference.

In this section, I read *Finnegans Wake* as primarily anecdotal in the way that Benjamin defines the term. In the last chapter we saw how Benjamin defines the anecdote as a space where experience can emerge with a striking and unexpected intimacy not found in the newspaper, and where history that threatens to become abstract can concretize on a human scale not often found in traditional historiography. The *Wake's* episodic structure can be viewed as a constellation of anecdotal shapes and forms. While it shares with news discourse an obsession with scandal, it unsettles the basically historicist reporting of news scandal as a collection of sensational facts and malefactors. Instead, the *Wake* springs scandal upon its readers anecdotally, in such a way that facts and actors remain primarily elusive but something of the experience of scandal is allowed to emerge with nearness. As the *OED* proposes that the etymological root of anecdote is both "things unpublished" and "to give out, to publish," suggesting that there is something simultaneously private or withheld and public or published about the anecdote, *Finnegans Wake* can be seen as a dialectic of the public and private dimensions of scandal played out at modernism's extreme experimental deep end.

Joyce's contemporaries were accustomed to viewing *Finnegans Wake* through the lens of the news. D. H. Lawrence records his reaction to a portion of *Finnegans Wake* published as *Work in Progress* in *transition* magazine in these terms: "My God, what a clumsy *olla putrida* James Joyce is! Nothing but old fags and cabbage-stumps of quotations from the Bible and the rest, stewed in the juice of deliberate, journalistic dirty-mindedness—what old and hard-worked staleness, masquerading as the all-new!"[14] While Lawrence admits little taste for Joyce's "Stew of the evening, booksyful stew" (268.14–15), and would distinguish the truly new from Joyce's "journalistic dirty-mindedness," he nonetheless implicitly expresses the way in which journalism and modernism converged and competed in their desire for the "all-new," and demonstrates just how easily the intentions of journalism and modernism suggested one another.

Eugene Jolas also measured the extent of Joyce's "Revolution of Language" in terms of its relative proximity to or distance from the news, suggesting that for Jolas as well news was the crucial touchtone for distinguishing the truly new from the merely novel. Unlike Lawrence, Jolas positions news language in contrast with the revolutionary new use of language in *Finnegans Wake*: "Words in modern literature are still being set side by side in the same banal and journalistic fashion as in preceding decades, and the inadequacy of worn-out verbal patterns for our more sensitized nervous systems seems to have struck only a small minority."[15] Lawrence's and Jolas's observations are apparently contrary to one another because Lawrence asserts continuity between news and *Finnegans Wake* while Jolas asserts a definitive break. In this sense, they differ only because Lawrence believes that Joyce has failed to break with news as definitively as Jolas does. Lawrence's and Jolas's terms of measure and their common imaginative connection between modernism and news, however, are highly convergent.

Their observations might be further reconciled by noting that Lawrence points to the salacious and sensationalistic attitudes common to both the news and the *Wake,* while Jolas is concerned with Joyce's departure from the "worn-out" language mode that most modern literature, in his view, has been content to share with news. For Jolas, the *Wake*'s language is not just thoroughly different from the language of the news, but takes its very identity from the distinct manner in which it differs *from* the news. Similarities and differences aside, however, Lawrence and Jolas both misread the project of *Finnegans Wake* when they claim that it fails to or succeeds in breaking from news, for such assertions of opposition between the *Wake* and news ignore the complex relationship between the two that operates on nearly every page of Joyce's book.

In order to elucidate this relationship, it is impossible to start other than by acknowledging the apparently immense differences between transmission and consumption of new discourse and *Wake* discourse. John Bishop elegantly articulates the slow process through which readers begin to explain what they read in *Finnegans Wake*:

> Impossible as it may be to fathom as an obscure totality, even at the level of a page, particles of immanent sense will stand out from the dark foil against which they are set, in turn to suggest connections with others, and still others, until—not necessarily in linear order—out of a web of items drawn together by association, a knot of *coherent* nonsense will begin to emerge; and upon this coherent nonsense, as upon the shards of a recollected dream, some interpretation will have to be practiced in order to discover an underlying sense.[16]

I am not aware of a better description of the process of reading *Finnegans Wake* than this one, and, on one hand, it will immediately suggest a contrast to the kind of streamlined, efficient reading experience that news facilitates and promotes. On the other hand, one's perception of great contrast must surely have something to do with one's training as a reader and one's conditioned reader expectations. For Bishop's description could be altered only slightly in order to express what a slow struggle it would be for a reader to construct meaningful connections *between* arbitrarily juxtaposed news stories, no matter how apparently coherent each is within itself. Further, to a similar extent that disparate though individually coherent news stories taken together become increasingly remote from self-evident meaning, disparate passages in the *Wake* do begin to take on some form of coherent story when taken in the aggregate. It is just, as Bishop says, that the story is patently nonsense.

Bishop's example of "coherent nonsense" is the common critical supposition that *Finnegans Wake* is about "a Nordic hunchback with the improbable name of Humphrey Chimpden Earwicker, who is married to someone even more improbably named Anna Livia Plurabelle, and who has committed an indistinct crime involving two temptresses, three soldiers, and unclear quantities of urine in Dublin's Phoenix Park."[17] As Bishop says, readers "cannot not notice"[18] that this scandal story is there once they have read enough of the book, but it is a completely absurd narrative, exactly the kind of thing one is too embarrassed to say at a cocktail party if *Finnegans Wake* comes up.

As another example of the kind of coherent nonsense that the *Wake* wrangles its critics into making, one could consider the recurring numbers 1, 2, and 3, and their association with HCE's crime in the park with two temptresses or three soldiers. While preposterous, such numeric explanations about *Finnegans Wake* remain tantalizing, because it is possible to render some sense of the scope of HCE's scandalous acts by tracking these numbers in their different incarnations. Partridge's *Dictionary of Slang and Unconventional English* reminds us that in late nineteenth and early twentieth-century nursery slang, "number one" denotes "urination," "number two," "defecation," and as a later extension of the first two, "number three" became low slang for "sexual relief, whether normal or self-induced."[19] This may be a useful way of imagining a consistent, but flexible schema that could account for the wide range of HCE's scandalous behavior, at turns heterosexual, homosexual, excretory, and onanistic, as represented in passages such as the following: "they found him guilty of their and those imputations of fornicolopulation with two of his albowcrural correlations" (557.16–17); "How they wore two madges on the makewater. And why there were treefellers in the shrubrubs" (420.07–08); "practising for unnatural coits with . . . two or three philadelphians" (572.24–25); "number two of our *acta legitima plebeia*, on the brink . . . of taking place upon a public seat" (85.12–14); "his

alpenstuck in his redhand, a highly commendable exercise" (85.11–12);
"He had laid violent hands on himself, it was brought in Fugger's Newslet-
ter" (97.30–32). (This last title would be a nice alternative for *Finnegans
Wake* expressed as a newspaper.) One thing we can be sure about, whatever the crime, it was "put in the newses what he did" (196.20): "Perousse
instate your *Weekly Standerd,* our verile organ that is ethelred by all
pressdom" (439.34–440.01).

But Bishop is finally too optimistic when he concludes that such
coherent nonsense is like a dream and, "like a dream . . . will clarify with
interpretation."[20] Perhaps it is slightly more accurate to say that the
Wake offers multiple and often competing narratives of coherent nonsense alongside or superimposed onto one another without often yielding
ground to interpretation or clarification. The very work of the book seems
to be to expose the literal level of narrative as nonsense, to dispel the illusion that scandalous experiences can be reported as easily as the newspaper
narrates them daily. Readers of *Finnegans Wake* are thus like reporters
inching into the smoke and fallout of a linguistic nuclear disaster, Joyce's
"*abnihilisation of the etym*" (353.23), which has exploded what was once
"as human a little story as paper could well carry" (115.36) into "atoms
and ifs" (455.17). Even if one catches a whiff of Adam and Eve's scandalous fall in the last phrase (which is like a simple scandal story that a
paper could carry), Joyce's abnihilisation makes one very skeptical of all
interpreters who would recuperate the little human story back from its
exploded atoms and tentative "ifs" into something so tidy as the human
interest story of Genesis. It seems axiomatic for the *Wake* that the more
strongly a critic asserts a literal level of meaning, reordering the atoms
and ifs into a neat "nuclear" family with a supporting cast, the more completely he or she has betrayed the necessarily atomic experience of reading
the book.

It should not be overlooked how extraordinary it is for a book to make
readers feel that literal explanations of represented experiences are ridiculous, for these are the narratives and plots that we rely upon to order the
multitudinous events and sensations that comprise everyday life. Yet this
is exactly what *Finnegans Wake* does through its creative relationship to
news narratives, by assuming news forms and by deforming them with
content that defies reportage. The more we become aware that you can
only "Wipe your glosses with what you know" (304.F3), the less inclined
we are to accept assertions and stories that "wash" and "wipe" away the
distance between experience and representation, stories that purport to
read the world without any "glasses" or "glosses" on at all. Imagine what
might result if the newspaper generated the same skepticism of its own
basic explanatory narratives that the *Wake* does. *Finnegans Wake* makes

the world of literal reportage seem like nonsense, dramatically reassigning the parts of the text that we think of as a "dream" to the coherent nonsense of explanation, and assigning to the murky representations of experience a sense of reality.

As Joyce told Max Eastman,

> In writing of the night, I really could not, I felt I could not, use words in their ordinary connections. Used that way they do not express how things are in the night, in the different stages—conscious, then semi-conscious, then unconscious. I found that it could not be done with words in their ordinary relations and connections. When morning comes of course everything will be clear again.... I'll give them back their English language. I'm not destroying it for good.[21]

Building upon this principle, Bishop seizes upon the passage in which ALP is depicted "reading her Evening World" (28.20) in order to develop a brilliant mode of reading *Finnegans Wake* as a "book of the dark,"[22] yet he does not pursue the possibility that the *Wake* is itself an *Evening World*, that is, an explicit revision of the *Daily World*, published by a "latter-press" (356.21), which, "in the hurry of the times ... will cocommend the widest circulation and a reputation coextensive with its merits" (356.27–28). *Finnegans Wake* can be understood as a revision of the ubiquitous language of the news, which has monopolized representations of the day, by a *Wake* language, reportage of the night, and as a creative rewriting of the news through the medium of unreportable scandal. We should thus take *Finnegans Wake* seriously when, in one of its many self-reflexive moments, it calls itself "This nonday diary, this allnights newseryreel" (489.35). Indeed, it is a great place "for the seek of Senders Newslaters" (389.36–390.01).

Hugh Kenner, on the other hand, has noted the prominence of the *Wake* as news, suggesting that, "the looking-glass through which the reader of *Finnegans Wake* is conducted is the *Daily Mirror*."[23] However, Bishop's qualification that the looking-glass is dark needs to be added to Kenner's account. Reading *Finnegans Wake* is like trying to read the newspaper through a glass darkly, squinting at lines of newsprint without being able to delineate event or character, or even to tell whether one's eyes have unknowingly drifted into another column or story. Kenner also omits the most consistent theme between the news and the *Wake* by overlooking how replete both are with scandal. Adulterous acts both heterosexual and homosexual, love triangles (and probably quadrangles, too), indecent exposure, incest, masturbation, miscegenation, primal scenes, the scandalous vision of father on the chamber pot, or the revelation of mother's genitals, the Fall of Adam and Eve ("the case of Mr Adams what was in all the sundays" (39.24–25) or "reporterage on Der Fall Adams for the Frankofurto Siding, a Fastland payrodicule" (70.05–06))—the capaciously scandalous *Wake* contains all of these and many more. Although it is by now well established that scandal and guilt are major themes of the book, the relationship of *Finnegans Wake* to the scandal culture of the news has not received enough attention. Collier argues persuasively that *Ulysses* was deeply shaped by divorce reporting,[24] but it has not been sufficiently recognized the extent to which *Finnegans Wake* offers itself as a series of variations on scandalous newspaper themes: "the homedromed and enliventh performance of problem passion play of the millentury, running strong since creation, A Royal Divorce" (32.31–33). The *Wake* is thus "Like the newcasters in their old plyable of *A Royenne Devours*" (388.07).

While the story sung in the *Wake*'s *Night Express* is a story of scandal, revealed but also concealed in all of its varieties, unlike the scandalous material in *Ulysses*, the edges of scandal are blurred in the *Wake*. As Margot Norris argues, "The difficulty of distinguishing 'self' and 'other' makes the status of guilt extremely problematic in the *Wake*. Insofar as Wakean figures are often projections of themselves, the 'other' can be regarded as the guilty self, and the characters' attitudes and comments toward others are often unconsciously self-reflexive."[25] *Finnegans Wake* constantly makes "private linen public" (196.18), negotiating between public outrage and private guilt, between the dominant morality and immoral desire, but in the *Wake* these are not oppositions of self and other. For instance, because *Finnegans Wake* revolves around public outrage over HCE's magnificently diverse disgraces and offense, we are not surprised to find among those gathered to hear Hosty's slanderous "Ballad of Persse O'Reilly" "a halted cockney car with its quotal of Hardmuth's hacks" (42.27–28), nosing around for a good scandal "*From the Buffalo Times of bysone days*" (275.L3) like Harmsworth's reporters. But, consistent with Norris's argument, we *may* be surprised to find that the ballad was produced on "the licensed boosiness primises" (497.24) of "Hosty's and Co, Exports" (497.26), that is, by the boozy innkeeper HCE himself. "[H]e's been slanderising himself" (463.28–29), which raises an interesting question: if one publishes "subtaile ... schlangder" (270.15) behind one's own back, like the subtle serpent in the garden, who may be "shoed for slender" (255.36)? In *Finnegans Wake,* publisher and published-about are often indistinguishable, so scandal is a snake that bites its own tail.

Scandal is a constant preoccupation in *Finnegans Wake*. Students and aficionados of scandal or anybody who merely "adores a scandal when the last post's gone by" (28.17) will run to *Finnegans Wake* as to a "whole school for scamper" (80.35). Its pages may be profitably "skand for schooling" (223.33), because the more one scans for scandal, the more types of scandal one is likely to learn about. Joyce offers a broad education about scandal in its inexhaustible permutations, a veritable compendium of scandal forms and the "pupup publication of libel" (534.17), a "newseryreel" in which scene by scandalous scene rolls through our twilit field of vision without explanation or framing. The four books of *Finnegans Wake* are themselves arranged "In four tubbloids" (219.17–18) and every chapter in each "tubbloid" positions its noteworthy stories in relation to the news. In the name *Finnegans Wake* itself we are perhaps licensed to hear "*Finnegans Week*," or even *Finnegans Weekly*: "Such wear a frillick for my comic strip, Mons Meg's Monthly, comes out aich Fanagan's Weck" (537.33–34).

While Joyce shows that the "Evilling chimbes is smutsick rivulverblott" (538.31), obsessed with scandal [*Revolverblatt* is German for scandal sheet], one can also read of other kinds of news in the *Evening Times* of *Finnegans Wake*. "[G]ossipaceous Anna Livia" (195.04) peruses the paper,

> To see is it smarts, full lengths or swaggers. News, news, all the news. Death, a leopard, kills fellah in Fez. Angry scenes at Stormount. Stilla Star with her lucky in goingaways. Opportunity fair with the China floods and we hear rosy rumours. Ding Tams he noise about all same Harry chap. She's seeking her way, a chickle a chuckle, in and out of their serial story. (28.20–26)

This catalog recalls the diversity of New Journalism as reflected in Chalaby's survey of two pages of the *Daily Mirror*. Like the *Daily Mirror* or *Daily World*, Joyce's *Evening World* contains fashion news, international news, Irish news, entertainment news, market news, news about every Tom, Dick, and Harry, and even a serial story. Elsewhere we find the weather forecast: "Welter focussed. Wind from the nordth. Warmer towards muffinbell, Lull" (324.24–25), or the forecast for Eden: "It is perfect degrees excelsius" (597.31). There are sports updates: "*the first sports report of Loundin Reginald has now been afterthoughtfully colliberated by the saggind spurts flash*" (342.34–36). Of course, it is punctuated ("All halt! Sponsor programme" (531.27)) with occasional advertisements: "Johns is a different butcher's. Next place you are up town pay him a visit. Or better still, come tobuy" (172.05–06) or "When you're coaching through Lucalised, on the sulphur spa to visit, it's safer to hit than miss it, stop at his inn!" (565.33–34). There are even personal ads that are perhaps a little *too* personal: "Jymes wishes to hear from wearers of abandoned female costumes, gratefully received, wadmel jumper, rather full pair of culottes and onthergarmenteries, to start city life together. His jymes is out of job, would sit and write" (181.27–30). Because characters can "check their debths in that mormon's thames" (198.36–199.01) as well as "berths in their toiling moil" (199.02), Joyce's *Evening World* seems to offer everything within the range of the *Morning Times* and the *Daily Mail,* everything between birth and death, tidal information included. All of the newspaper's favorite stories, ad-pitches, themes, and contests are well represented on almost every page: "old the news of the great big world" (194.23–24).

In *Finnegans Wake,* news is truly global and scandal spreads quickly all over the world, representative of technological developments in news dissemination: "In this wireless age any owl rooster can peck up bostoons" (489.36–490.01).[26] The world is made smaller by communication technology and international news, and it is as easy to pick up the news as it is for a rooster to peck up feed. Indeed, in *Finnegans Wake* news takes flight during the night as the "owl globe wheels in view" (6.29–30), and we are not surprised to see a "picture...shown in Morning post as from Boston transcripped" (617.22–23). If there "is an openear secret" (425.16), it "falls easily upon the earopen" (419.15), intent upon "picking up airs from th'other over th'ether" (452.13). Characters constantly "ear the passon" (39.23), hearing stories of passion, and passing them on. In every direction one sails in *Finnegans Wake* (as on the globe), one is bound to land eventually "on the labious banks of their swensewn snewwesner" (372.16–17). That is, you will hear the whispers about "so and so" whether you travel North, East, West, or South across the world or over the lines of the *Wake,* where "The new world presses" (387.36).

Scandal is almost always linked to the news forms that give scandal its structure. In *Finnegans Wake* where there is a scandal, there is a newspaper, newsreel, wireless, or radio nearby. The *Wake* keeps its ears open "allnights" to listen for "the bells of scandal" (483.06) and "to learn from any on the airse, like Tass with much thanks" (489.08–09). It constructs its "newseryreel," invented by Jacques Pathé, as "a nice pathetic notice" (421.33) or as a "Moviefigure on in scenic section. By Patathicus" (602.27) used to "roll away the reel world, the reel world, the reel world" (64.25–26). It also maintains close connection with the radio: "Here! Here! Tass... Havv... Rutter" (593.05–06). There are frequent updates, "As I hourly learn from Rooters and Havers through Gilligan's maypoles" (421.31–32) and "according to rider" (313.11) and other wire services whose reports are anonymous and perhaps annoying: a "wreuter of annoyimgmost letters" (495.02). At times, news is more than annoying, but rather a modern tyrant: "the best tyrent of ourish times" (497.36–498.01).

Joyce is equally concerned with the proprietors of the news who profit from the publication of scandal stories. *Finnegans Wake* is rife with at least "*semperal scandal stinkmakers*" (342.08), who make scandals as readily and routinely as candlestick makers make candles. Chief among the "scandal stinkmakers" in the *Wake* is Alfred Harmsworth, Lord Northcliffe. In *Finnegans Wake,* Harmsworth's *Daily Mail* is read with the devotion of morning prayer ("*Daily Maily, fullup Lace!*" (177.05–06), "Bring us this days our maily bag!" (603.07–08)), an exercise as regular as that of one "who runs his duly mile" (150.05–06), even if it is a "toiling moil" (199.02) because "I'll be so curiose to see in the Homesworth breakfast tablotts" (458.22–23) and to read "the horrible necessity of scandalisang" (188.21).

Finnegans Wake is set in a profitable time to let a "scandleloose" (343.24) for "simple scandalmongers" (514.01) and for "all the scandalmunkers" (95.34) who resembled Harmsworth, but he remains emblematic of all of the others in *Finnegans Wake*. Sometimes the *Wake* refers to the proprietor of the *Daily Mail* by his title, as in "Our pigeons pair are flewn for northcliffs" (10.36). But more often, Joyce plays on malevolent associations of his surname: "felixed is who culpas does and harm's worth healing" (246.31–32). The healing of reputations will surely be required when newspapers graduate from mere "Scandiknavery" (47.21) into harmful "depredations of Scandalknivery" (510.28), a real media hatchet job. "In *Finnegans Wake*, a scandal maker like Harmsworth 'pours a laughsworth of his ill information over a larmsworth of salt'" (137.34–35), so much so that it is worth to be cautious when meeting strangers: "is it any harm to ask, was this hackney man in the coombe, a papersalor...?" (529.18–19).

Finnegans Wake consistently links the news to profit motives. On the street one sees "them newnesboys pearcin screaming off their armsworths" (363.06). Joyce also contrasts the sales figures for newspapers and literature, expressing some envy for the newspaper's sales: "If all theMacCrawls would only handle virgils like Armsworks, Limited!" (618.01–02), suggesting perhaps that if those of his country bought the books of writers like Virgil at the rate they bought the newspapers of publishers like Harmsworth and Newnes, Joyce might be a very rich writer indeed. Shaun scolds Shem for squandering his earning potential by choosing a literary career over a more profitable newspaper career back when he was "a youth those reporters so pettitily wanted as gamefellow" (191.19).

What all of these examples might suggest is that this book, which above most, if not all, others resists explanation, relentlessly references, compares itself to, and holds itself up as form of news. But because *Finnegans Wake* simultaneously shatters the assumption that a reportable level of narrative exists within or may be extracted from its multifarious and enigmatic representations of scandal experience, it stakes out a new space and language for literature relative to news and news technologies. As Wollaeger defines modernism, *Finnegans Wake* attempts to clear a space in the media ecology for more authentic modes of communication. It embarrasses the desire of news to extract reportable events from personal experience, and instead would bring scandal from the distant spheres of news into the intimate space of readers.

Scandalous experiences in *Finnegans Wake* resist generalization or summary and remain singularly and stubbornly localized and particular, like the anecdote for which there can be no mediating context. If readers of *Finnegans Wake* are to give its scandalous particularities their due, they must struggle in individual acts of reading without recourse to generalization or reportage of event or plot. This struggle is anticipated in the book itself. Whereas the *Wake* famously calls for "that ideal reader suffering from an ideal insomnia" (120.13–14), for Joyce the ideal newspaper reader ("if you wil excuse for me this informal leading down of illexpressibles" (357.27–28)), is best situated "whilst . . . idylly turmbing over the loose looves leaflefts jaggled casuallty on the lamatory" (357.20–22). In contrast to stories that might be read in the lavatory, *Finnegans Wake* requires "patience; and remember patience is the great thing, and above all things else we much avoid anything like being or becoming out of patience" (108.08–10).

Instead of feeling, as news readers might, that context and event come more clearly into focus as a news story unfolds, the slow progress of the *Wake* is likely to blur contexts, events, and characters. The news form does all it can to assert that its stories and reports perfectly coincide with experiences and reality. The form of *Finnegans Wake* does all it can to fit a wedge between the experiences it vaguely represents, the experience of reading these representations, and all forms of reportage or accounting for these experiences, whether they are articulated by the *Wake* itself or by readers. Perhaps more than any other book, *Finnegans Wake* impoverishes the level of literal meaning and transfers the burden of coming to terms with the represented particularity of experience to readers. These particular and peculiar experiences must be brought (with difficulty) into the reader's intimate space. The next two sections explore the ways in which *Finnegans Wake* translates the anecdotal concealment and disclosure of scandal into a matter of spatial relations between readers and the experiences of others.

"BY THE WATERS OF BABALONG" (103.12)

In *Conversations with James Joyce,* Arthur Power recalls James Joyce's interest in the Bywaters-Thompson adultery scandal and murder trial:

"Like everybody else Joyce was very interested in the Bywaters and Thompson case of which the English papers were full in December 1922, even *The Times* giving it a detailed report."[27] Frederick Bywaters was a ship's steward and a family friend of Edith Thompson, who was eight years Bywaters's senior and unhappily married to Percy Thompson. Bywaters and Thompson's affair, punctuated by long stretches during which Bywaters was at sea, generated a large volume of letters, mixing the style and feeling of the sensational novels that the couples shared, in some of which Thompson describes secretly administering poison to her husband. After Bywaters returned from his last voyage in October 1922, he surprised the Thompsons on the street and stabbed Percy Thompson to death. When Thompson's letters were discovered, she was tried along with Bywaters for attempted murder, even though an autopsy found no trace of poison in Percy Thompson. Indeed, Joyce, who could be sympathetic about literary fantasy, defends Thompson to Power, painting her as a kind of Madame Bovary: ". . . at the trial she swore she had given her husband nothing, and it was all fantasy written by Bywaters, for her mind was evidently full of the stuff she had been reading, while she wrote those letters to make her seem romantic in his eyes because in turn he used to taunt her with descriptions of his life while on his voyages."[28] Both Bywaters and Thompson were convicted and sentenced to hang. Although Bywaters unquestionably murdered Thompson, the public sympathized with him and saw him as an unwitting pawn of the older Mrs. Thompson. Some newspapers petitioned for a reprieve for Bywaters, but to no avail.[29]

Adaline Glasheen and Clive Hart long ago identified references to Bywaters and Thompson in *Finnegans Wake*,[30] but Vincent Deane has more recently discovered the striking fact that the long stretch of narrative that Joyce referred to as the "plebiscite" (58.23–61.27) "was transcribed directly from an article in the *Daily Sketch* for 14 December 1922, which launched the petition for the [Bywaters] reprieve"[31] into one of Joyce's earliest *Finnegans Wake* notebooks.[32] Readers of the *Wake*, accustomed to scattered references to a given source, are likely to be startled by how extensive Joyce's use of the *Daily Sketch* article was, which gave a full page of "person-on-the-street" reaction to Bywaters's case and sentence.

Not enough has been said about Joyce's rather extraordinary use of a *news* source for so comparatively vast a stretch of *Finnegans Wake*. What does it mean for an author to use newspapers in this way, not simply as a basis for fictional stories, but as an actual structural source? What does it mean to use a relatively disposable and topical source as the basis for a work intended to be monumental as *Finnegans Wake* was, perhaps the first of a new breed of "presswritten epics" (438.18)? How are Joyce's distortions of the source meaningful in ways that reflect upon the news in relation to the *Wake*? As we turn to *Finnegans Wake*'s creative revision of this article, it is crucial to remind oneself of how strange Joyce's transcription and translation of the newspaper should seem. For one thing, its length and extent is out of character with Joyce's usual treatment of sources. As James S. Atherton notes, "[The larger class of Joyce's sources consists of] books from which Joyce took a few words, perhaps only a single word, perhaps a phrase, or perhaps—from some books—as much as a page or two."[33] But the larger problem that the newspaper source poses has to do with the recoverability of information. Atherton concerns himself with literary sources, with *Finnegans Wake* as one literary monument referring to others. But references to Shakespeare, to take an example of a writer whose works are relatively permanent, are drastically different from references to direct phrases and quotations from relatively ephemeral sources such as newspapers in the early days of twentieth century.

More recent genetic study of *Finnegans Wake* has revealed the great extent to which Joyce built his work upon just such ephemeral sources. As Luca Crispi, Sam Slote, and Dirk Van Hulle write, "A great deal of the *Wake*'s verbiage derives from notes taken from a variety of sources (newspapers, books, overheard conversations, etc.). . . . It appears that Joyce was amassing a heterogeneous stockpile of phrases in order to litter his work with all sorts of echoes of the world around him (of course, these echoes are almost impossible to identify without recourse to the notebooks)."[34] This compositional fact raises a number of questions about the extent to which Joyce imagined the sources of these echoes would be recoverable. Did Joyce imagine that his insomniac reader could or would track down references to such ephemeral echoes, or were these sources merely structural scaffoldings for Joyce and meant to fade, like the newspaper itself, out of existence? I think that this is a question that must be left open and allowed to remain suspended over inquiries about Joyce's news sources. However, it seems fair to say that Joyce's compositional practice is deeply conservationist in character, not merely stockpiling phrases that were instrumental for his work, but also creating an idiosyncratic, but perhaps loving, archive or collection of journalistic ephemera in the very same spot where its sources are obscured and forgotten. Here is something of Derrida's repression as "archiving otherwise."

Deane focuses attention on what information the discovery yields about "the origins and nature of Joyce's radically unspontaneous compositional process," but gives less attention to interpretation in the context of *Finnegans Wake*: "Even if we leave aside the intrinsic importance of the Bywaters and Thompson trial and its bearing on our interpretation of the finished text of the *Wake,* Joyce's use of it has implications of fundamental importance of any account of the genesis of the drafts through the notebooks."[35] Bill Cadbury similarly emphasizes the composition and development of this passage, asking "did [Joyce] develop the text in a way that amplifies the Bywaters echoes, beyond preserving the broad overlap of themes?"[36] Cadbury comes to the conclusion (consistent with Joyce's method of addition) that as he reworked his material, "the thematic implications are enriched in ways which also move us away from Bywaters and strictly into the world of the *Wake* itself."[37] However, in an important sense Joyce's revisions never cease to operate in conversation with the scandal culture of news, and, contrary to Cadbury's view, each revision can just as easily be seen as a specific intervention in the media treatment of the Bywaters scandal and related stories.

Published on page three of the *Daily Sketch* for December 14, 1922, the Bywaters article operates through a curious mixture of simultaneous specificity and generality.[38] Of the 22 opinions given (counting the three soldiers as a single unit), only two are identified by name: the dustman, Churches, and the actress, Miss Sheila Courtenay. The actress's name is used, at least in part, to advertise her latest project, "The Car and the Canary" at the Shaftsbury Theatre. However, it is difficult to understand why the paper names Churches, the dustman. We find a similar wrinkle in the logic of identification in the photographs and captions contained in the article. The photographs depict specific individuals, but the captions identify each one by occupation instead of by name: Waitress, Mannequin, Soldier, Sailor, Chef, and so on. On the one hand, the photographs and the occasional proper name seem intended to document the actual existence of the opinion givers, to humanize them, and to legitimize the *Daily Sketch*'s report on the "Remarkable Expression of Public Feeling." On the other hand, the opinion givers' anonymity and the way in which they are identified generically by occupation seems to support the *Sketch*'s pro-Bywaters case in another way, because opinions are prevented from appearing too narrowly those of particular individuals. Rather, they are held up as representative types from all classes in society, from dustmen named Churches to prominent Civil Servants who remain nameless. We find here a pattern of specificity and generality used to support the *Sketch*'s cause, where these qualities are used to balance one another and to mitigate the rhetorical danger of asserting too strongly either the specific or the general. It is, in Benjamin's terms, a newspaper crusade for generating empathy and abstract feeling for Bywaters.

Within the article, "What They Think," passive and active constructions fluctuate in a similar way, emphasizing the strong pronouncements of the opinion givers and deemphasizing the editorial actions of the *Sketch*:

> Opinions were collected by the *Daily Sketch* yesterday from people chosen at random in the City and suburbs, the region of the clubs and the poorer neighbourhoods of the East. Three out of four of those spoken to declared themselves at once heartily in sympathy with the petition.[39]

Strong active verbs apply to the people on the street—They *think,* Three out of four . . . *declared* themselves—while the actions of the *Sketch* shrink from view: were collected by, chosen at random, spoken to. Calling as little attention as possible to the *Sketch*'s active shaping of opinion, it still tries to assert the randomness of the people chosen and the fairness of their geographical distribution, both City and suburb, club region and poorer neighborhoods. One tacit mark of the *Sketch*'s active arrangement is the complete omission of the one-quarter opinion that was, presumably, heartily unsympathetic with the petition.

The *Sketch* uses the opinions to demonstrate sympathy for the petition, but these opinions differ or diverge from the *Sketch*'s instrumental purpose. The commissionaire, the solicitor, and the omnibus driver are the only ones who explicitly support the petition: "Every one will be glad to sign the *Daily Sketch* petition." "Time is short, and your readers should make a point of signing the petition at once." "I heartily support the petition."[40] But several respondents, such as the commercial traveler, the taxi driver, the barmaid, and the chef, say little more than that Bywaters should not die: "I do not believe in the capital sentence." "Bywaters is a silly young fellow, but he ought not to pay the full penalty."[41]

What the *Sketch* relies most heavily upon, however, is a slippage that equates the public's animosity toward Mrs. Thompson with support for Bywaters's petition. In the article's logic, support for the petition means blaming the deceptive older woman for manipulating Bywaters. Most of the evidence that the *Sketch* uses to show support for the petition comes in the form of anti-Thompson feeling and the assumption that the older woman was the puppeteer of an innocent Bywaters, "the unfortunate dupe of an unscrupulous woman."[42] It seems clear, however, that there is a circular route through the newspaper between reporting and recording public opinion. As Deane notes, the newspapers consistently referred to Bywaters in their reports as "the boy."[43] It is unsurprising that the *Sketch* should find so much animosity toward Mrs. Thompson when its reports probably helped to shape this feeling.

The hotel manager provides a good example of the circular nature of scandal reporting, opinion formation, and the reporting of opinion:

> When I read the *Daily Sketch* this morning I was struck with its humanitarian attitude. Personally I believe in the abolition of capital punishment. I hope that Bywaters and Mrs. Thompson will be reprieved, although it is obvious to everyone that the youth was drawn into the crime by the irresistible influence of his lover.[44]

We might say that the *Sketch* first structures its narrative of the Bywaters case to fit into an existing complex of possibly misogynist conceptions and public prejudices, and that what it subsequently records as support for the petition is actually just a measure of how readily the story dissolves into this complex.

In what significant ways, then, does Joyce transform the Bywaters material from the *Sketch*? Cadbury writes, "in its later [draft] versions the plebiscite comes in overall effect to feel more coolly critical of its object than it did in early drafts, embodying far more the public ambiguity about HCE than the way ordinary people on the street felt generally sympathetic to Bywaters and hostile to Edith Thompson."[45] Joyce offers a more richly variegated spectrum of opinion and reaction than the *Sketch* does, refusing to omit one-quarter of the responses for the sake of consistency or for the purpose of swaying readers. But Joyce does not merely create an ambiguous tangle of "jostling judgements of those . . . malrecapturable days" (58.21–22). More importantly, he also modifies the speech and opinions of each person to correspond to his or her special occupation or preoccupation. The *Sketch,* as we have seen, uses specificity only to the degree that it must in order to guarantee that its general assertions rest squarely upon individual thoughts and feelings. In the *Sketch,* it hardly matters whether or not it is a chef who claims, "I do not believe in capital punishment, and I certainly do not think that this boy deserves it."[46] His title, "Chef" only helps to demonstrate the overwhelming solidarity of opinion among different occupations and classes. In the *Wake,* however, each individual is fully pictured in language. The *Wake* attunes one to how uncomfortably the chef's remarks would suit the *Sketch* article if his speech were more germane to and resonant with his individual identity. The chef's individuality and singularity seems to take the fore in Joyce's revision:

> Eiskaffier said (Louigi's, you know that man's, brillant Savourain): *Mon foie,* you wish to ave some homelette, yes, lady! Good, mein leber! Your hegg he must break himself. See, I crack, so, he sit in the poele, umbedimbt! (59.29–32)

Joyce imagines that a chef such as Escoffier, or a devotee of Brillat-Savarin, one who has broken many eggs for the sake of an omelet and who thinks in the idiom of cuisine, might take a more accepting view of the crime than the *Sketch*'s generic chef does. Joyce's chef speaks in his own idiom, however parodic, fulfilling the specificity and the particularity that the *Sketch* gestures toward without really desiring or having any use for it in its larger intentions. In fact, Joyce's chef doesn't tell us much of anything that could contribute to an argument for or against either Bywaters or HCE. His response to whatever instrumental questions have been posed to him is to crack an egg into a frying pan. The anecdotal action embodies an attitude of individual idiosyncrasy, but it never quite assumes the specificity of opinion. Joyce's chef has been asked about the broken egg (HCE is sometimes represented as Humpty-Dumpty), but he responds, as a chef might, by returning an omelet.

In this sense, the chef's opinion is rather useless, but useless in a positive, noninstrumental way. The response might be considered anecdotal because it insists on particularities so tied to the individual character that it resists abstraction or universalization, especially the empathetic and abstract mediating context of the *Sketch* article. Eiskaffier is so much a parody of a chef, so much himself, that his comments cannot be used to support any "side" of an issue at all. In contrast to the highly pragmatic and programmatic news story, which in order to "save" the life of the real person, Frederick Bywaters, the *Sketch* must imaginatively sacrifice so many others, *Finnegans Wake* is deeply noninstrumental in its use of its sources and materials. As one of the "rewritemen" (59.27) of the news, Joyce foregrounds a deep conflict in news between representing real events and representing real people. The *Wake* at times employs the forms, content, and language of the news, but they are all held in suspension. To a degree almost incomprehensible, it assembles information and sources in a way that supports no stable, literal, or reportable narrative, and fulfills no single discernible project or agenda. It is perhaps the ultimate anecdotal text.

Finnegans Wake adopts and adapts the formal course set by the *Daily Sketch,* but it wanders far from its purposes, getting lost in the humor and uniqueness of the existing characters, and creating new characters to fit in among them. The *Wake* mimics the artfully arranged *Sketch* story, but it divorces that arrangement from its original logic of empathetic intention. That is, the *Sketch* offers a form highly charged and driven by specific goals, but Joyce, like the chef who returns an omelet when given an egg, reproduces the form only to undermine the logic that shaped it. Joyce empties out the form of the *Sketch* article by making it useless, unmediated, and incapable of supporting any argument or reportable level of narrative. In Joyce's "plebiscite" the opinion givers are individualized (or anecdotalized) to an extent that their cumulative utterances support no consistent viewpoint or abstraction.

But one of the consequences of this individual complexity is that no clear sense of HCE's specific offense or scandalous behavior can emerge without being contradicted or negated by a competing hypothesis. The same is true for public reaction, ranging from complete condemnation to total exoneration, which prevents any consistent public response from forming. Scandal is evoked only to be held suspended forever, as are its public effects, each held in abeyance as part of a literal level of narrative that *Finnegans Wake* avoids ever establishing.

"YOU'LL DIE WHEN YOU HEAR" (196.05–06): A PATHOS OF SCANDAL

If the development of the "plebiscite" section shifts emphasis from the events of HCE's scandal and its public reception toward a preoccupation with language and the anecdotal representation of character, it also draws the subjects of scandal closer to readers. In the last section we saw the anecdote as resisting the empathy and abstraction of the *Sketch*'s press crusade. Here we find the other crucial function of Benjamin's anecdote: bringing experience into the intimate space of the reader, and thereby setting up the conditions for a pathos of nearness. Consider Joyce's treatment of and continuing sensitivity to one particular subject of scandal, Edith Thompson. The *Sketch* vilifies Thompson at the expense of Frederick Bywaters, but her worst crimes seem to have been like those of Emma Bovary: adultery, and an indulgence in literary fantasy. In 1931, nine years after Joyce took his first notes from the newspapers about the Bywaters case, and long after Bywaters and Thompson were hanged, Joyce returned to the case by incorporating into his notes and into the *Wake* many elements from *The Trial of Frederick Bywaters and Edith Thompson,* which contained a transcript of the public trial and the couple's letters.[47]

Much of this material was compressed into a passage in which Glugg (Shem) and Issy play the parts of Dante's Paolo and Francesca. They enact the roles of Dantean lovers seduced by a book, as Bywaters and Thompson shared sensational novels, but both speak in language that originates almost entirely in Bywaters and Thompson's intimate letters. Joyce thus draws a strong parallel between the literary fantasies of the two adulterous couples. The editors of Joyce's notebooks demonstrate the density of allusion in *Finnegans Wake* to their correspondence by quoting pertinent passages from the Bywaters-Thompson letters:

> I could shake him—no go—no initiative of his own [. . .] oh an ass nothing more.

and all Saturday evening I was thinking about you—I was just with you in a big arm chair in front of a great big fire feeling all the time how much I had won [...] It seems like a great welling up of love—of feeling—of inertia, just as if I am wax in your hands—to do with as you will [...] Darlingest when you are rough, I go dead—try not to be please.[48]

In *Finnegans Wake* these become:

As for she could shake him. An oaf, no more. Still he'd be good tutor two in his big armchair lerningstoel and she be waxen in his hands. Turning up and fingering over the most dantellising peaches in the lingerous longerous book of the dark. Look at this passage about Galilleotto! I know it is difficult but when your goche I go dead. Turn now to this patch upon Smacchiavelluti! (251.21–27)

Joyce cobbles the language of Edith Thompson's letters together with the scene in which Paolo and Francesca commit adultery after reading about Lancelot and Guinevere.[49] Joyce rewrites "Lancelot" as "Galilleotto," evoking Galileo, and thereby adding to the scene of seduction an overtone of amazed discovery, as Galileo must have felt when he discovered new moons. The scene is similar in manner to the way in which Bywaters and Thompson shared romance novels and seemed to fall in love through them, and for both couples, "Love brought us to one death," as Francesca tells Dante.[50] Joyce stresses the crucial place of language in Thompson and Bywaters's romance, emphasizing that they conducted their affair by writing letters and by reading novels in common. In fact, Joyce seems drawn to the extent to which Bywaters and Thompson were readers who let fiction come powerfully close to their lives.

When Dante hears Francesca's story, he is so moved that he swoons and falls. The line in which Dante falls is famous for its imitative, hard-falling consonants: "E caddi come corpo morto cade" [and fell as a dead body falls].[51] Joyce includes an imitative device that resembles Dante's own, perhaps in direct allusion, for the sentences leading up to it strongly recall the blowing winds of Canto V: "As he was queering his shoolthers. So was I. And as I was cleansing my fausties. So was he. And as way ware puffing our blowbags. Souwouyou" (251.36–252.03). He and she both square their shoulders and clench their fists against the wind, recalling Dante's lovers, both accepting the consequences of the Faustian deal they have struck and resembling now the very letters they sent each other, as they blow in the wind ("letters be blowed!" (251.31)), as Paolo and Francesca do. But instead of a hard fall, Joyce's verbal effects evoke a "swoon" that is as soft and pitying as Dante's fall is hard and stunning.

It is well known that Canto V of *Inferno* was among Joyce's favorites in Dante, one of the *Divine Comedy*'s most "dantellising peaches." He memorized long passages from Dante's work and was apparently moved to tears by them, as Alessandro Francini Bruni recalls: "I saw him many times with tears in his eyes after such a reading."[52] Joyce was a reader who let represented experiences into his intimate space. He was perhaps more affected by the pathos of Paolo and Francesca's story than many contemporary news consumers were by the much more proximate story of Edith Thompson and Frederick Bywaters. Accordingly, Joyce removes Thompson and Bywaters from the news reports and reframes them with reference to Dante's sad lovers, putting the news account in close relation to Dante's piteous representation. The effect is a literary echo chamber of swoons within swoons, as Joyce combines Bywaters and Thompson with Dante's Paola and Francesca, both couples originally moved by powerful reactions to romance stories. Joyce thus assembles a series of nested books, each of which opens out to another as readers respond to the pathos of stories and are in turn written about by other writers: it is books, romance and adultery, readers, and pathos all the way down.

Joyce imaginatively connects two scandalous stories that compelled him and stirred his pity in Bywaters and Thompson and Paolo and Francesca. They are structurally parallel narrative situations, each comprised of a record of intimate experience on the one hand, and on the other, an observer, either the character, Dante, or Joyce's narrator, who is surprised to be so suddenly moved by that experience. In each there exists a moment of pathos in which reports and events fall away and leave unframed experiences in their stead, experiences that creep up and spring upon swooning observers. Joyce's recasting of Bywaters and Thompson as Paolo and Francesca models just such a response to the subjects of contemporary news scandal.

But Joyce does more than model the sudden feeling of pity and grief for these subjects. He also invites readers to occupy the observer's position within the model just described. The reader is implicitly next in line in a chain of observers that connects Dante to Joyce, Paolo and Francesca to Bywaters, and Thompson to Glugg and Issy. Here again we might have recourse to Benjamin's pathos of nearness in order to imagine the mechanism of the sudden swoon, to think about how the story of Bywaters and Thompson strikes the narrator with such immediacy, but then opens toward readers as well, offering them the experience of the swoon if they choose to take Glugg and Issy's story into their imaginative space. We can imagine a nested sequence of observer/swooners responding to lovers in which pathos is passed forward through anecdotal episodes like a baton, as depicted in figure 2.1.

Lancelot & Guinevere	Paolo & Francesca	Bywaters & Thompson	Glugg & Issy
↓	↓	↓	↓
Paolo & Francesca →	Dante →	Joyce →	[reader]

Figure 2.1   Nested Reader Responses

The passage gestures outward, toward the reader—"Souwouyou"—evoking at once "swoon," but also a more ominous "so will/would you." In contrast to the empathy in which news culminates (and which the *Sketch* article cultivates), here we are presented with the opportunity for a feeling of immediate experience and pathos. Like Joyce's "Souwouyou," such moments of pathos result when the experiences of others suddenly find their way into one's own space, without buffers of explanation, context, or mediation. The "Souwouyou" is the position that is always offered and the promise always extended to readers of *Finnegans Wake*. But it is also a threat. The "Souwouyou" is the threat of immediate pathos, of erasing the empathetic, abstract, and safe distance of report, and of falling uncomfortably into grief. It has long been a truism that there's lots of fun at *Finnegans Wake* in spite of its obvious reference to death and falling, and while that is certainly often the case, it has not been well enough acknowledged that the premise of the "grand funferall" (111.14–15) lies in the fact that scandalous "partners lovesoftfun at Finnegan's Wake" (607.16), and thus "fell upong one another: and themselves they have fallen" (15.19). In other works, *Finnegans Wake* is as much about grief as gaiety.

More than in any other way, what *Finnegans Wake* offers in relation to the news discourse of scandal, which reports events at a safe but titillating distance, is the invitation to experience and respond strongly to close particulars. The *Wake* writes scandal because scandal is located in the same place that intense personal experience lies; but it removes scandal from its safe distance, requiring that we draw every alien word toward us, into our space and imagination, before we even know what it might mean, to wrestle with it when it provokes our desire to understand it, to let it live in our space for many hours, until flash by little flash, experiences are represented to comprehension, always tentatively, but never without a second and reciprocal experience of reading that brings what the *Wake* reports vertiginously near.

CHAPTER 3

CHARACTER

FINNEGANS WAKE RESPONDS TO NEWS SCANDAL IN PART by liquidating literary character. If it is difficult to tell what scandal has occurred, it is even more difficult to say who was responsible for it. Joyce replaces character with conceptual category, overlapping sets of signifiers, and even, in his notebooks and from time to time in the *Wake,* symbolic figures or sigla. Joyce is singular in the extent of his liquidation of character. Most modernist novelists did not take such extreme measures in this regard. Instead of more or less abandoning it, they were forced to share the category of character within a media ecology where characters were represented with greater and greater profusion every day. This was a challenge of which Woolf was well aware, to return to her for a moment. In her ostensible disputation with Wells, Galsworthy, and Bennett, Woolf positions character as the primary and most necessary ground of modernist innovation.[1] Woolf acknowledges "character-making power" as a central category of cultural production and represents the novel as "a very remarkable machine for the creation of human character."[2] At first glance, she appears to treat the crisis of character to which modernism must respond as primarily a literary problem, suggesting of Edwardian novels that "in none of them are we given a man or woman whom we know."[3] However, her understanding of the challenges confronting modernism are insistently historical rather than merely literary historical, and it is possible to detect material causes that stand behind literary problems. Indeed, even though she represents the Edwardian novelists as culprits, Woolf says, "Our minds fly straight to King Edward," and she cites his period as "the fatal age . . . when character disappeared or was mysteriously engulfed."[4]

The character-creating machine that consolidated its "character-making power" most during this age was not the Edwardian novel, of course, but the press. Of all the ways that the New Journalism emerged to challenge the traditional territories of literary representation, the category of character stands out as a centrally contested space. The press became a major component of what contemporaries began to perceive as a huge character machine, selling visions of character as much as it did reports of world events or political news, often in ways that made representations of character appear inseparable from certain kinds of news and events. Here we can look ahead in the following chapters to Gertrude Stein, who, surveying the dilemmas of the contemporary novelist in 1935, lamented, "since there is so much publicity so many characters are being created every minute of every day that nobody is really interested in personality enough to dream about personalities."[5] Stein seems to privilege personality over character, as though character had once been a mere route to a deeper and richer territory of personality but through the mechanisms of mass media has now become an end in itself. Although it is easy enough to detect irony in Stein's pronouncement, not least because she was so expert at dreaming her own personality in multiple forms in her work, the novelist's dilemma is nonetheless palpable. In the space of character, modernist fiction seems forced to confront its own inescapable part in market economies of supply and demand. The news media floods the market with character, and as a result the market for personalities that the novelist was traditionally privileged to dream about and offer to the public begins to dry up. What is left is a shared media space where character is a key representation to be negotiated in a tense but subtle tug of war.

Of all the modernist novelists, none experimented more closely with the representation of character in news discourse than John Dos Passos. Rather than abandoning character or plumbing psychological depths beyond the purview of newspaper character, Dos Passos experimented with the new forms of character that were becoming pervasive in the media ecology. Dos Passos's *U.S.A.* trilogy can be understood as a major experimental intervention in and disputation with the newspaper's new character economy. Indeed, Dos Passos writes character right on the edge of the news. In the following, I read *U.S.A.* as engaged in a complex and continuous negotiation and power struggle with news discourse over the language of character in the media ecology, one that finally opens out into a class struggle over the language of America itself.

Dos Passos stages an ambitious experiment that imagines what a coherent and sustained novel narrative would look like if it were narrated in the news style. The very length and scope of the project reveals dimensions of news narratives that would perhaps be invisible in any other form, if only because news accounts, while theoretically comprehensive in scope, emerge only piecemeal in newspapers. It is thus difficult to track the aggregate effect of the newspaper's coverage of the world. In contrast, in *U.S.A.* Dos Passos envisions an entire fictional world of characters represented through the reportorial style of news discourse. In this way, the novel estranges readers from its characters' intimate experiences and critiques the overall vision of the world that news discourse slowly overlays upon reality day by day. By making extensive use of news style on the stage of the novel, Dos Passos measures and performs the inadequacy of news discourse for representing character, while also suggesting new possibilities for modernist fiction to articulate experience within a radically transformed marketplace.

There is, of course, a long critical tradition that would account for the perceived "flatness" of characters in John Dos Passos's *U.S.A.* by appealing to the trilogy's stylistic and thematic affinities with news media. Reviewing 1919 for the *New York Times,* John Chamberlain heralded Dos Passos's "Experiment With the 'News' Novel," observing that " '1919' is primarily a 'news' novel. ... It is able to stick as close to the headlines of the newspapers as it does because its characters, after the manner of so many Americans, live in and by the news. ... Because of their living in and by the headlines, Mr. Dos Passos's characters are, sometimes, very flat and transparent."[6] Chamberlain sees Dos Passos as the first novelist to register the extent to which the daily newspaper had percolated into the "universal solvent" for life in the 1930s, replacing the old values of community and church with the daily rhythms of the stock market pages and with rumors of war—in short, with new ways of regulating life and giving it meaning. For Chamberlain, the representations of characters' lives "reflect no deep meaning; even their tragedies pass away as a new crop of headlines calls the world to new news."[7]

Nearly 70 years later, novelist E.L. Doctorow observes that Dos Passos's characters live "below the headlines" in a manner that elaborates upon Chamberlain's own:

> they're presented as ordinaries: their lives can intersect, they can sometimes be charming or sympathetic, but they are always seen from above, as in satire, and all their irresolution, self-deceit, and haplessness, and their failure to find empowerment in love or social rebellion, is unconsoled by the moral structure of a plot. *U.S.A.* has no plot, only the movement forward of its multiple narratives under the presiding circumstances of history.[8]

Doctorow's observation that *U.S.A.* seems plotless, or propelled forward only by historical circumstances, corresponds to Benedict Anderson's argument that the newspaper is a collection of arbitrarily arranged items, which, as we have seen, primarily represents what Benjamin calls the "steady onward clocking of homogeneous, empty time."[9] We might say then that Dos Passos's first intervention in the discourse of character is to sever his characters from the "consolations" of plot that traditionally give characters meaning in novels. This is not to say that *U.S.A.* is truly plotless, for indeed it seems to teem with plot, but rather that Dos Passos does much to cultivate a feeling that his characters exist in isolation from all structures of meaning except for historical contingency, as do the characters in the homogeneous, empty space of the newspaper's columns.

Doctorow and Chamberlain agree that the characters live in relation to the headlines, and there is a sense in which this is literally true. Because the trilogy begins with the first of 68 "Newsreel" sections, when readers begin *U.S.A.* they encounter news headlines and snippets of news stories before any of the narrative content. Melvin Landsberg insists that the Newsreel, Biography, and Camera Eye sections merely enhance the character narratives, viewing these three modes as "supplementing" and "auxiliary devices,"[10] but we may gain much by reversing this hierarchy and understanding the characters as supplementary and auxiliary devices for the Newsreels that dominate from the first page of the trilogy.[11] Instead of merely attending upon the main narratives, the Newsreels "represent a border area where the fictional events within the trilogy shade into the passage of history," as David Seed argues.[12] For Seed, "the Newsreels entangle the reader in a plethora of news-items which resembles the mesh of circumstances that drag down the trilogy's characters."[13]

The Newsreels also represent a much larger and more varied spectrum of historical events and reference points than the other three modes of *U.S.A.* can, increasing the trilogy's field of ironic possibility. For, as Donald Pizer observes, "The juxtapositional richness of the trilogy is ... almost infinite. A modal segment ... may obliquely refer to immediately adjacent different modal segments, to similar kinds of experience in biographies elsewhere in the trilogy, or to similar kinds of experience in other modes elsewhere in the trilogy."[14] Among these modes, the Newsreels represent the greatest number of possible opportunities for "juxtapositional richness" of an historical character. The very sequential arrangement that puts the "Newsreel" first presents the possibility that everything that follows in the trilogy takes place somehow in, by, and below the world of the Newsreel. To this extent, the Newsreels literally as well as figuratively represent the epistemological horizon of the world of the characters.

However, Dos Passos's deepest engagement with news discourse occurs not in the Newsreel sections but rather in the narrative segments of *U.S.A.* Dos Passos experiments by staging a creative confrontation between the overlapping language and conventions of both news and novels, and in effect transforms both. The narrative segments call for us to see the trilogy as a modernist "news novel" whose narrative mode represents the violence or at least distortions that news discourse does to traditional novelistic conventions of character. Thus, what Chamberlain and others have described as the "flat and transparent" quality of Dos Passos's characters in *U.S.A.* only indexes the extent to which news discourse defamiliarizes the qualities of roundness and opacity we are accustomed to in the novel, as well as one's expectation that it will represent life in a way one finds recognizable. The changes in the novel in turn render visible the changes in the use of the American language in the media that Dos Passos wished to expose, which readers come to expect every morning, perhaps without realizing how inadequate it has become for representing character on a recognizably human scale. Here Benjamin's anecdotal terms are again useful. If *Finnegans Wake* denies all abstract contexts that would remove experience from its human scale, then Dos Passos's strategy is much the opposite. Practically nothing is represented on a human scale in *U.S.A.* Instead, characters are seen from Doctorow's great height, almost as mere side effects of news and history. However, it produces an effect that is disorienting and shocking in its own right.

Jean-Paul Sartre offers a brilliant reading of this kind. When Sartre argues, "I regard Dos Passos as the greatest writer of our time,"[15] he does so upon the strength of Dos Passos's engagement with news form, history, and ideology. At first Sartre senses only an "unrelieved stifling" in Dos Passos, making one feel that, "In capitalist society, men do not have lives, they have only destinies."[16] But soon Sartre makes a connection between this effect in Dos Passos and its cause:

> I open *Paris-Soir* and read, "*From our special correspondent*: Charlie Chaplin declares that he has put an end to Charlie." Now I have it! Dos Passos reports all his characters' utterances to us in the style of a statement to the Press.[17]

By writing a novel in the style of a press statement, Dos Passos shapes his characters' experiences into a form that cuts them off from their own humanity, denying them the anecdotal scale that could communicate their experiences to readers. But there is not only a denial of the anecdotal, but also a fatal internalization of the news media's approach to character. News representations of character begin to seep into the language of self-conceptualization. Sartre's example from the *Paris-Soir* about Charlie Chaplin declaring an end to Charlie poignantly illustrates this. Here an actor declares an end to his persona, but it might as well be a person dispassionately declaring the end of his own life.

For Sartre, then, Dos Passos represents a paradoxical world because his characters are at once inside and strangely outside of the "mirror" of fiction.[18] He values Dos Passos's work because it draws us into the mirror with the characters and suddenly casts us out, forcing us to confront how the characters' lives look with and without their own illusions, how they are changed and deadened the farther from their own spaces we are positioned.[19] Dos Passos responds to the dominance of news narratives by importing their style into the novel, the very place we expect to find experience represented. He does so, according to Sartre, because, "He wants to show us this world, our own—to *show* it only, without explanations or comment."[20] Of course, it is difficult to imagine one's life so flattened; but for Sartre, that is Dos Passos's unique achievement. For Sartre, one's life *is* so flattened, and the way in which Dos Passos engages the style of news makes one know it, "until we feel like smashing our destinies."[21]

However, by overemphasizing the extent to which *U.S.A.* coincides with the news style Sartre risks totalizing the narrative operation. What he does not account for in Dos Passos's representation of character are glimmers of intense experience that shine through the news style. These anecdotal glints of experience constitute crucial moments of disorienting "juxtapositional richness" by which Dos Passos intervenes in the representation of character. For instance, Brian McHale demonstrates that in Dos Passos's free indirect discourse there is often a "gap between the characters' perspectives and the mediating discourse," in which we observe that "the voices that speak the characters' stories are understood to have originated in no personified voice, no subject, but in the modes of social discourse themselves and in the socio-cultural situations to which they correspond."[22] So far this is consistent with Sartre's judgment. However, McHale usefully identifies a remainder, a leftover that inheres after we have sorted the voices according to their "modes of social discourse," or "non-literary registers": "Once its situational voices have been isolated and identified, certain residues remain, segments which manifest a specifically 'aesthetic' perspective or sensibility, and are indices of a specifically 'literary' discourse."[23] This is the anecdotal remainder that Sartre ignores, yet it functions to intensify the very effects on character that he was attempting to chart.

It is precisely within this intimate remainder (after the other modes of social discourse are accounted for) that we can identify fleeting attempts to represent the immediate experiences and feelings of characters whose lives are otherwise reported from a great height. The narrative is constituted as reportage shot through with often grim motes of experience and sensory detail; this describes the effect that accrues in moments when we read, perhaps, of a trickle of cold sweat running down the back of a character who is in every other way distant from us. To meet with such an anecdotally rendered detail or sensory effect in a news report would be out of the ordinary; to find it among the pages of a novel should be mundane, but among the character reportage in *U.S.A.* it is arresting or shocking. Dos Passos writes the narrative portions of *U.S.A.* in the language of the newspaper, but shot through with the very language of experience that news discourse and its related discourses of power threaten through both representation and internalization. The narrative mode of *U.S.A.* thus constantly marks the conflict between literary and news discourse in Dos Passos's time, a strategic, premeditated, desperate, and cunning negotiation of reportage and experience.

TWO MORE IN THE CAMPAGNA

Through this negotiation, scenes of sexual excitement emerge as a special type of anecdotal description in *U.S.A.* Such scenes seem to hover between flat reportage and poetical or sensual representation of the kind that McHale characterizes as the literary residue of the trilogy. All characters, regardless of class or situation, may be subject to this mode of narration. Janey Williams: "let her head droop on his shoulder, her lips against his neck. His arms were burning hot round her shoulders, she could feel his ribs through his shirt pressing against her";[24] J.W. Moorehouse: "She used some kind of musky perfume and the smell of it and the slight rankness of cigarettesmoke in her hair made him dizzy and feverish when he danced with her" (165); Charley Anderson: "After he'd given her a rough last kiss, feeling her tongue in his mouth and his nostrils full of her hair and the taste of her mouth in his mouth he'd walk home with his ears ringing, feeling sick and weak" (328).

There are many factors that minimize the significance of such moments of literary residue and anecdotal description. For instance, in *U.S.A.*, sexual encounters almost always result in unwanted pregnancy, venereal disease, or just plain disappointment and loneliness. The descriptions themselves tend to be ambivalent to the extent that readers are usually offered little guidance or perspective to help judge the encounters. Although it is true that there is a higher quotient of sensory detail at such moments than one meets with elsewhere, this is arguably unremarkable to the extent that for the subject of sensual experience it is largely unavoidable. Readers may even feel that these descriptions simply perpetuate and extend the flatness of narrative norm: "well, look what they're up to now." Moreover, Dos Passos almost always minimizes the impact of sensory impressions through polysyndeton, the use of successive conjunctions that in *U.S.A.* tends to flatten and ironize whatever is reported, even sensual descriptions. However, in spite of the ways in which Dos Passos qualifies and reduces the sensual content of such scenes, they remain conspicuous moments of intimate experience and liveliness marked out from otherwise largely flat character narration.

We can dismiss such moments, then, as a special class of description, exemption, or anomaly, but to do so would ignore their important function with respect to the rest of the narrative portions. In order to arrive at a sense of this function, let us consider the scenes between Dick Savage and Daughter that bookend the climactic scene in 1919 in which Dick gets a close glimpse of Woodrow Wilson in Rome. As is so often the case in *U.S.A.*, a scene of great public significance is paired with a private encounter. In this sequence, Dick and Daughter meet outside of Rome, then Dick sees Wilson in Rome, and finally Dick and Daughter meet again, though this time in a way that has been utterly transformed and mediated through the prism of Dick's vision of Wilson.

In the first scene, Dick and Daughter have made a solitary excursion into the countryside outside of Rome. Dos Passos's precedent for this scene seems almost certainly to be Robert Browning's "Two in the Campagna," which also finds a speaker and his love among the wildflowers and the ruins of ancient Rome. The Campagna has already been staked out as a literary site, and Dos Passos recalls, extends, and satirizes this tradition, setting his scene with many of the same trappings that are found in Browning's poem, for instance, a feeling of pastoral removal: "They went up a path over the hills above the town and soon found themselves walking through wet pastures and oakwoods with the Campagna stretching lightbrown below them and the roofs of Tivoli picked out with black cypresses like exclamation points" (674). We seem firmly within the literary mode of Dos Passos's descriptive spectrum, and what follows are attempts at rendering experience in that mode. The narrator becomes the rough equivalent of Browning's speaker, both of whom search for language that can encapsulate sensual experience. Like a poet, Dos Passos engages the senses: Dick and Daughter see the showers moving in, feel the sprinkle of light rain on their hair, and smell the red cyclamens:

> He could smell her sandy hair and warm body and the sweetness of the cyclamens. He pulled her to her feet and held her against his body and kissed her on the mouth; their tongues touched. He dragged her through a break in the hedge into the next field. The ground was too wet. Across the field was a little hut made of brush. They staggered as they walked with their arms around each other's waists, their thighs grinding stiffly together.... They lay squirming together among the dry crackling cornfodder. She lay on her back with her eyes closed, her lips tightly pursed.

He had one hand under her head and with the other was trying to undo her clothes; something tore under his hand. She began pushing him away. (675)

This passage represents a common way in which Dos Passos describes sensual experience. It contains detailed sensory data (the smell of hair and flowers, tongues touching, wet ground, thighs grinding), but retains something of the reporter's distanced accounting (the matter-of-fact narration, the distancing use of conjunctions). The scene itself is already a falling off from the idealized setting of "Two in the Campagna." The ground is too wet for lovers, a nuisance that necessitates a retreat from the natural setting into a considerably less Romantic little brush hut.

Once indoors the scene cannot unfold as it does in Browning's poem. Dick tears Daughter's underwear and she pushes him away, but then promises to give Dick her virginity when they get back to Rome: "They plodded along down the hill through the downpour that gradually slackened to a cold drizzle. Dick felt tired out and sodden; the rain was beginning to get down his neck. Anne Elizabeth had dropped her bunch of cyclamens" (675–76). While the flower is symbolically plucked in Browning ("I pluck the rose/And love it more than tongue can speak"[25]), in Dos Passos it is merely dropped. While for Browning's speaker "the good minute goes," for Dick and Daughter it never even came. And yet the scene has been a short but comparatively paradisiacal sensory respite from the flat urban scenes and talk of the war and its aftermath that dominate this part of 1919. Perhaps it is even fair to say that this is as close to Eden as one gets in Dos Passos, an Eden seen through relatively distant reportage, sensual residue, and ironic anticlimax, yet still evocative of some anecdotal experience that leaves its mark.

But this scene must been taken in relation to the one that follows in order to understand how Dos Passos patiently builds what Pizer calls "juxtapostional richness." The following scene involving President Wilson crucially inverts the orders of experience and mediation that normally govern the narrative world of *U.S.A.* Wilson is primarily a Newsreel and biography figure. Indeed, Dos Passos reserves for Wilson his most unrestrained and bitter satire and disapproval, playing a central role in *U.S.A.* that Landsberg identifies as "Satan in Dos Passos' epic."[26] In the "Meester Veelson" biography, Wilson is (along with Georges Clemenceau and Lloyd George) one of the

Three old men shuffling the pack,
dealing out the cards (570)

The biography of the Unknown Soldier that concludes *1919,* "The Body of An American," is one of Dos Passos's most effective sardonic biographies, alternating between gory descriptions of the anonymous soldier's war-torn body and homey American platitudes. The portrait concludes, "Woodrow Wilson brought a bouquet of poppies" (761).

Along with his appearances in the "Meester Veelson" and "The Body of an American" biographies, Wilson is mentioned frequently in the Newsreel sections: "after a long conference with a secretary of war and the secretary of state President Wilson returned to the White House this afternoon apparently highly pleased that events are steadily pursuing the course which he had felt they would take" (510); "PRESIDENT HAS SLIGHT COLD AT SEA" (572); "the mistiness of the weather hid the gunboat from sight soon after it left the dock, but the President continued to wave his hat and smile...." (643); "PRESIDENT EVOKES CRY OF THE DEAD" (649); "2000 passengers held up at Havre from which Mr. Wilson embarked to review the Pacific fleet, but thousands were massed on each side of the street seemingly satisfied merely to get a glimpse of the President" (745).

Of this handful of headlines, the most important one for my purposes concerns the thousands of people "seemingly satisfied merely to get a glimpse of the President." "Seemingly satisfied" admits that it is not absolutely clear what onlookers feel when a figure such as the president, who to most people is primarily a media figure, enters into the intimate space of one's own lived experience. The ambiguity evidences uncertainty about what exactly happens when the world of news reportage, from which, in Benjamin's terms, the empathetic newspaper reader imaginatively travels out, instead suddenly intrudes with unexpected nearness into one's intimate space. The headline thus calls attention to the very mediation of experience in which Dos Passos wishes to intervene on a much larger level, and it is significant that just after the ironic Eden scene between Daughter and Dick, he positions Dick as a presidential onlooker during Wilson's visit to Rome. As such he assumes a position identical to the one the Newsreel headline evokes, but while in the newspaper the position is revealed as an epistemological limit for the journalist, in *U.S.A.* Dos Passos can interrogate this ambiguity:

> Mr. Wilson's silk hat stood up very straight against all the time-eaten columns and the endless courses of dressed stone. "Yes," replied Mr. Wilson, "it is the greatest pride of Americans to have demonstrated the immense love of humanity which they bear in their hearts." As the President spoke Dick caught sight of his face past the cocksfeathers of some Italian generals. It was a grey stony cold face grooved like the columns,

very long under the silk hat. The little smile around the mouth looked as
if it had been painted on afterwards. The group moved on and passed out
of earshot. (677)

Here the world that is normally mediated, abstract, and reported converges with Dick's intimate world to form an experience, but it is one
first of disorientation and later of terror. Wilson's silk hat stands out conspicuously against the columns and the dressed stone, which contrasts
further with Wilson himself, whose face is "grey stony cold" under the
hat. There are contradictions between Wilson's appearance and his words
as well. He speaks of the immense love of humanity that the Americans
have demonstrated, but he seems to lack any human qualities himself;
his face is grooved like the time-eaten columns and his smile appears like
something painted on afterward. The description of the smile—"a little
smile around the mouth"—contains an odd dislocation, as though the
smile and the mouth are neither physiologically connected nor animated
by human intention. Dick's sense that Wilson's smile has been painted on
afterward conjures powerful feelings in him of artifice, lifelessness, and
deception. There is an unsettling retrospection suggested in "afterward"
in a scene narrated entirely from the perspective of the present. But the
smile may be even more terrifying than fraudulent or unsettling because
the grotesque image contrasts the warmth we associate with smiles with
the lifeless face of the president. The president who is empowered to evoke
the cries of the dead in the newspaper and to bring a bouquet of poppies to the Unknown Soldier's funeral appears in Dick's space rather like
an inanimate thing, neither living nor dead, with the flesh of a stone
column.

Dick has had the chilling experience of encountering a figure
whose actions and powers are continuously evoked as real in the daily
news, only to discover that the figure is reptilian in person. He is
shocked by his unmediated experience of the president's appearance and
speech. To Daughter in the following scene he describes, "A terrifying
face, I swear it's a reptile's face, not warmblooded" (677). He implores
Daughter, "Oh, Christ, let's stay human as long as we can . . . not get reptile's eyes and stone faces and ink in our veins instead of blood" (677–78),
evoking perhaps another Victorian poem, this time Matthew Arnold's
"Dover Beach": "Ah, love, let us be true/To one another! for the world,
which seems/To lie before us like a land of dreams,/. . . Hath really neither joy, nor love, nor light."[27] When Dick observes that the president has
ink in his veins instead of blood, he comes close to articulating that what
gives the president the appearance of life, his substance, is mediation or
newsprint itself.

If Dick has just learned that reportage makes the reptile appear human, readers of *U.S.A.* have known all along that the opposite is also true. Dos Passos's reportorial mode makes human characters into reptiles, and the scene in which Dick's sexual desire for Daughter is finally realized is narrated in reptilian fashion:

> "To hell with them all," said Dick, throwing his arms around her.
>
> In spite of the hot rum, Dick was very nervous when he took his clothes off. She was trembling when he came to her on the bed. It was all right, but she bled a good deal and they didn't have a very good time. At supper afterwards they couldn't seem to find anything to say to each other. She went home early and Dick wandered desolately around the streets among the excited crowds and the flags and the illuminations and the uniforms. (678)

Despite all of its disappointments and its ironic contrast to Browning's love scene in the Campagna, the scene directly preceding Dick's vision of Wilson is far richer in sensory detail and more evocative of intimate experience than this impoverished scene that directly follows the vision. Here, Dick's nervousness and excitement from seeing the reptilian Wilson seeps into his sexual encounter with Daughter and even outlasts this encounter, spilling out into the "excited crowds" in the streets of Rome; it is a reptilian form of excitement that seems to run through Dick and the entire city. Although Dick has just implored Daughter to stay human as long as they can and to keep blood in their veins instead of ink, their sexual encounter as described is little more than a bloodletting. It is as though Dick has internalized the newspaper's conception of character, as Sartre recognized in Chaplin.

Dos Passos's defiance of what one expects of character description and narration in fiction helps to uncover exactly what one does and does not expect from newspapers. For instance, if there is a disparity in news discourse between what is experienced and what is reported, we may attribute that to the pragmatic character of news discourse. It would be foolish, the thinking goes, to expect news discourse to be responsive and attentive to the minutiae of experience in the fashion of a novel. We may compartmentalize the representation of experience into generic categories: we expect novels to shape themselves faithfully around the contours of experience, while we accept that news discourse will reasonably reduce experience into supposedly manageable accounts. But *U.S.A.* exposes the roots of such rationalization by pointing out the spurious distinction between news and novels. Dos Passos demonstrates that news and novels cannot be differentiated, and that we only try to do so at our own peril. He shows that our expectations are rooted in a false binary that may only finally condition us to accept narratives that erase experience. By constructing the novel as a supplementary repository for experience, we tacitly assent to the bleeding out of experience in the public sphere of news discourse. Benjamin, as we have seen, argues that this process begins to restrict the ability to have meaningful experiences in the first instance, and Dos Passos represents this with horrific effect in the Dick and Daughter Rome sequence, and elsewhere in *U.S.A.*

Dos Passos's interrogation of the "seeming satisfaction" of the onlookers who glimpse the president makes an ideological intervention as well. Precisely because we expect so little experiential content in news discourse, ideological realities can all the more easily pass through realistic narratives such as the news narratives in order to appear identical with reality. In other words, the narrative expectations we have for impoverished experience in news open a space for ideological contingencies to materialize as actual and inevitable, reifying them, in Lukács's terms. Like Wilson's stone face, which will resemble flesh in the photographs of the next day's newspaper, ideologies attached to news characters can be represented on the same experientially impoverished narrative plane on which every other facet of daily reality gets narrated and reproduced. Drawing deeply on the conventions of realistic character description, news allows ideologies associated with news figures to appear to inhabit the same plane of reality in which events and experiences unfold and within which we imagine ourselves to exist. It is only in rare moments of shock and disjuncture that the nonidentity of reified character and experience opens to momentary view.

U.S.A. intervenes in the rationalizing and enabling binary between news and novels by forcing the realization that there are no intrinsic ways of distinguishing news from literary representation. No matter how deeply we might rely on the generic distinction or how strongly it might condition our narrative and experiential expectations, the distinction is an illusion that we maintain at potentially disastrous expense. Thus, while Juan A. Suárez can, on one level, convincingly argue that Dos Passos sought to "muffle [the] noise" of everyday life and popular culture and found in commercial culture only "alienation, uprootedness, and mass deception,"[28] on another level, Dos Passos dismantles the false distinctions between the novelistic and the commercial or popular upon which such contentions rely. A more accurate way of describing Dos Passos's project may be to say, as Michael North does, "Dos Passos was thus politically and socially mistrustful of the very techniques he put to such innovative use in *U.S.A.* His ambivalence presents an opportunity, however, to investigate the complex relationship of aesthetic modernism to the larger modernity of which it was a part and which it helped in turn to shape."[29] By collapsing his narrative mode with the conventions of news, or rather, by falling just short of collapsing them in such a way that one recognizes an anecdotal residue that can only be described as vestigially novelistic or sensuous, Dos Passos grounds both news and modernist fiction in a single, indivisible, and irreducible language whose tensions can, at its best moments, generate productive shock. By carefully engulfing novelistic character in *Erlebnis* and simultaneously investing news character with unsettling glimmers of *Erfahrung*, Dos Passos's equation for the modernist novel is capable of producing a terrible pathos of nearness that he represents through the very process and using the very means of its own diminishment.

SACCO AND VANZETTI MUST DIE

For Dos Passos the idea that the language of character can be shaped either in complicity with or resistance to the impoverishment of experience or *Erlebnis* finally maps onto a larger analysis of language that considers the determining institutional and ideological conditions themselves. The struggle over the language of character within the new media ecology does not merely define the position of the modernist novelist, but it also represents a linguistic and ideological struggle at the heart of class conflict itself. That is, the modernist novelist's struggle to use language in this media ecology parallels Dos Passos's representation of class conflict in America; both may be understood as the relentless struggle by the powerful and the powerless alike to wield and control a single, unstable language. For Dos Passos, the powerful continue to pervert the radically and distressingly malleable language of America for the purposes of domination, while the powerless seek to reinforce and rebuild the language of freedom upon which America was said to be founded. To the extent that access to the power to shape the language of America is obviously unequal, Dos Passos represents those who live "below the headlines" in intense struggle with government and corporate power and their linguistic complicity with news discourse. For Dos Passos, literary struggle and class struggle find a kind of equivalency in the imperative to intervene in increasingly mass-mediated language. In this way, Dos Passos's narrative technique looks much like Benjamin's theory of art. Both believe that ideologically destructive uses of language undermine meaningful experience and its potential communication, and both believe that revolutionary interventions in the ecology of language can provoke a shock that is the precondition of awakening and, thereafter, potential amelioration.

Nowhere is the complicity of government and corporate power with news discourse more apparent than toward the close of *The Big Money*, when the Newsreels, Camera Eye, and narrative portions converge around the Sacco and Vanzetti case. Here, Dos Passos illuminates America as two unequal nations whose relationship can only be negotiated through a common language, one that is assumed to bind them, yet no longer does, and is more often used to occlude injustice and inequality than to expose it. Camera Eye 49 thus concludes with Dos Passos's autobiographical persona desiring and intending to

> rebuild the ruined words worn slimy in the mouths of lawyers district-tattorneys collegepresidents judges without the old words the immigrants haters of oppression brought to Plymouth how can you know who are your betrayers America. (1136)

Here different authority figures are bound together because each betrays the language of liberty and revolution upon which the speaker imagines America was founded. The project he envisions is one of linguistic reappropriation and reconstruction.

One of the "collegepresidents" Dos Passos has in mind is surely Woodrow Wilson, onetime president of Princeton University, elected to the U.S. Presidency after he promised to keep America out of World War I. But the more proximate referent for "collegepresidents" above is A. Lawrence Lowell, president of Dos Passos's alma mater, Harvard University. Lowell was part of the advisory committee assembled by the governor of Massachusetts to determine whether Sacco and Vanzetti deserved a new trial. When the committee advised against a new trial, Dos Passos published "An Open Letter to President Lowell" in the *New York Times* and the *Nation*. The case, he wrote, "has become part of the world struggle between the capitalist class and the working class, between those who have power and those who are struggling to get it. . . . Are you going to prove by bloody reprisal that the radical contention that a man holding unpopular ideas cannot get a free trial in our courts is true?"[30] By combining Wilson and Lowell into "collegepresidents" who contribute to the "ruined words," Dos Passos allows the betrayals of 1919 surrounding World War I to echo and reverberate forward through the years to merge with the betrayals of *The Big Money* surrounding the Sacco and Vanzetti case.

There are other significant intermodal juxtapositions among the sections that comprise the Sacco and Vanzetti sequence. The Camera Eye section that concludes with America's "ruined words" is followed by

Newsreel LXV, the last item of which reports at length the grotesque fate of a factory worker employed to test the viscosity of a lubricating oil:

> One morning about a year later Smythe cut his face while shaving and noticed that the blood flowed for hours in copious quantities from the tiny wound. His teeth also began to bleed when he brushed them and when the flow failed to stop after several days he consulted a doctor. The diagnosis was that the benzol fumes had broken down the walls of his blood vessels. (1137)

The account goes on to detail Smythe's unimaginable fate, which culminates in 18 months of transfusions and unstanchable bleeding, during which, "up to eight hours before his death, the complaint recited, he was conscious and in pain" (1137). Only the graphic description of the Unknown Soldier's mauled body in the concluding biography of 1919 compares with the description of Symthe's condition: "The blood ran into the ground, the brains oozed out of the cracked skull and were licked up by the trenchrats, the belly swelled and raised a generation of bluebottle flies" (760). Running blood merges the fates of the soldier who dies in a war fought to "save the Morgan loans" (89) and the fate of the factory worker who is sacrificed to industry in the postwar Big Money boom.[31]

Through these juxtapositions, Dos Passos builds a vision of language and power through shocking adjacencies, but a major element of his analysis also involves representing the rapid character change of Mary French from an art gallery attendant to a social activist who struggles to save Sacco and Vanzetti. Just after the grotesque and prolonged description of Smythe's sad fate ends, the narrative jarringly turns to Mary French, and her section commences this way:

> The first job Mary French got in New York she got through one of Ada's friends. It was sitting all day in an artgallery on Eighth Street where there was an exposition of sculpture and answering the questions of ladies in flowing batiks who came in in the afternoons to be seen appreciating art. After two weeks of that the girl she was replacing came back and Mary who kept telling herself she wanted to be connected to something real went and got herself a job in the ladies' and misses' clothing department at Bloomingdale's. (1137)

Most readers will be unable to ignore the ironic juxtaposition of an industrial accident with privileged women in an art gallery, but like arbitrarily juxtaposed items in a newspaper, the significance of the connections seem at first intangible. Yet the Smythe passage and this one connect through adjacency, and they also startlingly juxtapose through the word "flow."

Smythe's "blood flowed for hours in copious quantities" and the "flow failed to stop after several days." Mary French, slowly becoming sensitized to labor injustice and gradually moving away from her mother's complacent world, ministers to the ladies in "flowing batiks" in the art gallery. That the dresses are "batiks" seems especially significant in the context of Dos Passos's Smythe/French grouping. Batik cloth is selectively treated with wax before it is dyed. The waxed portions resist the dye in what is known as a "resist technique," resulting in a patterned cloth that might be characterized as decoration by imperviousness. It is tempting to read batik as a textile metaphor that glosses the insulated art gallery in which Mary French works, one selectively buffered into pleasant patterns. Mary French senses a reality beneath the wax of her own insulated existence, but she comes no closer to scratching through it when she exchanges her gallery job for a job at Bloomingdale's.

However, in the course of this Mary French section, Mary is transformed from a Bloomingdale's worker with a guilty conscience to an outspoken activist and publicist, determined to save Sacco and Vanzetti. Mary French's struggle is represented in large measure as a struggle with the language of the justice system and the press that condemn Sacco and Vanzetti. Her primary attempts to intervene come, not surprisingly, through writing and speaking: "She wrote articles, she talked to politicians and ministers and argued with editors, she made speeches in unionhalls. She wrote her mother pitiful humiliating letters to get money out of her on all sorts of pretexts" (1148). The challenges and difficulties that Mary French now faces are strange to her, and they trickle from her days to disturb her dreams. In one dream, scraps of a typewritten sheet contain a crucial message she cannot decipher: "she was trying to put together pieces of a torn typewritten sheet, the telegram was of the greatest importance" (1149). This nightmare and Mary French's urgent speaking and writing chimes suggestively with the image of "ruined words" in Camera Eye 49:

> pencil scrawls in my notebook the scraps of recollection the broken half-phrases the effort to intersect word with word to dovetail clause with clause to rebuild out of mangled memories unshakably (Oh Pontius Pilate) the truth. (1135)

Like Mary French's struggle with language and the torn typewritten telegram in her dream, the scraps of recollection, broken halfphrases, and mangled memories frustrate the Camera Eye persona's efforts to write what he imagines to be the truth. Mirroring Mary French in his total commitment to saving Sacco and Vanzetti from execution, the Dos Passos persona must try to write "truthfully" in face of all the institutions that wield language more powerfully than he can, those who have "ruined" the words that once were used by America's immigrant "haters of oppression." Like the broken materials of Mary French's dreams, "scrawls" and "scraps" are the materials out of which the Camera Eye persona must rebuild the shattered image of the America. The struggles of Camera Eye, or the authorial persona, thus begin to parallel more and more exactly the struggle that takes place on the level of character, and these levels seem ever more closely connected and equivalent through the struggle for representational power that *U.S.A.* stages simultaneously and multidimensionally.

In Camera Eye 50 one finally feels the full weight of newsprint over scraps and scrawls:

> they have clubbed us off the streets they are stronger they are rich they hire and fire the politicians the newspapereditors the judges the small men with reputations the collegepresidents.... (1156)

At this point, the worlds of the Camera Eye and Mary French seem more than merely parallel or equivalent. Improbably, parallel lines converge: the different narrative sections are not only held together by the Newsreel that cements their themes and interests together, but also by the suggestion that the Camera Eye persona has protested alongside Mary French and was clubbed off the same streets from which she too had been clubbed: "A cop was cracking her on the hand with his club" (1155). The two parallel but usually separate worlds of the Camera Eye and the main narratives are brought together here through the cracking of a club. The violence of the police officers and the execution of Sacco and Vanzetti seem literally to warp the narrative levels and spaces in *U.S.A.* until the Mary French narrative, the Newsreels, and the Camera Eye sections seem much more than merely juxtaposed; rather, they seem vividly simultaneous, as the exigency of the historical experience they recount pulls them into spatial and temporal coincidence. Although facts and elements of history are collected and deposited in various ways in the subjective memory of the Camera Eye, in the imaginative recasting of history in the Mary French narrative, and in the actual historical headlines of the Newsreels, it is in the extent to which these carefully delineated narrative worlds finally collapse into one another under the weight and pressure of historical catastrophe that history seems most powerfully constellated in *U.S.A.* as well as accessible to the reader's experience. The smashing together of narrative levels is calculated to unsettle readers where they sit.

At the precise moment in which the Camera Eye, Mary French, and the Newsreel sections collapse into one, the United States is torn in two. That is, when *U.S.A.* seems at its most highly integrated, its sections mashed together by the catastrophe of Sacco and Vanzetti's deaths, Dos Passos reveals the cleft between strata of power in the trilogy's namesake, America: "they have clubbed *us* off the streets," begins Camera Eye 50 [emphasis added]. This "us" unites the hitherto separate and parallel modes of the trilogy. It may also be a play on the theme of this Camera Eye section, that there are two Americas, one rich and one poor, one triumphant and one beaten. *U.S.A.* fractures into US and us, upper and lower cases, upper and lower classes: "all right we are two nations" (1157). The two nations inhabit different spaces and they have different relationships to language: "the men of the conquering nation are not to be seen on the streets [...] the streets belong to the beaten nation [...] we stand defeated America" (1158). The conquering nation has "turned our language inside out" and "have taken the clean words our fathers spoke and made them slimy and foul" (1157). But just as Sacco and Vanzetti's executions have drawn together Dos Passos's separate language modes in the trilogy, they also reinvigorate the words of the beaten nation, words descended from "the old American speech of the haters of oppression" (1157): "the men in the deathhouse made the old words new before they died" (1158). Because the language of America is deceptively self-identical, cases like Sacco and Vanzetti's can bring the differences within the common language and between its different users to light.

So this powerful Camera Eye section is inconclusive because language itself is always being negotiated, but it is also literally inconclusive because, like many of the Camera Eye sections, it is unpunctuated:

we stand defeated America

This remarkable attempt at a conclusion stands alone, trying to force a moment of recognition, to settle the negotiation of language, to freeze the trilogy in the instant of its deepest nadir. But the language of the Camera Eye and the language of the news are a common language. They bleed together, and *U.S.A.* continues to illustrate the endlessness of linguistic negotiation. The Camera Eye persona cannot stem the tide of this language, and it slips out of his grasp and control and runs into a statement to the press that Newsreel LXVII joins already in progress:

when things are upset, there's always chaos, said Mr. Ford. Work can accomplish wonders and overcome chaotic conditions. When the Russian

masses will learn to want more than they have, when they will want
white collars, soap, better clothes, better shoes, better housing, better living
conditions

> *I lift up my finger and I say tweet tweet*
>> *shush shush*
>>> *now now*
>>>> *come come* (1159)

The momentarily and temporarily powerful voice of the Camera Eye persona morphs into the voice of Henry Ford, the figure emblematic of the
Big Money era and ethos who casts a long shadow from the early narrative
and Newsreel sections of *The Big Money*, and from the biography, "*Tin
Lizzie*." All of a sudden, "things" are merely "upset." But there is little
cause for concern, because the American work ethic and economic system can and will provide for everybody, even the distant Russian masses
and their anticipated consumerist desires, who here simply displace the
protesters freshly beaten off of the Boston streets. The place where things
are upset is pushed off, distanced, exported half the world away. In the
transition to the ensuing song lyric, it is almost as though Mr. Ford
becomes the "I" and explicitly urges everybody to "shush shush" with
his finger to his lips. Those upset people are now addressed as children,
implored to be quiet with an appeal to self-evident common sense: "now
now/come come."

   The renegotiation and containment of the decisive but fleeting Camera
Eye pronouncement of defeat continues into the subsequent biography section. "*Poor Little Rich Boy*," the biography of William Randolph
Hearst, which finally culminates the sequence revolving around Sacco
and Vanzetti. Placed here, the biography reinforces the coercive power
of news when it repeats the words of authority, and it also represents
the American language as a field of common language that means different and even opposite things according to the class and wealth of its
speakers. Dos Passos represents Hearst as an outsider to the real world
precisely because of his extraordinary wealth: "All his life Mrs. Hearst's
boy was to hanker after that world/hidden from him by the mist of
millions" (1162). The "gilded apronstrings" (1162) condemn Hearst
to separation, suggesting that Hearst's wealth dominates him like the
overbearing mother of a poor little rich boy. Hearst is drawn to the news
industry precisely because, "Newspapermen were part of the sharpcon-
toured world he wanted to see clear, the reallife world he saw distorted by
a haze of millions, the ungraded lowlife world of American Democracy"
(1163).

The news industry seems like a lens that might bring the world into focus for Hearst, but rather than providing an objective entrance into the real world, it is a lens that changes the very subject upon which it is trained. Every attempt to reflect the world produces instead a mere representation of the world, and the news representation of the world changes the world and pushes it even farther away from Hearst. For example, consonant with Harmsworth's ambitions, Hearst's papers appear to touch every point in the lives of the lower classes from which Dos Passos pictures Hearst barred and for which he lusts; the papers represent the

> lowest common denominator;
> manure to grow a career in,
> the rot of democracy; Out of it grew rankly an empire of print. (1164)

Hearst even democratically ran "revelations about Standard Oil," exposing that "the trusts were greasing the palms of politicians in a big way" (1166–67):

> (His fellowmillionaires felt he was a traitor to his class but when he was taxed with his treason he answered:
> *You know I believe in property, and you know where I stand on personal fortunes, but isn't it better that I should represent in this country the dissatisfied than have somebody else do it who might not have the same real property relations that I may have?*) (1167)

What appears to be a representation of and for the dissatisfied turns out to be a representation to the dissatisfied. Hearst's exposés would seem to make him a class traitor, but Dos Passos reveals Hearst as a hidden patriot for the winning half of a divided America.

The representation of struggle between powerful and powerless reaches its peak between the final Camera Eye section (dealing with the Harlan County miners' strike) and the biography of energy baron Samuel Insull, in which the final unpunctuated line of the Camera Eye runs into the biography's title after a short blank space: "we have only words against/*Power Superpower*" (1210). Donald Pizer reads "[t]he startling thrust of meaning across the modal barrier" as a privileged point with purchase upon the entire trilogy's meaning, "a crystallization of theme and form in the work as a whole": "Words are all we have against power, and power extends through the economic and political system from a county sheriff to an Insull."[32] It is a powerful moment of modal crossing, but Pizer perhaps overemphasizes it because the unpunctuated Camera Eye and some Newsreel sections frequently spill over into other sections, as we have seen when Camera Eye 50 runs into the Newsreel that begins with Henry Ford's press statement. To privilege this particular crossing as a crystallization of the theme in *U.S.A.* may be harmfully to hypostatize language and power in an oppositional fashion that is often resonant at the level of the trilogy's theme, but at odds with Dos Passos's underlying method. This method, as we have seen, relies upon the crucial tension between, on the one hand, "words against/*Power Superpower*" and on the other "strangers who have turned our language inside out who have taken the clean words our fathers spoke and made them slimy and foul" (1157); in other words, while there may be only words against power and superpower, it is the same language that *Power Superpower* also simultaneously speaks, co-opts, and corrupts.

Thus, while *U.S.A.* represents an oppositional relationship between these two countries on the narrative level, the trilogy's form and modes of representation are not reproductive of this opposition. Rather, we see different strata of power productively engaged in struggle and disputation of the same single language, in the same way that Dos Passos self-consciously sculpts his narrative out of the common language and media space he shares with the news. While the narrative may represent Hearst in starkly oppositional terms, the narration is built upon an ongoing engagement with the language Hearst represents. We can here draw a thread through Benjamin, Joyce, Woolf, and Dos Passos, and ahead to Stein, for despite occasional claims or representations of opposition to news discourse in their texts, each is in reality sensitively engaged in a deliberate and necessary negotiation with news within a shared media sphere, and, moreover, motivated at all points by a desire to intervene strategically in the place and kind of experience represented there.

MARY FRENCH, C'EST MOI

As we have seen with Woolf and Joyce in their different ways, Dos Passos intervenes in the contested ground of character that drew modernist fiction into ever-greater contact and competition with news discourse in the early twentieth century. He does so by drawing upon the reportorial style of the newspaper to describe characters over an extended length of narrative fiction. *U.S.A.* achieves its disorienting and sometimes shocking effects at once through Dos Passos's draining of the traditional experiential content readers expect in character narratives, but also by maintaining just enough (or more strictly speaking just too much or just too little) residue of anecdotal experience so that the narrative portions become doubly unsettling. By doing so, Dos Passos not only exposes the impossibility of making generic distinctions between newspapers and fiction, but also demonstrates how cultural expectations have been destructively conditioned, internalized, and reproduced by these generic expectations. To the extent that generic distinctions help to parcel experience out to novels and allot to news discourse a reportage drained of experience, these distinctions radically lower cultural expectations about the relative priority, place, and necessity of experience in the public sphere, thus contributing to what Benjamin sees as part of the overall reduction in all forms of meaningful experience.

Moreover, the literary modernist's struggle with news over the language of character is closely paralleled to the larger class struggle in America, a crucial dimension of which is represented as the power to define what the language of America means and how it will be used. This language itself— of freedom, justice, and equality—is tied fundamentally to categories of human experience, and to this extent at least, Dos Passos's struggle for the language of character and experience finds its equivalency in the American class struggle to guarantee an experiential understanding and practice of the democratic language of America. Dos Passos's own practice comes full circle as *U.S.A.* finally collapses the worlds of the authorial Camera Eye persona and narrative sections of Mary French, reinforcing Dos Passos's vision of their convergent goals, as well as his identification with the condition of his own experientially impoverished characters.

CHAPTER 4

IDENTITY

IF THE CATEGORY OF IDENTITY UNDERLIES AND INFORMS the representation of character in Dos Passos, it is explicit and thematized in the work of Stein. No literary modernist was more attuned to the effects that news media were beginning to have on identity than Gertrude Stein. Stein's preoccupation with archiving her own past and projecting a public identity, but also, crucially, with suppressing or repressing certain features of her past and identity that may have troubled her, helped sensitize Stein to the peculiar pattern of representation and suppression that she identified at the base of assertions of identity in the newspaper. After the success of *The Autobiography of Alice B. Toklas,* Stein began to make a distinction between entities, which she defined as autonomous, and identities, which were seen as troublingly relational: "[People] know they are they because their little dog knows them, and so they are not an entity but an identity."[1] This distinction formed a platform for a series of opposed terms with positive and negative charges that Stein began to use more or less interchangeably. As Bob Perelman summarizes, "On one side there was genius, the masterpiece, the present, entity, the human mind, and on the other, society, newspaper writing, memory, identity, human nature."[2] This chapter argues that Stein's rejection of identity in her 1930s writing, and especially in *Everybody's Autobiography,* can be accounted for in her own rereading of *The Autobiography of Alice B. Toklas* side by side with the daily newspaper and her subsequent recognition that modern identity has become structured like a news story.

Stein was particularly attuned to deep problems of identity, temporality, and narration that she eventually observed in common in both news discourse and in her own autobiographical efforts. Stein discovers shared problems of archivization, temporality, and identity between newspapers and *The Autobiography of Alice B. Toklas,* both of which she comes to view as efforts to maintain the illusion of stable identities by suppressing temporal differences. After examining these commonalities in the first part of this chapter, I then turn to *Everybody's Autobiography,* viewing it as Stein's reorientation of the autobiographical form as a particular and deliberate intervention in the concept of identity that seeped out of news discourse and began to trouble her autobiographical practice and her own sense of identity. In response to both news identities and *The Autobiography of Alice B. Toklas,* Stein experiments with new autobiographical practices in *Everybody's Autobiography,* inventing a narrative of process, discovery, particularity, and nonidentity rather than product and identity, of existing and changing rather than merely happening, and of detection and investigation in which strong personalities can break through events in ways that cannot be "smoothed over" or "recovered from."[3]

WHAT WILL HAVE BEEN OF *THE AUTOBIOGRAPHY OF ALICE B. TOKLAS*

Identity and temporality are at issue in Stein's third "Narration" lecture of 1935 when she addresses the newspaper's desire to erase the time between events and their reportage:

> This is really what the newspaper has to say that everything that has happened has happened on that day but really this is not true because everything that has happened on that day on the newspaper day has really happened the day before and that makes all the trouble that there is with the newspaper as it is and in every way they try to destroy this day the day between the day before and the day the newspaper day.[4]

The concept seems simple and familiar: news stories are written about the events of one day and published the next day but are presented as "today's" news. However, for Stein this seemingly simple fact "makes all the trouble," the trouble, as we shall see, with temporality and identity in the process of archiving and anarchiving. Stein emphasizes the way in which newspaper stories retrospectively report events by eliding or ignoring the temporal difference between the event and its reportage. As such, the identities produced in newspapers rely for their stable appearance on the suppression of the temporal difference that defines and simultaneously plagues reportage. The newspaper is thus doubly motivated to report and to withhold, to conserve and to forget, to archive and to anarchive, all inseparably and irreducibly in the exact same location.

To observe a similar constellation of identity, temporality, archivization, and anarchivization, one need only consider Stein's autobiographical

practice in *The Autobiography of Alice B. Toklas* in order. There, in response
to Etta Cone's confidence "that she could forgive but never forget," Alice
B. Toklas reports, "for myself I could forget but not forgive."[5] This
insistence upon forgetting but not forgiving is a perfect formulation of
Stein's autobiographical strategy. Motivated at all points by suppressed or
repressed grievances that she has not forgiven, Stein's text forgets or erases
these grievances by constructing a narrative whose lack of tension and air
of pleasantness are conspicuous, embodying "an optimism that gives the
story of [Stein's] life the character of a fairy tale," as Janet Malcolm puts
it.[6] At the same time, the grievances that have been meticulously omitted
from the archive seem constitutive of the process of remembering itself.
The grievances are palpable in their very denial or absence, as when Stein
refuses to be persuaded by Picasso that she "is as unhappy as he is" (738),
suggesting a deep unhappiness by its very disavowal.

The *Autobiography* is overt about Stein's "bad memory for names"
(796), and perhaps no name is more forgotten than that of "Gertrude
Stein's brother," Leo Stein. Stein's life was transformed by the agoniz-
ing conflict with her brother that commenced (or came to a final point)
when Alice Toklas moved into 27 Rue de Fleurus and culminated in Leo's
departure, but in the *Autobiography* their break is casually overlooked:
"During the winter Gertrude Stein's brother decided that he would go to
Florence to live. They divided the pictures that they had bought together,
between them" (801). Stein, who used commas sparingly, places one conspicuously here, but it is only in the silent punctuation that reinforces the
division of "together" and "between" that we can read the absent traces
of Stein's "bad memory" of her falling out with Leo. Pronouns also hint
subtly at Leo's absence and the new presence of Alice in Stein's life. After
"*they* divided" what "*they* had bought," a new paragraph abounds with
so many "we" statements that the effect may be one of intoxicated triumph or celebration of Stein and Toklas's partnership: "*We* planned that
we would have a little passage way made . . . *we* decided that *we* would
paint the atelier. . . . *We* proceeded to have all this done" (801, emphasis
added).

The oblique celebration hinted by the repeated "we" that "the old life
was over" (802) reminds us that Stein not only forgets what she cannot
forgive, but also forgets what she cannot admit, perhaps most importantly her love and sexual relationship with Alice Toklas. This is what
Catharine R. Stimpson calls the "lesbian lie" of the *Autobiography* that
"insists that no lesbians abed here."[7] In more private texts such as "Lifting
Belly," of course, Stein does openly represent and celebrate her erotic relationship with Toklas—"I love cherish idolise adore and worship you. You
are so sweet so tender and so perfect"[8]—making the *Autobiography* seem

excessively muted by contrast. At the same time, it is possible to trace the archive of Stein's love for and even perhaps lovemaking with Toklas in the very places in the *Autobiography* that are calculated as erasures. In a curious passage that describes a walk to Assisi taken during Toklas's first summer with Stein and Leo in Italy, the Toklas narrator says, "I alas have only one favorite saint, Saint Anthony of Padua because it is he who finds lost objects and as Gertrude Stein's elder brother once said of me, if I were a general I would never lose a battle, I would only mislay it" (750). If there is a saint from whom the forgetful *Autobiography* could have used a blessing, the narrative playfully self-reflects, it would be the saint of lost objects. However, Alice (doubly present as narrator and in the pun "alas," which also marks her difference from the writing Stein) suggests that the apparently lost things in the *Autobiography* are only "mislaid." To mislay something is not to lose it forever, but merely temporarily. "Mislay" itself might be a word that finds something temporarily lost by the narrative, especially if we think of it as a sexual pun on "laying" a "miss" "wrongly" or "unsuitably," that is, as a lesbian. This in turn helps to find what the next paragraph goes on to lose, which seems to be the oblique recording of a sexual encounter:

> It was a very hot italian day and we started as usual about noon, that being Gertrude Stein's favourite walking hour, because it was hottest.... We started from Perugia across the hot valley. I gradually undressed, in those days one wore many more clothes than one does now, I even, which was most unconventional in those days, took off my stockings, but even so I dropped a few tears before we arrived and we did arrive. (750)

The description of the heat, the undressing of clothes and stockings, and the stress on "arrive" as a displaced synonym for "come"—indeed, Toklas's "few tears" even seem to conjure lost virginity—all suggest that repression is not the opposite of archivization, but rather, as Derrida puts it, "to archive *otherwise*."[9]

In fact, the whole shape of Stein's *Autobiography* seems to confirm what Derrida points to as the temporality of the archive, which is not, as one might think, directed toward the past or present, but rather to the future. The temporality of the archive is "what *will have been*."[10] From the perspective of 1932, Stein attempts to contextualize and control the archive of "what will have been" of her past. This is a process at work in miniature within the narrative itself. Stein's narrative is insistently proleptic, shuttling forward in time to an explicit or implied "later on" in order to reflect back and recontextualize the past as it is being narrated. This is evident when she playfully suggests that Picasso's and Matisse's paintings, "in those days...had no value" (666). Picasso's portrait of Stein is even set up to mirror Stein's own *Autobiography* in such a way that both point to "what will have been": "everybody says that she does not look like [her portrait] but that does not make an difference, she will, [Picasso] said" (669); that is, Picasso's portrait of Stein ensures that she will have looked as the portrait represented her.

To a large extent, Stein would continue to employ the autobiographical tactic of forgetting but not admitting or forgiving through her entire writing life, and any discussion of identity and autobiography in Stein's writing could always be put in the larger context of Stein's enduring tendency to "decontextuate" the private roots of her writing, as Ulla Dydo terms it.[11] However, after the *Autobiography*'s success and her own media celebrity, Stein seems to have become more aware of media constructions of identity and to have been confronted and unsettled by the similar pattern of suppression and elision to be found in her own writing and in news discourse. *Everybody's Autobiography* records Stein's subsequent identity crisis and writer's block,[12] both of which centered around Stein's observation, as we shall see, that the *Autobiography of Alice B. Toklas* was essentially a newspaper.

THE BEING EXISTING OF *EVERYBODY'S AUTOBIOGRAPHY*

Looking back at *The Autobiography of Alice B. Toklas,* Stein suspects that it collapses into the conventions of news identities. What Stein says of newspapers could now equally apply to the *Autobiography*: "I said newspapers make things too easy and I said that once to a reporter and he said you have no idea I am sure how terribly hard we work. Yes I said but after you have done all that hard work you have to write it up as it would be if you had known it all beforehand.... There is no discovery...."[13] In contrast, Stein tells Thornton Wilder that she now intends to break from her earlier methods and "simply say what was happening":

> ... the first autobiography was not that, it was description and a creation of something that having happened was in a way happening not again but as it had been which is history which is newspaper which is illustration but is not a simple narrative of what is happening not as if it had happened not as if it is happening but as if it is existing simply that thing. And now in this book I have done it if I have done it.[14]

Stein groups *The Autobiography of Alice B. Toklas* with the narrative modes of newspapers and what amounts to historicist historiography ("as it had been"). All of these describe things that have happened in the near or distant past and are narrated with a feeling of what had been (history) or with a feeling of what "is" right now (news). Instead, Stein wants narrative to express a thing without creating the false impression that it had happened in some disconnected past or that it is happening now in some equally independent present. She neither seeks the "had been" of the past seen from the present, nor the news illusion that what has happened yesterday is really identical with today. The past is in some way neither remote nor recurring, and Stein desires a way of representing this. *Everybody's Autobiography* is to be a realistic representation of that which Stein calls "being existing" within the dimension of temporal continuity. This mode differs from the "what will have been" of the *Autobiography* and as well as from the "continuous present" of her earliest writing.[15]

As such, Stein moves away from the programmatic "what will have been" of the *Autobiography* in order to capture "what merely is," but in a form in which temporality is never collapsed to project falsely stable identities. In "Narration," Stein reflected on the ways in which newspapers create a feeling of happening without change:

> A newspaper man is trained to make this easy by never changing, nothing must ever be changing, things are happening but nothing must ever be changing about their being happening, the newspaper must never give to any one reading it a feeling that anything is changing about something being always happening, if it ever could or would or should then any one would come to have some suspicion that there might be a beginning and ending to anything and if there is a beginning and ending to anything then it destroys the simplicity of something always happening.[16]

This is precisely how Stein now sees the *Autobiography*: as falsely asserting a stable identity to whom things happen without ever admitting changes to identity. For Stein, this problem is not merely one of narration or even of identity, but rather implicates the effects of mass culture on both language and identity. In a discussion of spoken and written language with an Egyptian man, Stein claims, "everybody talks as the newspapers and movies and radios tell them to talk the spoken language is no longer interesting and so gradually the written language says something and says it differently than the spoken language" (13). For Stein, it is no longer useful to approximate spoken English in writing because the spoken language has become compromised and dominated by the language of newspapers, movies, and radio. Stein characterizes this language as both aggressive and coercive when she emphasizes that everybody talks as they are told to talk.

Like Dos Passos, Stein ties this observation about language to a larger cultural and political phenomenon, in this case a contemporary desire for organization and a strong inclination to be controlled or enslaved. For Stein everybody wishes to be enslaved primarily in order to avoid consciousness of passing time:

> The only reason why people work or run around, and naturally everybody does all of one or the other of them is that they will not know that time is something and that time can pass. That is the only reason for working or for running around. (60)

People insulate themselves from the fact that time passes by finding occupation in work or leisure. Perhaps Stein's post-*Autobiography* inactivity as a writer, her return to "everybody" status, makes her newly sensitive to passing time and to the occupations that everybody else uses to avoid thinking about the passage of time. For Stein, the immediate effect of time unconsciousness is an increasingly homogenized, collective identity for everybody, and she feels herself to have to some extent lapsed into it. The constant "Gertrude Stein" of *The Autobiography* has become in *Everybody's Autobiography* a generic "I" with resemblances to "everybody," or even "anybody." After she recounts how she was named "Gertrude Stein," Stein concludes with little fanfare, "All right that is my name" (119). Elsewhere she admits, "I used to think the name of anybody was very important and the name made you and I have often said so. Perhaps I still think so but still there are so many names and anybody nowadays can call anybody any name they like" (10). To the extent that mass media has homogenized identities, then, we can for now suggest that Stein's autobiography might very well be renamed *Anybody's Autobiography*.

Stein feels that her identity, anybody's or everybody's identity, works similarly to the retrospective reportage of the newspaper. The newspaper provides the essential temporality for time unconsciousness, which encourages homogenized identities. As we have seen, the newspaper reports events that have happened a day ago but tries to erase the temporal distance between event and report in order to give the appearance that event and report are identical and simultaneous. It also suppresses the consciousness that time passes by mistaking the present of writing as a point of stable identity that can smooth over temporal contingencies. News discourse is structured to deny differences between event and reportage, falsely reconciling the vicissitudes of identity at different times and avoiding altogether the challenges posed to the concept of stable identity by time. Crucially conditioned by news reports, identity for Stein has come to rely upon a similar temporal structure: modern identity has become structured like a news report.

For Stein, identity is exposed as only the illusion that the self in retrospect is identical to the present self. This was a painful lesson that her own success seems to have taught her. Now a bestseller and a celebrity, Stein finds her writing joined to the economic order, and her identity becomes as thoroughly defined from without, through the orders of publicity, as she had once defined herself from within.[17] The publicity and the money that attended this success seem to have contributed to new uncertainties for Stein about her own writing and her identity.

> And identity is funny being yourself is funny as you are never yourself to yourself except as you remember yourself and then of course you do not believe yourself. That is really the trouble with an autobiography you do not of course you do not really believe yourself why should you, you know so well so very well that it is not yourself, it could not be yourself because you cannot remember right and if you do remember right it does not sound right and of course it does not sound right because it is not right. You are of course never yourself. (70)

Here in *Everybody's Autobiography*, the language of "trouble" creeps into her discussion of autobiography as elsewhere we have seen it in reference to newspapers. Stein accuses autobiography of bankruptcy because it amounts to deception not only for reader, but for writer as well. The autobiographer's position is analogous to that of the journalist Stein describes in her "Narration" lecture; each consciously produces deceptive or illusory identities that collapse temporal differences, writing as though each had known the outcome all along. Moreover, the autobiographer cannot help but be aware of the deception with respect to identity in the very act of narrating the self: "you do not really believe yourself."

In spite or perhaps because of this, Stein seems compelled to alternate between autobiographical recounting and self-conscious meditation on identity in *Everybody's Autobiography*, between passages that reflect upon the deception of identity construction and ones that conduct the day-to-day narrative work of autobiography, such as this passage that immediately follows Stein's claim that "You are of course never yourself": "Well anyway I did tell all about myself, telling about my brother was telling about myself being a genius and it was a natural thing to tell it all to Seabrook" (70–71). Here Stein not only continues the account of the conversation she had with an admirer, but her account includes a speech about her identity that elides, even makes a show of eliding, any of the instabilities or inconsistencies upon which Stein has just meditated at length. In order to proceed past her reflection on the deceptiveness of autobiographical identity, she must make a bridge back to the narrative that admits her ambivalence about the way in which she is about to contradict herself: "Well anyway." Stein thus juxtaposes self-conscious reflection with autobiographical narrative so that their contradictions might be seen more starkly. It is one strategy of several in *Everybody's Autobiography* for coming to terms with the effects of news language upon identity and autobiography. In the next section, I examine a central strategy that Stein uses to disrupt the narrative tendency in autobiography and in newspapers to smooth over nonidentical effects.

WRITING THE SELF AGAINST THE GRAIN OF AUTOBIOGRAPHY

Is it any longer possible to represent a "Gertrude Stein" instead of an "everybody"? Is there even a "Gertrude Stein" to represent now that she has become "everybody" herself? Stein means to test or to put pressure on the inevitability of the title *Everybody's Autobiography*, by asking how the resemblance between newspapers and autobiographies, and thus the autobiographical subject's false identity, can be shattered. Stein suggests an answer to this in her "Narration" lecture, and again, it is articulated through an analysis of news discourse that seems to parallel her self-reflection on autobiography in *Everybody's Autobiography*:

> It is very curious in a newspaper that sometimes really sometimes a personality breaks through an event, it takes a tremendously strong personality to break through the events in a newspaper and when they do well it is soon over it is soon smoothed over and even history wishes to change it into something that any one could recover from.
>
> In a novel in a play no matter what it is that happens it is hoped that nothing will be smoothed over that every minute of that novel there is a beginning and an ending that always any personality that any one has there is one that no one can ever change into something that any one can recover from.[18]

Under normal conditions, news subsumes personality into the contour of the event and forces it to conform to the grain of the report. News narratives invert the novelistic priority given to personality by subordinating personality to the narration of events, or "what happens," but strong personality challenges the illusion that events succeed one another without the constant beginnings and endings that expose identities in flux. When a strong personality does manage to break through a reported event, challenging the smooth contour of the report and exposing the illusion of stable identity, news desires to smooth it back into the surface and to recover from the "break" or rupture, just as historiography can turn ruptures into smooth reports. Stein maintains the parallel she draws between news and history, each wishing to "recover" from the traumatic moments in their smooth narratives when strong personalities break through the surface and assert personality at the expense of a sense of narrative continuity.

For Stein, then, autobiography functions in yet another way like the newspaper, smoothing personality over into the happenings of the autobiographical narrative and into conformity with an atemporal auto-biographical identity, the supposedly consistent and stable retrospective consciousness that organizes the past and is itself free from internal tem-poral divisions. Like news discourse and conventional historiography, autobiographies have a smooth narrative grain that subordinates strong personality to event and identity. In contrast, Stein wants to reclaim autobiography as a space for strong personality, to write autobiography against the news-like grain of autobiography. The language of "break-ing" and "recovery" is crucial. Narratives such as autobiographies and news stories tenaciously assert and reassert identity, which becomes the conceptual category into which all events across a given temporal spec-trum can be subsumed and organized. To have a personality for Stein is thus to insist upon inassimilable particularities that break out of the tena-cious pattern that subordinates personality to identity. To be committed to personality is to embrace an aesthetic of disruption rather than identi-fication. As in Benjamin's anecdotal model, Stein grasps for ways in which to bring personality out of the abstraction of identity and into the reader's space.

To claim autobiography as a space for nonidentical personality, Stein must find an alternate narrative model that she can adapt in *Every-body's Autobiography* in order to produce the shock effects of person-ality. Stein finds special leverage against news discourse and traditional autobiography in the form of the detective story:

> In the newspaper thing it is the crime it is the criminal that is interest-ing, in the story it is the story about the crime that is interesting. Now think, you will perfectly realize that the newspaper practically never tells anything about detecting, a little in the case of Dillinger, a little in the case of Hauptmann but still really very little and in lesser crimes not at all the emphasis is entirely upon the crime and not upon the detecting and in

the written story it is impossible to hold the attention by telling about the crime you can only hold the attention by telling about detecting.[19]

Stein's describes the detective story's dual narrative in a manner that resembles the structuralist account of the genre given by Tzvetan Todorov, in which detective novels contain two stories, that of the crime and that of its investigation:

> The first, that of the crime, is in fact the story of an absence: its most accurate characteristic is that it cannot be immediately present in the book. In other words, the narrator cannot transmit directly the conversations of the characters who are implicated, nor describe their actions: to do so, he must necessarily employ the intermediary of another (or the same) character who will report, in the second story, the words heard or the actions observed."[20] Newspapers usually hide the fact that there has been investigation of the crime. They wish to assert the transparent facts of the crime itself and, unless the story of the investigation holds particular public interest, they wish to suppress the investigation altogether, preferring to replace the crime with its report. While newspapers would prefer the illusion that there is as little mediation as possible, the detective story holds attention by emphasizing the detecting and thus the very mediation of the crime itself; to represent the crime itself would be to give the narrative game away before it even begins.[21]

In effect Stein transforms the autobiography into a special form of the whodunit. Just as the newspaper does, traditional autobiography makes the fatal mistake of trying to narrate the crime. Instead, Stein wants to narrate the detection of the crime in the manner of the detective story. At the same time, she also wants to avoid letting the detection finally lapse into the same false identity as the newspaper's narration of the crime. After all, the detective story genre is as conventional as news or autobiography. The crime eventually becomes a fixed identity in the mystery story after the detection is over, and can thus be said to lapse back into the newspaper in the final analysis. Stein will not just mechanically adopt one set of conventions in place of another. In Stein's own detective story, *Blood on the Dining-Room Floor*, written between *The Autobiography of Alice B. Toklas* and *Everybody's Autobiography*, "there is no solving of the crime," as Harriet Scott Chessman stresses.[22] Stein's approach to autobiography remains as unconventional as her approach to detective fiction. What Chessman argues about *Blood on the Dining-Room Floor* applies equally to Stein's experimental adaptation of the detective story to autobiography: "it reminds us of the rituals of this genre, even as it completely transforms the genre itself."[23]

Most importantly, detective stories set up the shock of unsettling discoveries, whether of the corpse, the motive, the means of murder, or the exposure of the murderer. Stein's experimental autobiography is thus a detective story in which the autobiographer must simultaneously play both detective and criminal, bringing the mystery of her own personality as surprisingly to light as when the detective points to the criminal and instantly produces in the reader feelings of discovery, recognition, and shock. In the next section I turn to the ways in which Stein tries to achieve this break or shock through the anecdotal structure of *Everybody's Autobiography*, which, like Benjamin's formulation of the anecdote, creates spaces for unmediated experience out of which personality can potentially break, perhaps without being recovered from or smoothed over.

THREE ANECDOTES OF AMERICA

Critics have noted the anecdotal structure of *Everybody's Autobiography*. Richard Bridgman describes Stein's digression along paths of association, which permit "flashbacks in time [and] ... the connection of subjects that would normally be separated in a continuous narrative, even though they were actually linked in the author's mind."[24] The "Introduction" to *Everybody's Autobiography* exemplifies this associative technique, consisting of "five anecdotes, each pegged to a specific person, and each carrying a thematic burden."[25] Shirley Neuman calls *Everybody's Autobiography* a "meta-autobiography," in which theory and illustration are fused in the anecdotes Stein retells:

> Stein's use of anecdote is comparable to [the] deduction from a single case which had characterized certain schools of psychology since William James and Sigmund Freud. To use anecdote in literature as the experiential basis of a 'knowledge' manifested in generalization is to abstract it from its usual historical function. ... It is impersonal and no longer embedded in chronology.[26]

Bridgman and Neuman both note the way in which Stein uses anecdotal forms to break chronology into experimental narrative spaces.

Stein's visit to America presents the occasion for her to rethink identity through national temperament, personal history, and celebrity culture. Stein returns to America after 30 years, and she approaches the identity of the country as she approaches personal identity: "You are never yourself to yourself except as you remember yourself" (70). Would America be as she remembered it? What would she discover about herself when she returned? Would she be identical to the person who left there or will she have changed? Stein's America is the country of self-creation and space,[27] exactly the right place for the process, discovery, and movement that will characterize her new mode of autobiography. It is the place to set her own personality into relief by comparing the self that she is to the self that she remembers, as well as to the self made famous by *The Autobiography of Alice B. Toklas*: "I used to say that I would not go to America until I was a real lion a real celebrity at that time of course I did not really think I was going to be one.... In America everybody is but some are more than others. I was more than others" (173). America, then, is itself an experimental space for Stein. It is also the place that exposes the discontinuity of identity, as when Stein revisits the site of her childhood, Oakland, and powerfully reflects that "there is no there there" (298).

I will now turn to three anecdotal moments generated through the experimental space of America that emblematize Stein's experimental negotiation of fixed identity and powerful, disruptive personality. The first of these three anecdotes does not demonstrate personality breaking through the narrative grain, but rather its opposite, showing the process by which personality is normally subsumed by fixed identity in news discourse and conventional autobiography and historiography. Not surprisingly, this set piece derives from Stein's encounters with the press in America, specifically a photographer's visit to Stein's hotel room:

> I liked the photographers, there is one who came in and said he was sent to **do** a layout of me. A layout, I said yes he said what is that I said oh he said it is four or five pictures of you **doing** something. All right I said what **do** you want me to **do**. Why he said there is your airplane bag suppose you unpack it, oh I said Miss Toklas always **does** that oh no I could not **do** that, well he said there is the telephone suppose you telephone well I said yes but I never **do** Miss Toklas always **does** that, well he said what can you **do**, well I said I can put my hat on and take my hat off and I can put my coat on and I can take my coat off and I like water I can drink a glass of water all right he said **do** that so I **did** that and he photographed while I **did** that and the next morning there was the layout and I **had done** it. (225)

In this unforgettable passage, I have marked Stein's emphasis on "doing" in bold print in order to highlight Stein's representation of action and process that subsequently becomes fixed as static moments in the printed layout of next morning's newspaper. In contrast to the way in which the "doings" of taking on and off the hat and coat and drinking water are hypostatized as images on the next day's page, the passage itself keeps moving: it is an eruption of energetic verb forms for "do." Stein's anecdote conveys the rich interplay of what the photographer wants Stein to do, what Alice always does, what Stein never does or could do, what she can do, does, and did—but these actions contrast with the static layout of the newspaper page, ending the bright anecdote coldly in the past perfect tense, "had done." Stein slyly suggests that not until her layout appears in the paper had she "done" the shoot, stressing the ways in which identities are fixed retrospectively in the newspaper, though this anecdote might just as easily stand as a self-critique of *The Autobiography of Alice B. Toklas,* which, as we have seen, Stein also associates with retrospective and false identification. The final photographic layout not only ends the various "doings" that it attempts to represent, but it collapses the experience of the shoot into appearance of the layout itself, as though the publication rather than the posing of yesterday's photos constitutes the "had done" of the layout. This is thus an anecdote about the way in which experience becomes hypostatized as a reported identity in the morning after of both news and autobiography. Stein dramatizes the very temporal elision that she complains of in the newspaper's equation of event with report when she repositions herself as spectator of the layout instead of as its model. It is only from the perspective of a spectator that Stein's experience of the day before begins to take its lasting identity, just as the conventional autobiographer can be a mere spectator of a smooth progression of facts.

Thus Stein's personality does not finally break through the smooth surface of the photo layout. Her lively and comical routine of drinking water and doffing and donning her hat is flattened into two dimensions. Sometimes in *Everybody's Autobiography,* however, we do glimpse personalities that break through events in ways that cannot be smoothed over, and now we might move to the second anecdote I would like to examine. In the passage from "Narration" in which she compares detective fiction to crime reporting, Stein alludes to the newspaper treatment of the Hauptmann trial. Bruno Richard Hauptmann was accused of kidnapping and murdering Charles and Anne Lindbergh's infant son and stood trial in New Jersey in early 1935, coinciding with Stein's trip to New York. During the trial Stein had lunch with the actor Katherine Cornell, and Stein is deeply impressed by the story of her husband's spectatorship at the Hauptmann trial:

I always remember the husband of Katherine Cornell and the Hauptmann trial. Everybody was going there we did not, I like to read detective stories but really not see them, to know what they are but not to sit with them at least I have never sat perhaps I would like to anyway I did not.

The husband of Katherine Cornell had gone every day and then he did not go any more, and he said the reason why was that he could not go any

more because the day before coming back in the train Mrs. Hauptmann
was there in front of him and she said to some one I wonder if it is going
to snow or if there is going to be any skating. The naturalness of her saying
this to some one suddenly made it that he could not go again and he did
not go again. (227–228)

In this anecdote, Stein dramatizes the personality of Mrs. Hauptmann
breaking through the spectacle of the Hauptmann trial in the near space
of one of its spectators. Stein says that she does not like to "really see"
or "sit with" detective stories, but this is exactly what Cornell's husband
is forced to do on the train. The spectacular trial was unfolding *as* news
at the same time that it was as event, almost as a single identity, and for
spectators in the courtroom, the trial and the news must have seemed
strangely simultaneous. However, Hauptmann's wife breaks through the
events of the trial for Cornell's husband in a way from which he could
neither recover nor smooth over; after he "sits with" and "really sees" her
speech on the train, he does not return again to watch the trial unfold
as news. It is neither a grand nor a very violent gesture that disrupts his
spectatorship, but merely Mrs. Hauptmann's offhand comments about
the weather and the probability of skating, which are enough to uncou-
ple the events of the trial from the narrative grain into which Cornell's
husband had fit both it and perhaps even his own experience of observing
the trial. Mrs. Hauptmann's naturalness is a shock to Cornell's husband's
own experience of the trial. The mundane, the trivial, and the quotidian dimensions of experience reveal the experiential poverty of his
spectatorship.

To put it in Benjamin's terms, Cornell's husband is transformed from
the empathetic newspaper reader to one who experiences a pathos of nearness. Recall that in the empathetic gesture one moves imaginatively out
toward the object to meet it on abstract grounds different from one's own.
Cornell's husband literally acts out the empathetic movement, leaving his
home each morning to watch the news and trial unfold at the courthouse.
The trial and its participants do not exist for him or strike him outside
the distancing and abstracting relationship of empathy. But this empathetic relationship is overturned when Cornell's husband "sits with" and
"really sees" Mrs. Hauptmann in the train, the transitional space between
abstract courthouse and intimate home. It is not what Mrs. Hauptmann
says so much as where she says it, and the fact that what she says can
be understood by Cornell's husband as full of "naturalness," that matters
most. This is quite like the inverse of Dick's vision of Woodrow Wilson.
For a thing to seem natural it must have been absorbed into intimate
space, and, for Cornell's husband, this is a place in which that experience

cannot be recovered from or smoothed over by the narratives and appeals to empathy that hold potentially unsettling things at a safe distance. The pathos of nearness means suddenly and unexpectedly finding the hitherto empathetic object *in* one's space, and having to come to terms with it, like Cornell's husband, on his way home rather than in some abstract and distant elsewhere represented by the courthouse. One can no longer simply go home when one's interest is exhausted. Cornell's husband cannot, let us say, look at a photograph of Mrs. Hauptmann in the paper the next day and be comfortably returned to the position of spectator as we saw in Stein's own ironic dramatization of herself as spectator of Gertrude Stein.

This brings us to the final anecdote I would like to examine in which personalities are dramatized as breaking through narratives of identity. The personality it concerns is perhaps the most vivid in *Everybody's Autobiography*: Alice Toklas's umbrella. Placed strategically just before Stein recounts her experiences in America, the following anecdote about transatlantic circulation, personality, and the illusion of retrospective reporting at once models Stein's writing of personality in relation to identity in autobiography and newspapers, as well as cautions about the seductiveness of identity and reportage:

> So we had everything made [in preparation for going to America] and we stayed at Bilignin until we left for Paris. And in Paris we only stayed a few weeks and [our servant] Trac came back and Alice Toklas bought an umbrella, this was later left at a restaurant in Central California and after she wrote for it sent to San Francisco and by that time we had left America and it was sent to Carl Van Vechten in New York and just this week Eddie Wassermann has brought it over to her. She is sorry about it because she says if it had stayed over there it would have been something to go back to get. And in between she had bought another just like it at any rate we both thought it was just like it but now the other one has come back we see that the handle is different. (169–170)

On the verge of Stein's narration of America, Alice's umbrella, bought on the eve of their departure from Paris, returns from America. The previous sentence is purposely choppy because it tries to render the crossing paths of Stein and Alice's experiences and their subsequent accounts, including Alice's umbrella and its inexact replacement. This symmetrical circulation of objects, memory, and narration cautions Stein and subsequently her readers about how imperfectly umbrellas are remembered and how easily they are replaced with umbrellas that seem exactly the same as the lost one. Indeed, the replacement umbrella is desirable for far more than its rain-repelling ability; it is desirable because, although it fails to reproduce or replace the lost original, it does appear to replace and satisfy a lack. But whatever handle Stein and Alice think they have upon the remembered umbrella, the handle they grasp is slightly different from the one they remember.

The homecoming of Alice's umbrella dramatizes the danger of replacing the past with retrospective reports or identities. Here history returns as it rarely does, a perfect artifact, an object from the past that can be placed next to the object that replaces it, where it will insist upon the differences that have been blurred by the process of replacement or identification. The seductive stand-in umbrella (that prophylactic against bad weather and, for Alice, loss) is a model for identity in traditional autobiography, suppressing difference, but also denying and protecting one from the terrible loss of a sheltering identity. Here, in contrast, although Stein narrates from the perspective of having been to and returned from America, the umbrella can intrude to remind her that "just this week" the past might still strike one and return with an unsettling difference. Thus, Stein stresses past and present "being existing" together, always within potential striking distance. Unlike *The Autobiography of Alice B. Toklas,* in which the past is archived as a strategic identification of "what will have been," and more specifically "*who* will have been," in *Everybody's Autobiography* past selves return to the present self as so many drops of rain in a thunderstorm from which there is only an illusion of shelter.

ENDING AN AUTOBIOGRAPHY WITHOUT IDENTITY

If the "what will have been" of *The Autobiography of Alice B. Toklas* gives way to "being existing" in *Everybody's Autobiography,* then ending such an autobiography becomes a special challenge. One way to end an autobiography is implicitly or explicitly to round out the representation of one's identity, taken as a whole and as the culmination of all the events and feelings that have built it. This culmination is now impossible for Stein. Her experiences have shown her that stable identities are illusions. Identities are made only by smoothing over differences in past and present selves, by feeling confident that subsequent reports do justice to diffuse experiences. *The Autobiography of Alice B. Toklas* ended with the stunning *coup de théâtre* in which Stein revealed herself as the writer of Toklas's autobiography—"I am going to write it for you" (913)—asserting at once Stein's identity as author as well as fixing the identity of Stein and Toklas's relationship as an implicit and eternal marriage. As powerful an ending as this is, it relies upon a retrospective fixing of identities that Stein distrusts by the time she has become a celebrity, experienced writer's block, and lost her old umbrella of identity. Further, although Stein wants to draw upon the conventions of detecting from the mystery story, she must also avoid establishing or fixing the identity of the criminal at the end book, which is where detective fiction, like autobiography, usually takes false refuge from the storm of crime.

As she approaches the end of the book, Stein thus begins to incorporate more and more disruptions into her narrative that expose the exact moment and perspective from which she writes as contingent rather than fixed. For instance, she increasingly admits markers of the present of the composition process, such as "just this week," into her narration of the past. She reminds us that the past is something whose facts might strike one *right now*, like an umbrella returned from America that one thought was long lost and satisfactorily replaced. Stein purposely breaks the false illusion that one can be situated somewhere other than in a contingent and never-completed present when one writes about the past. In this passage, for instance, Stein allows the present moment of writing to break the grain of her narration of the past:

> For the first time they were making arrangements that did not please me and I was beginning to say so, and the long distance telephoning that we had heard that everybody did began.
>
> Some one has just sent me a Camel pen from America, you fill it with water and it writes ink. But you have to press hard on it to make it write ink if you fill it with water and as I like to press lightly when I write I began to fill it with ink. Well yes ink is better than water. So we went on struggling. I said I would not go unless they arranged it the way we wanted it and there we were. (194–195)

Stein interrupts the narrative about lecture negotiations in Chicago to mention not only the moment of composition but to stress the physical act of writing as well. We imagine that when the pen physically interrupts or stalls the writing process, it prompts Stein to digress about her gift (another object sent from America that intrudes upon Stein's narrative). We imagine Stein having to stop and get up, to fill the pen with ink, though she knows that it is designed to take water and that she slightly misuses it, to think about who sent the pen to her and where it was sent from, and to consider her preferences about how hard she likes to press on the page when she writes. With the pen refilled, Stein sits down to resume writing, but she cannot resist mentioning the unusual convergence of the American narrative, the American gift, and the present of composition. She tries to duplicate for her readers the intercession in the present of an object from the place that Stein writes about as belonging to the past. The alchemical novelty pen, a pen that magically transmutes water into ink, provides the equally novel occasion for Stein's transmutation of time. It is appropriate that the digression occurs in the middle of a discussion about struggle and negotiation: "So we went on struggling." Now when Stein says this it refers not only to the lecture arrangements, but to the composition of *Everybody's Autobiography* as well. It refers to the difficulty of narrating in such a way that neither distances the past nor denies the consciousness that time passes, and foregrounds for the reader Stein's awareness of and commitment to this difficult task. How lightly, indeed, can she press?

The other ending strategy that Stein incorporates is to shuttle the past right into the present without ever fixing the present as a completed identity or product of the past. After Stein and Toklas return from America, *Everybody's Autobiography* begins to appear in the narrative itself: "So we had a good time in England and then we came back to Paris again, that was a month before we were leaving for Bilignin and I began writing this book but I was hesitating whether it was the narrative about which I had talked to Thornton" (314). The autobiography appears as a work in progress, and the writing of the autobiography becomes a part of the autobiography as it is written. In writing so Stein implies that autobiographical composition is subject to the passage of time and hence is a process and an act of becoming that does not resolve into a product or identity without suppressing or repressing the temporal dimension of experience.

Stein's conclusion to *Everybody's Autobiography* centers upon the London premiere of the ballet, *A Wedding Bouquet,* based upon Stein's play, "They Must. Be Wedded. To Their Wife." This premiere becomes the last retrospective event to be narrated before the autobiography reaches the contemporary and simultaneous point of its final composition: "And so our winter went on and now it is spring, and next Friday we go to London to see The Wedding Bouquet put on.... But first we are going to London to see The Wedding Bouquet and then it will be today" (324). Stein writes from the perspective of the day after the premiere and anticipates her narrative catching up to her present moment. In "so our winter went on and now it is spring," Stein signals that the spring of the narrative is the same as the spring of the composition. Finally, when she says "now it is spring," it applies equally to the events of the narrative past and the present of composition. Further toward the end of the autobiography, Stein writes, "It was tomorrow which was yesterday and it was exciting..." (327). It might be noted that here Stein has supplied herself with the same temporal elements that the newspaper uses when it narrates events, but she has strategically rearranged these elements. Because the newspaper tells events from the previous day as though they were today, for the newspaper, "tomorrow" is today, "yesterday" is two days ago, and "today" is yesterday. In Stein's autobiographical variation, "tomorrow" represents the eve of the premiere two days ago, "yesterday" is the day of the premiere, which actually *was* yesterday, and the implied "today" is the day after the day of the premiere, which is the present of writing to which the narrative is quickly catching up. In contrast to Stein's complaint about the temporal destructions of newspaper narration, *Everybody's Autobiography* will finally establish yesterday as yesterday and today as today.

If we look carefully we will be able to see the past coincide with the present of the writing—"and then it will be today"—but at that concluding moment Stein crucially resists identification:

> . . . perhaps I am not I even if my little dog knows me but anyway I like what I have and now it is today. (328)

Stein admits that "perhaps I am not I" even if her dogs Basket or Pépé still recognize her. However, whereas once this recognition was the cause of difficulty—"It is not extremely difficult not to have an identity but it is extremely difficult the knowing not having identity"[28]—Stein now seems comfortable with this irresolution and even to embrace it: "but anyway I like what I have." Nor does she seem to rely on the idea of autonomous entity, which finally may only have been an unsuccessful attempt on Stein's part to return an autonomous sense of identity through the back door.

This conclusion could be seen as the very antithesis of the strong identifications made at the end of *The Autobiography of Alice B. Toklas*. In place of identity we have an anecdotal assemblage of experiences, which is what Stein has tried to narrate and yet prevent from becoming concretized as identities right up to the minute that she finishes writing. Identity is the toll that is paid along the path that leads back to experience. I suggested earlier that one way to read the title of *Everybody's Autobiography* is as an expression of Stein's new feeling of identity loss and of thus becoming a generic "anybody." Seen from another perspective, however, the title also suggests that autobiographical subjects are always multiple "everybodies": the "I" is not one but rather the illusion that tries (but cannot succeed) to stabilize the "everybody" that the autobiographical subject is revealed to already have been. Thus the archival and absolutely singular "one who will have been" of *The Autobiography of Alice B. Toklas* is revealed as the "everybody one has been" of *Everybody's Autobiography* to absolutely singular effect. In this way, Stein responds to her perception that modern identity has conformed to the temporality and structure of newspaper identities, attempting to craft an autobiographical subject who breaks forth from the contours of retrospective narration in order to represent intimate experience otherwise.

CHAPTER 5

WAR

As I anticipated in the introduction, if nearness of experience is the broad category of modernist fiction's engagement with news discourse within their shared media ecology, then war reporting is a limit case. In this chapter, I trace the implications of endings in Gertrude Stein's final memoir, *Wars I Have Seen*, through its close relation to the vivid and descriptive war reporting of World War II. Just as *Everybody's Autobiography* is a species of autobiography that attempts to reconfigure its genre as a narrative of existing rather than of events and happenings, *Wars I Have Seen* operates as a species of war reporting that reflects Stein's desire to represent war beyond the level of "happening," which she sees as a limitation of war reporting. Instead, she develops an experimental form of reportage that attempts to represent "being existing," during wartime. In her third "Narration" lecture, Stein argues that the ability to represent "being existing" rather than mere "happening" hinges crucially upon beginnings and endings: "if there is a beginning and ending to anything then it destroys the simplicity of something always happening."[1] Stein's observation seems simple: the news never ends. As she writes, "there is no beginning and ending because every day is the same that is that every day has anything that it has happening."[2]

For Stein, this conflict between news form (what we have been calling the continuous clocking of homogeneous, empty time) and content (the reporting of individual news items) impoverishes the ability of news to represent the devastating experiences of war. This is the case because in the news there are no formal means of arresting the tumbling forth of happenings in order to isolate and assimilate experience in intimate space. News never comes, in Benjamin's terms, to a standstill. In contrast, *Wars I Have Seen* represents the experience of life during war as a veritable series of endings, a strategy with which Stein experiments and which she adopts as a consequence of her vision of news narrative, with the aim of drawing the experience of war nearer to readers. *Wars I Have Seen* writes the experience of witnessing and waiting out World War II by investing in that which news cannot: endings of all kinds—of stories, lives, the war, and, finally, *Wars I Have Seen* itself, which Stein vows to abandon when the war ends.

GERTRUDE STEIN'S LIFE DURING WARTIME

I choose to focus this war-themed chapter not through texts that represent warfare but instead through a text that seeks to represent the experience of life during wartime. The overwhelming audience to whom newspapers represent war are people who merely live during wartime. Thus, one might expect to find the richest negotiation with war reporting in a text written from the perspective of the addressee of war reportage, a writer like Stein who anxiously awaits and relies upon war news even as she attempts to represent experience in her own terms. Woolf's "The Mark on the Wall," as we have seen, also fits in this context and can be seen as a species of war story. My selection is also driven by the fact that many of Stein's pre-World War II texts can be understood as war stories in ways that productively expand our sense of what constitutes the genre of the war story. Harriet Chessman, for instance, connects Stein's erotic poem "Lifting Belly" to the World War I context in which it was composed: "As with most of Stein's writing of the early war period . . . 'Lifting Belly' is a love poem."[3] Thus, amid the elaborate discourse of love in "Lifting Belly," when Stein writes, "Lifting Belly is anxious./Not about Verdun./Oh dear no,"[4] she disavows anxiety about the war only to simultaneously provoke questions about the extent to which a love poem can also be a war poem, or the ways in which the erotic might be a significant response to the anxiety of war.

Parts of *The Autobiography of Alice B. Toklas* can similarly be read as war stories even though they are set at a certain distance from warfare. In fact, the war provides a relatively rare occasion in the *Autobiography* to glimpse a textual "tender button" between Stein and Toklas that Stein was otherwise so scrupulous to limit. During an alarm one night, Stein wakes Toklas and asks her to come downstairs:

> Give me your hand and I will get you down and you can go to sleep down stairs on the couch. I came. It was very dark. I sat down on the couch and then I said, I'm sure I don't know what is the matter with me but my knees are knocking together. Gertrude Stein burst out laughing, wait a minute, I will get you a blanket, she said. No don't leave me, I said.[5]

Although this passage does very little to clarify the ambiguous preposition in Toklas's "twenty-five years with Gertrude Stein,"[6] it stands out as an affectionate and even loving moment. Importantly, not only the moment but its representation in the text seems to be stimulated by the war. Just as the moment is produced as an effect of the war, the necessity of representing the stress of war seems to produce this textual exception to the way in which Stein depicts her relationship with Toklas. Stein expands our sense of what a war story is, but we might also say that the war marks her texts in ways that sometimes depart from Stein's anarchiving practices. For this reason, war may shed special light on Stein's representational practices and modes of archivization and anarchivization.

To write about *Wars I Have Seen* is also necessarily to enter into a larger discussion of Stein's wartime survival in occupied France and her connections to Nazi collaborator Bernard Fäy. These years received coherent treatment in 1996 in an appendix to a volume of Stein's letters and eventually received attention from Janet Malcolm in three *New Yorker* articles, and then later as a nationally reviewed monograph.[7] Malcolm thus brought the controversy from an appendix to the very center of Stein's life in such a way that one cannot write now about a text like *Wars I Have Seen* without thinking about its archive fever, its simultaneous desire to record experience and to erase its own archive of reactionary politics, questionable relationships, and alignments. My contribution to this discussion is limited here to the ability to reflect on the debate itself through some central terms of this book: experience, identity, news, and archivization. This may in turn help to shift the current emphasis in the discussion from retrospective identities and narratives of "happenings" during the war toward terms that better reflect Stein's own textual practice and experiential vision. In other words, Stein's understanding of "happening" versus "existing" seems already to reflect on the questions that have now emerged about her past, which often take Stein's life as a sequence of "happenings" understood retrospectively rather than as a state of "being existing" propelled forward in time. As Derrida argues, archives are like answering machines that always say the same things, except a little bit differently depending on the asker, question, and context. I thus begin with a short discussion of how Stein's terms and textual strategies might help us to reflect on the ways in which the controversy has been framed by Malcolm's *Two Lives*.

Whereas Stein's experimental foray into literary autobiography is conspicuously pleasant and surprisingly devoid of the narrative tensions or mysteries that usually keep readers reading books, *Two Lives* insists upon the elements of Stein's life to which Stein herself seldom, if ever, admitted or confessed. Malcolm's signal question—"How had the elderly

pair of Jewish lesbians escaped the Nazis?"[8]—indicates Malcolm's general orientation toward Stein, which is to wonder about all that Stein
would not or could not confess: her sexual identity, her Jewishness,
the agonies of her adolescence, the devastating loss of her mother,
her fierce need for fame and public acclaim, her connections to Fäy,
and more. Malcolm skillfully opens the doors of the Stein's archival
texts and lets the light shine on Stein's hermetically closed work and
life.[9]

However, Malcolm's central question—"How had the elderly pair of
Jewish lesbians escaped the Nazis?"—presumes and relies upon various
supposedly stable identities: elderly, Jewish, and lesbian. As we saw in the
last chapter, Stein works to intervene in the formation of these very kinds
of identities as they all too often concretize in autobiography, newspapers,
and history. To write history through identity is to give retrospective shape
to an at-best semi-coherent mass of experiences—of "being existing" in
occupied France as elderly, Jewish, and lesbian. It is also to smooth this
"existing" into a grain of narrative "happenings": "during the war, Stein
the elderly, Jewish lesbian did this then this then this." This orientation
toward identity at the expense of lived experience in some sense defines
Malcolm's discussion of Stein's war years, and it is thus premised upon
and structured by certain symptomatic repressions and suppressions of
its own.

Let us consider a moment that can perhaps be considered symptomatic
of this identity-oriented approach to biography and history. While Stein
is writing *Wars I Have Seen,* she is told that she and Alice must either
leave for Switzerland or go to a concentration camp. The startling fact
that they never left for Switzerland seems to raise with great intensity
Malcolm's central question about their decisions and the means of their
survival. Malcolm searches for evidence of their decisions and means in
the passage in *Wars I Have Seen* in which Stein and Alice resolve not to
leave France. Here is the passage as Malcolm cites it:

> We are not moving tomorrow we are going to Switzerland . . . and Alice
> Toklas and I sat down to supper. We both felt funny and then I said. No, I
> am not going we are not going, it is better to go regularly wherever we are
> sent than to go irregularly where nobody can help us if we are in trouble,
> no I said, they are always trying to get us to leave France but here we are
> and here we stay. What do you think, I said, and we thought and I said we
> will walk down to Belley and see the lawyer and tell him no . . . the lawyer
> said perhaps we had better go and then he said he had a house way up in
> the mountains and there nobody would know, and I said well perhaps later
> but now I said to-morrow we are going to move to Culoz, with our large
> comfortable new house with two good servants and a nice big park with

trees, and we all went home, and we did move the next day. It took us some weeks to get over it but we finally did.[10]

Malcolm's account seizes on the mention of their staying where somebody could "help us if we are in trouble," and concludes by quoting and italicizing Stein's words from much earlier in *Wars I Have Seen*—"*Nobody can do anything but take care of you*"[11]—presumably implying that Stein decided to stay in France because she was going to be taken care of by Fäy, just as she is always taken care of by someone, usually Stein's "worker bee,"[12] Toklas.

However, Malcolm's second ellipsis in her quotation of Stein omits a "tender button" of experience that argues for the poverty of historical identification in this account: "We walked down to Belley it was night it was dark but I am always out walking at night, I like it, and I took Alice Toklas by the arm because she has not the habit of walking at night."[13] This moment bears a strong resemblance to the moment in the *Autobiography* in which Stein consoles Toklas and her shaking knees, both as a rare articulation of intimate experience between the two women in Stein's autobiographies and as a representation prompted by the exceptional circumstances and stress of wartime. Although Malcolm uses this passage to make the point that someone always took care of Stein, the omitted section shows Stein taking care of "worker bee" Alice instead. It is a quiet moment of experience during wartime in the dark, and Stein again comforts Alice, who is unused to walking out alone at night. Similarly to the moment in the *Autobiography*, this representation seems to materialize in the text through the extreme stress of Stein and Toklas's experiences, exactly that category of experience that Malcolm accuses Stein of evading in her writing but then chisels out of her own account.

The excision of a rarely represented tender moment between Stein and Toklas at the instant of their crucial decision to stay in France cuts deep.[14] It is to do as traditional autobiography, newspapers, and history do according to Stein, reporting Stein's story retrospectively, as though her experiences could simply be understood *as* history rather than *in* history. In fact, such moments may be by definition what can be omitted from a historical narrative without doing any damage to the identities it asserts, yet what is contained within these moments may pose an anecdotal challenge to narratives of identity. Such historical or biographical narratives presume a point of stable identity that can finesse the experience of "being existing" forward in time into an account of "happening" that tries to narrate history without acknowledging temporality or change. Indeed, Stein's strategy in *Wars I Have Seen* may be seen as a kind of anecdotal response to such erasures of everyday experience during wartime. As Phoebe Stein

Davis writes, "Although a number of critics have argued, as I will here, that Stein's textual 'sorties' rewrite traditional conceptions of history to include the everyday experiences of those who lived in small towns in France during the war, these readings often reassert an opposition between history and the everyday that Stein's war writings work to undermine."[15] "Being existing," or experience, is erased when one plucks out a tender moment between Gertrude and Alice in the night, on their way to declare that they will continue to live just as they have lived for as long as they can live that way, despite consequences and what from their perspective, though not from ours, was the unknown.

To a greater extent than *The Autobiography of Alice B. Toklas* and even *Everybody's Autobiography, Wars I Have Seen* records "being existing" as it is propelled forward into the unknown. Organizationally, *Wars I Have Seen* thus resembles war reportage by trying to record complex and intense experiences of war neither as they have happened in some near or distant past nor from a fixed point of retrospective identity and finished knowledge, but precisely as they unfold, however unmanageable or unspeakable these experiences may be. This perhaps makes *Wars I Have Seen* more like a war journal than an autobiography, and indeed, the packaging of *Wars I Have Seen* when it was published in 1945 markets Stein's book more as war reportage than as autobiography. At the same time, it trades on Stein's identity as a celebrity autobiographer and experimental genius in order to make its sales pitch for her brand of reportage.

This marketing warrants close attention because it represents the uncomfortably hybrid form of Stein's project itself, one that draws upon and intervenes strategically in war reportage but crucially differs from it as well. Random House President Bennett Cerf introduces Gertrude Stein in the front flap of the dustjacket by positioning her as at once extraordinary and ordinary, playing on the differences, or aberrations, that have come to characterize Stein's texts, all the while assuring potential readers that *Wars I Have Seen* will abide by the same contract that the *Autobiography* did:

> Gertrude Stein proved in her *Autobiography of Alice B. Toklas* that, when she wants to, she can write straightforward English that any average high-school student can understand. *Wars I Have Seen,* with a few very minor aberrations, is another such book.[16]

But Cerf quickly qualifies the similarity between autobiographies, because the historical context for *Wars I Have Seen* creates an entirely different set of concerns, constraints, and expectations. These historical exigencies account for some differences from the *Autobiography,* but they are differences that make *Wars I Have Seen* even more accessible and of greater general interest to a wider range of readers, the class of readers interested more in war reporting than in the eccentric autobiographies of modernist expatriates:

> Bear in mind that this entire book was written in longhand under the very noses of the Nazis. After they were driven out of France, Alice Toklas typed the manuscript and Frank Gervasi, who moved in with General Patch's Seventh U.S. Army, brought it back with him to America. *Wars I Have Seen* is the on-the-spot story of what the common people of France endured from 1940 to September, 1944.[17]

Moments after invoking the uncommon Gertrude Stein, Cerf associates her with the common people of France and all they endured during the occupation. Cerf, then, promotes *Wars I Have Seen* as the work of a modernist celebrity, but he also advertises Stein's autobiography as a species of war journalism, an "on-the-spot story." On the one hand, this representation is reinforced by the red strip that runs underneath Stein's cover portrait: "A First-Hand Report of Four Years of Nazi Rule in France and the Joy of Liberation in 1944." On the other hand, the difference between "on-the-spot story" and "first-hand report" may be considered an external sign of the internal tension within *Wars I Have Seen* between story and reportage and the respective generic conventions and expectations of each.

Externally as well as internally, then, *Wars I Have Seen* is marked by the tension between personal journal and war report, but also by the tension between representations of war as experience ("first-hand," "on-the-spot") and the tendency to reduce war retrospectively to a narrative of happenings and abstract identities ("Nazi Rule in France," "The Joy of Liberation"). *Wars I Have Seen* responds to an imperative to conserve experience[18] by at once acting as a form of war reportage, but also by intervening in deep obstacles within war reportage that constantly undermine, erase, or qualify the experiences Stein wishes to archive. Stein's innovative narrative strategies in *Wars I Have Seen* aim to register World War II through a creative and combative relationship to the unending news discourse that Stein at once consumes, writes and overlaps with, and writes against.

During World War II, correspondents also attempted to conserve experience with immediacy unparalleled in the history of war coverage, reporting from close to the action and focusing on the common soldier and his everyday struggles. Not long after World War II, historian Joseph J. Mathews looked back at some of the changes in technique and technology that attempted to draw the news consumer nearer than ever before to the experience of war:

> The war-news consumer of the nineteen-forties was in one sense far closer to events on the battlefields than his grandfather, regardless of the actual distance he might be removed from active fighting. Technical developments in communications had cut the time of transmission, had made it possible to bring to him the sounds of battle by wireless, and the realistic sights of warfare by improved photography. But the great bulk of such news was of the incidental, segmental, and "human interest" variety. It is one of the paradoxes of war-news development that as the progressive mechanization of warfare reduced the relative importance of the individual soldier, the news became centered increasingly on him.[19]

The technology available to war reporters made it easier than ever before to render the senses of war, its sights and sounds, to news consumers, and these technological advancements were supplemented by narratives that emphasized individual soldiers, humanizing them by naming them, and even, as Mathews reports, sometimes supplying their home addresses and their girlfriends' names. Thus, while Stein was recording what the common people of France endured during occupation, reporters were attempting a seemingly parallel task of recording what common soldiers endured in combat.

One need only to look at a few samples of war reportage to verify Mathews's account of how vivid and intimate the details of experience seem to be rendered. Although the dispatches of a single war correspondent cannot represent World War II reportage in the aggregate, the close inspection of specific dispatches may suggest some of the preoccupations and narrative techniques that were favored and valued more generally at this time. Correspondent Ernie Pyle landed with American soldiers in Normandy during July and August of 1944, beginning the push through France that ends for Stein when the Americans finally arrive in Culoz. It is difficult to imagine a more lucid or vivid account of the American advance than the one Pyle paints in his daily dispatches for the Scripps-Howard news service. More than a mere observer, he is an actor in the drama he reports, talking to real life characters, such as Lieutenant Orion Shockley, about military plans and safety:

> "We don't know what we'll run into, and I don't want to stick you right out in front, so why don't you come along with me? We'll go in the middle of the company."

I said, "Okay." By this time I wasn't scared. You seldom are once you're into something. Anticipation is the worst. Fortunately this little foray came up so suddenly there wasn't time for much anticipation.[20]

Pyle reports literally from the middle of things, ready to tell a "first-hand report." In fact, the middle of things is shown to be the safest place to be. Pyle describes the awful anticipation. He draws the news consumer closer by talking about his own feelings and he uses the second person to generalize from his feelings, subtly engaging the addressed news reader in Pyle's experience.

Reviewing Pyle's other dispatches from this offensive, one finds that his intention is always to bring experience home to Americans. Of the men in the Heavy Ordnance Company, Pyle writes, "These men are not in much danger. . . . Compared with the infantry, their life is velvet and they know it and appreciate it. But compared with them your life is velvet. That's what I'd like for you to appreciate."[21] Here the "you" is no longer an abstracted "I," but rather a distinct news reader that Pyle locates along a continuum of relative "danger" and "velvet" that includes and implicates himself, the infantry, the ordnance company, and the American reader at home. Corporal Richard Kelso of the ordnance company, we learn, is 45 years old, and he could be at home "making big money," but "He too sleeps on the ground and works 16 hours a day, and is happy to do it—for boys who are dying are not 3000 miles away and abstract; they are 10 miles away and very, very real."[22] Pyle is aware of how abstract 3,000 miles can make war, soldiers, and death seem to his distant audience. In this example, as in the previous one, readers may be struck by a sudden awareness of their own tendency toward abstraction as Pyle forces them to recognize his dispatches as records of experience and to resist the abstraction that can accrue over great distances. His approach to representing perspective and sensory information is so disciplined that readers are constantly positioned in the space of the soldiers, with very little relief from this immediacy, such as might come from more distant accounts of political speeches, troop movements, and death tolls.

Dispatches such as Pyle's "The Universe Became Filled with a Gigantic Rattling" describe the massive bombing by German forces and contain vivid representations of the experience: "And then all of an instant the universe became filled with a gigantic rattling as of huge, dry seeds in a mammoth dry gourd. I doubt that any of us had ever heard that sound before, but instinct told us what it was. It was bombs by the hundred, hurtling down through the air above us."[23] Here, Pyle underscores his own and the soldier's limited horizon of experience as they encounter something new that exceeds their previous expectations; but their war-sensitized instincts quickly allow them to read the significance and to imagine the scale of bombing. Another dispatch describes how terribly the pilots must feel whose friendly fire killed many soldiers and almost killed Pyle himself (Pyle's own fate was to be shot by a Japanese gunman on an island off the coast of Okinawa less than a year later): "I'm sure that back in England that night other men—bomber crews—almost wept, and maybe they did really, in the awful knowledge that they had killed our own American troops. But I want to say this to them. . . . Any-body makes mistakes."[24] In the process of sending a consolatory message to the American bombers in England, Pyle sends an emotional message to his larger audience, asking them to empathize with the bombers' tears and grief. His reportage relies not upon factual evidence, for he never sees or meets those who dropped the bombs, but rather upon appeals to the capacity of readers to empathize with distant experiences. Pyle also does not turn his gaze from death. He shows his audience the "shell craters," "little pools of blood on the roadside," "burned-out tanks," "cows in the fields, lying grotesquely with their feet to the sky, so newly dead they have not begun to bloat or smell"; he records "the inhuman quiet," and "the men dead so recently that they seem to be merely asleep."[25] "There is nothing left behind but the remains—the lifeless debris, the sunshine and the flowers, and utter silence."[26]

In these vivid ways, carefully crafting description and attentive at all times to perspective, Ernie Pyle attempts to bring news consumers across a great distance to the sights and experiences of war. However, there is more in the news process and form for which to account before we can evaluate how successfully experience is communicated or preserved in such war dispatches. Again, looking back on the recent war coverage, Mathews also observes:

> In another sense the World War II citizen was further removed from the battlefields than his forbears. . . . Between the ordinary civilian and the war in its larger and more profound aspects there came into existence a varied array of middlemen and a host of governmental agencies . . . [that] selected, synthesized, summarized, and interpreted the news. No matter where the reader or listener resided, a great portion of the information that reached him had undergone a process of selection and refinement . . . .[27]

The attempt to render experience in news dispatches during World War II encounters barriers inherent to news organization and form. On the one hand, correspondents refined techniques of description, narration, and perspective that brought readers very near to the sounds and sights of warfare. But on the other hand, the technology of news and the growing scale and complexity of mass media mitigates this potential nearness. The mechanized and multiply-mediated forms and frames of news come into conflict with the correspondent's increasing closeness to the action and to the experience of war. Even the context in which Pyle's reports would eventually be published, alongside other stories determined largely by calendrical coincidence, mediates the vivid impressions of his accounts. Finally, we might notice how Pyle's dispatches terminate, as Benjamin argues newspaper reading does, in appeals to empathy that require readers to imagine events in distant spaces that they could hardly recognize as their own. The imaginative movement is always one in which the news consumer at home is asked to travel empathetically to the battlefields alongside vividly represented soldiers who remain, nonetheless, in a space apart.

"THERE ARE SO MANY ENDS TO STORIES THESE DAYS"

Stein is primarily concerned with a feature of news discourse that is different from any of these qualifications about war reportage. As we have seen, Stein identifies form as a central problem for news because it contains neither beginnings nor endings: "That is where the newspaper is interesting, there is of course no beginning and no ending to anything they are doing, it is when it is and in being when it is being there is no beginning and no ending."[28] By implication, although Ernie Pyle can hope for or anticipate the end of the war in his correspondence, the news itself neither hopes to end nor anticipates ending. This is precisely the problem that *Wars I Have Seen* engages by linking the ability to represent the nearness and pathos of experience with the narrative capacity of bringing an end to both narrative content and form. Recall that for Benjamin as well endings, and especially the finality of death, give experience communicable form and meaning. Given the specific historical and technological configuration of news, experience becomes elusive unless the stream of information itself can be productively arrested.

Before turning to examples of Stein's practice of ending, it is important to see how she peculiarly positions war news in the daily lives of those in the occupied French countryside. In *Wars I Have Seen* war news is a constant feature of life, but Stein notes that everybody seems to rely upon local word of mouth instead of the news that arrives through the radio. It is a fact that Stein at once marvels at and validates:

> That is what makes it so extraordinary, everybody listens to the radio, they listen all day long because almost everybody has one and if not there is their neighbor's and they listen to the voice from any country and yet what they really believe is not what they hear but the rumors in the town, by

word of mouth is always the most convincing, they do not believe the
newspapers nor the radio but they do believe what they tell each other and
that is natural enough, all official news is so deceiving, so why not believe
rumors... at any rate they have a chance of being true rumors have but
official news has no chance of being true none at all, of course not. (161)

For those within the occupied area, rumor supersedes official news. For
such people, rumors at least risk becoming true, while official news serves
little function for those who are actually subject to the forces of war. At
the same time, official news stubbornly adheres to daily life, a constant
feature of life in wartime. Even Stein goes to sleep each night listening to
the news on the radio, but she claims that it makes no impression upon
her; she does not even consider what the radio reports when she weighs
evidence for whether or not the Germans are returning to her region.

The quotidian signs of life in occupied France seem to produce better
knowledge for Stein than could be learned from the airwaves or read in
the newspapers. For instance, Stein notices that wild ducks, whose pop-
ulations had been hunted thin in years past, now fearlessly populate the
landscape. How quickly the ducks "form old habits again," Stein marvels
(101). Pushcarts, archaic in France before the war, are back in fashion,
as though automobiles had never succeeded them in the Parisian streets
(101–102). Life in occupied France as Stein represents it is a life against
the backdrop of wild ducks and pushcarts, which conveys more to Stein
than the background noises of radio and newspapers can about what
it is like to experience war and how to gather meaningful and reliable
intelligence about it.

A similar truth value might even inhere in the wild rumors that cir-
culate in the countryside, such as the rumor of an unnatural coupling
and birth that Stein hears from a woman whose niece had just been in a
maternity ward in Bourg:

> [The niece] told her that a woman in the Maternity in Bourg had just been
> brought to bed that is she just been delivered of six little puppy dogs, not
> possibly I said, but yes she said, not often but quite often, you see she said,
> in times like these women do console themselves with dogs and this does
> happen, of course the dogs dont survive they are kept in museums, but it
> does happen, not really I said, oh yes she said, in Bourg they once had it
> happen to a nun, and when the doctor went to see her the dog would not
> let him come near her. Did it really happen oh yes, she said it does happen
> and it did happen. (168)

For Stein, the experience of war can be crystallized in such anecdotal stories that, while certainly fictional, nonetheless represent the dislocations of

human experience on a recognizable scale and with uncanny or shocking intimacy. At first Stein resists the story of the woman who births a litter of pups, taking up a stance of biological realism, but neither Stein's skeptical "not possibly" nor "did it really" can shake the woman's belief in her story. Stein lets the woman have the last word, insisting to the end that "it does happen and it did happen," but though the content of the statement is the woman's, its form is typical of Stein's own style, a style such as in the sentence that ends the first paragraph of the book, "I did and I do." Thus, though Stein continues to disbelieve, perhaps she also joins her style to the woman's impossible claims in order to meet her halfway between credulity and incredulity. After all, the impossible rumor surely does not tell truth or fact, but it may articulate the intimate truth about the way it feels to live in conditions that everybody once imagined impossible. This anecdote might be compared to the first paragraph of *Wars I Have Seen* in which Stein narrates her own birth: "To begin with I was born, that I do not remember but I was told about it quite often" (3). Although she cannot remember it and must be told about it, Stein's birth is incontrovertibly true. But it raises the question with which *Wars I Have Seen* begins: "I do not know whether to put in the things I do not remember as well as the things I do remember" (3). Stein chooses to put her birth in, but because she cannot remember the experience it is treated summarily and ambivalently, ultimately conveying to herself and to her audience very little. On the other hand, the litter's birth, though fictional and thus also incapable of being directly experienced or strictly remembered, yet attaches through its anecdotal form to the experience the war, and perhaps reveals more and assumes greater substance in *Wars I Have Seen* than Stein's own birth.[29]

However, as much as Stein's practice differs from news by valuing rumor over report, it also mirrors news in significant ways. For instance, Stein's anecdotal collection of stories is grouped much like stories in the newspaper because, like the daily newspaper, she scrupulously registers whatever occurs with each uncertain passing month, and events are arranged primarily by calendrical coincidence. The stories themselves can duplicate this structure of temporal coincidence in their very content, which are often about the experience of war contingencies. For instance, on one of her daily walks Stein meets a peasant woman whose grandson, André, has been taken to a labor camp in Germany. The woman tells Stein how André had been sick when he was 12, but when he became 19 he had to be examined by the Germans to see whether he would be taken away: "The first visit they said no he did not need to go and the second visit they said no he did not need to go and the third visit they said go . . ." (85). Stein tries to register what it feels like when the decisions that most affect one's life are out of one's own hands, and when those who do decide seem unpredictable, unfair, or inexplicable:

> ... that is the horrifying thing about an occupied country, the uneasiness in the eyes of all young men and in the eyes of their fathers mothers sisters and brothers, and wives, that uneasiness because at any moment they can be taken away at any moment, their papers can be all in order and yet, and then papers can not be in order and also, and just now our neighbors were telling us of a young man we had known him very well in Belley and later here, and he would go out to the nearest town to buy bread, and his mother said no do not, and he said but mother my papers are in order and he went and he did not come back.... (156–157)

Some people with all of their papers in order are taken away, while others without papers in order are left as they are. Stein emphasizes that these events are sudden and immediate when she stresses that she and Alice have "just now" heard their neighbor's story. In the face of brutal and unpredictable power, it might as easily have happened just yesterday, or just tomorrow, or never. The experience of life comes to feel as contingent and startling as the very form of the newspaper itself and the contingent relationships among its parts.

Stein counsels the woman to "write him all the details of your daily life just the way we have been talking and how you remember him as a little boy that will comfort him ..." (85), suggesting that stories of everyday experience and memory can be consolatory or strengthening. In many ways, Stein's advice to the grieving grandmother characterizes her own project in *Wars I Have Seen*. She tells the woman to write her own *Wars I Have Seen* by selecting from what she experiences and what she remembers. *Wars I Have Seen* thus becomes a constellation or archive of the kinds of stories Stein suggests the woman should write to her grandson, recording the details of daily life.

In this sense, *Wars I Have Seen* implicitly takes up the question of the way in which the relationship between the history of war and experience should be imagined. Shall the history of war be construed as homogenous, empty wartime filled up with battles and names? Shall it be the determinist history of how the war sealed the fates of individuals thrown in its path? Or shall it be the continuous record of "being existing" during the war? For Stein, as much as the war seems to determine her experience and as much as her own life can be narrated through the scaffolding of military history—"From war to war" (190)—Stein seems to resist the definition of war as an outside force that shapes everybody's experiences. Instead, she catalogues the unique personal experiences that she sees and hears about in meticulous detail as a way of recording history on a human scale and using human-scaled stories. Accordingly, Stein's text is comprised of a series of anecdotes about Stein's life and the lives of the many "common" people she meets in occupied France during the war. Over and over, Stein emphasizes the endings of these stories, some of which are examined in the next section.

ANECDOTES OF ENDINGS

"There are so many ends to stories these days so many ends that it is not like it was there is nothing to be curious about except small things, food and the weather" (100). Stein differentiates her model of war history from the reporter's model by showing how often the reporter's continuous and overarching war really ends for individuals continuously. For example:

> We had a friend whose name was Gilbert and he was gone away and his wife followed him and the little girl Christine was left behind with some neighbors, we did not know them and one day a red-headed and active young fellow asked for me and I saw him and I said what and he said I have a message to you from Gilbert, ah I said is the little girl not well, oh yes he said she is all right she is staying with us, ah yes I said, do you need anything for her, I said and he said no she was all right and he was fiddling with a matchbox and I said well and he said the message is in here and I said you had better go, and he said are you afraid of me and I said no and you had better go and dont you want the message he said and I said no you had better go and he said I will go and he had tears in his eyes and he went out and told the servant that we had not received his message and a friend said were you not curious and I said no not. (100)

It seems clear enough that the Germans have taken Gilbert and his wife away. However, it is unclear what message the matchbox contains, how it came to contain a message, or how it came to be addressed to Stein. Has somebody in Germany sent a matchbox with news of either Gilbert's or his wife's death? If so, who sent it and why would the addressee be Stein and not the daughter's current guardians? Is it some request from Gilbert, perhaps for money? This seems unlikely because Stein rejects the matchbox but has just offered to help the daughter. Perhaps the message will ask her to try to intercede on Gilbert's behalf with connections such as Bernard Fäy? Whatever the case, Stein disavows being frightened or curious, and yet the passage seems to belie her word. She turns to verbal antidotes as some awful reality asserts itself: the rhythmic repetitions intensify, as do the frequency of rhyming words "no" and "go," which deny and repel the message in the matchbox. The passage models the way in which Stein contains the bad news coiled in this little matchbox by taking possession of the experience, sculpting it into a stylized narrative form and then asserting an ending to it.

The matchbox models the anecdote itself. Its diminutive form comes into Stein's intimate space carrying some intense potential experience. Stein feels helpless in the face of this intrusion of the message into her space. The arrival of the little container for experience leaves Stein unguarded by any mediating or abstracting contexts. She is not asked, as Pyle's news reader is, to empathetically imagine a distant experience; rather, that experience is brought home to her, hand delivered in the tiny container. In the course of modeling her denial of the matchbox's power, Stein in effect crafts her own experience into another anecdote, another textual matchbox in a series that line up in Stein's text to be delivered to her own readers with vivid and sometimes equally unsettling nearness.

Stein associates the ability to narrate, shape, and contain terrifying experiences with the ongoing struggle to maintain sanity. Soon after recounting the matchbox anecdote Stein remarks, "The funny part of it all is that relatively few people seem to go crazy" (100). For Stein, survival seems to mean the ability to exert control over what is often the only thing one *can* control—narrative—before madness intervenes and takes even narrative capability away. This is evident when Stein meets an "oldish woman" along the road and she tells Stein a species of "pleasant" story (106):

> Just the other day a camion came along and he ran over one of our chickens and he did not notice it he just went on but a little later another one came along and he noticed it and he stopped and got down and gathered in the chicken and went on, just then my nephew came out and saw him and as he went away he noticed the number so a little later when the camion came back again my nephew stopped him and said you have to pay me for that chicken that is to say not money I do not want money I want the chicken, and the man said not at all I will pay you but I will not give you the chicken . . . and he drove away and said I what did your nephew do, I have no nephew she said I only have a niece that is to say I only have a father-in-law, that is not my home where I live it belongs to my brother-in-law and just then our roads parted and we said good-bye. (107–108)

It is impossible to tell whether the woman's nephew has been killed, whether she is mad, or whether she has been driven mad because her nephew has been killed. Whatever the truth, her narrative records the mundane and quotidian dimensions of life and disconnects just short of reporting the event Stein has become curious about. What one receives in place of a satisfying account for the woman's story is a different sort of ending, one that reports nothing, but perhaps conveys quite a lot. It is not an ending that terminates in revelation or confirmation, but one that rather ends by diverging along a different path. The woman's anecdote ends with many endings: a chicken is killed, a nephew disappears, and the women's paths diverge. The story reports personal experience and seems saturated with endings, but here endings do not invite, but rather defer, the sense we expect and associate with ending. As in Stein's anecdote about the matchbox, this anecdote heightens the feeling of ending in the very process of evading conclusions.

Later in *Wars I Have Seen*, Stein's friend, a captain of the gendarmerie and the father of a little girl, "has just been carried off, whether by the mountain boys whether by the Germans nobody seems to know" (144). Under these conditions all accounts of the disappearance seem suspect, and rumors all seem to have equal possibility of being true, but may all be equally irrelevant:

> Whether it is to put down the mountain boys whether it is because a German colonel has been killed whether it is because they are afraid of a landing whether it is because they do not know what to do, whether it is because it is coming to an end and an end has to be like the end at the theatre when the piece comes to an end a state of confusion, whatever it is our good and gentle friend has been taken and we are very sad. (144)

Stein's transition from "whether" to "whatever" directs readers away from causes and toward effects. The language of "whether" and "because" moves in a direction away from the captain's disappearance. This is impersonal language and accounting, of putting down the Resistance, of killing a German colonel, of fear, and of the whole war coming to an end, a word that is repeated four times in the sentence. The shift to "whatever" near the end of the paragraph signals a transition to language of a more personal nature: "good," "gentle," "friend," and "very sad." The potential causes of the captain's disappearance shrink from importance, sinking into the passive form of "has been taken." Syntactically, Stein moves from sentences in which the potential agents of the captain's disappearance are awarded subject status to sentences in which the captain himself is restored as the subject and as the focus of Stein's attention and her grief. All three of these anecdotes to some extent use endings to shape, focus, and contain grief from life during wartime, representing Stein's consistent anecdotal strategy throughout *Wars I Have Seen*.

DESIRING THE END OF AUTOBIOGRAPHY

In *Wars I Have Seen*, it is not just individual stories that end, but the book desires its own end as well. Stein plots the duration of her narrative to match the exact duration of the war. When it ends, she will end her autobiography. The autobiography may be seen as an archive of personal anecdotes that thematize and wish for an end to the war itself. Stein sees evidence everywhere that the war will end soon in late 1943, but by the winter of 1944 she begins to fear that the war will never end at all. This uncertainty must help to account for Stein's anecdotal or episodic structure, but the experience of uncertainty is also registered in the shape of these anecdotes themselves, which can be seen as narrative expressions of uncertainty about when and how the war will end.

Stein explicitly ties the end of her story to the end of the war, and, in the act of writing, she looks forward to the end of writing: "then that will finish the book the first American tank and surely it will be coming along, one week or two weeks the pessimists say three weeks" (233). Stein's daily writing is a form of waiting, a writing whose goal is to cease writing, and Liberation is in part the realization of the goal of arresting writing:

> What a day what a day of days, I always did say that I would end this book with the first American that came to Culoz, and to-day oh happy day yesterday and to-day the first of September 1944. (244)

Stein gives a quick, almost perfunctorily patriotic account of meeting the first American soldiers and then, with the exception the epilogue, her narrative is ended.

In conclusion, we can count the many resemblances between Stein's autobiography and Ernie Pyle's reportage, demonstrating the affinity and commensurability of their projects. Like Stein, Ernie Pyle used description and perspective to capture the experiences of individual soldiers and to draw an empathetic audience across a great distance to be remarkably close to the sounds, sights, and feelings of the war. Like Stein, Ernie Pyle could break the abstraction of war into a series of smaller wars, as the title of his dispatch "Each One Is a Separate Little War" suggests.[30] Like Stein, Pyle could also conceivably wish for an end to the war. But this is as close as the structure of news can come to ending. News itself has no desire to end and can never wish for its own end. In this way, there is always a potential tension between the necessarily limited structure of news (the system of selection, synthesizing, summary, juxtaposition, dissemination, and interpretation) and its nearly limitless range of potential content upon, as we have seen, "extend[ing] its purview to life as a whole."[31]

When Stein writes in creative relation to reportage, she negotiates this tension within news by stressing endings and deferring report and explanation. Further, she correlates anecdotes that end with a wish for the war to end with the ending of her book. Wish, content, and form converge in a constellation of different figurations of experience. As "A First-Hand Report of Four Years of Nazi Rule in France and the Joy of Liberation in 1944," *Wars I Have Seen* both misses and exceeds the mark. She reports Nazi rule not as an identity or event itself, but as daily life during war, a life in which Nazi rule could at turns seem background for personal experience or could just as quickly snatch a family member or a neighbor away. While Stein's description of liberation has joyful elements, more than any other function, liberation serves to put an end to *Wars I Have Seen.* Liberation frees Stein from the burden of her own book and the grave obligation to report experience.

Here we can circle back to Benjamin, who, like Stein, also recognized the value of "a messianic arrest of happening."[32] "The historical materialist," Benjamin writes, "cannot do without the notion of a present which is not a transition, but in which time takes a stand [*einsteht*] and has come to a standstill. For this notion defines the very present in which he himself is writing history."[33] The techniques we have observed in modernist fiction for isolating experience from the stream of information through anecdotal nearness and shock finds its complement in the materialist historiographer's intervention in the seemingly endless transitions and happenings of historicism in the form of a revealing and revelatory standstill. Here too, the standstill is associated with shock: "Thinking involves not only the movement of thoughts but their arrest as well. Where thinking suddenly comes to a stop in a constellation saturated with tensions, it gives that constellation a shock, by which thinking is crystallized as a monad."[34] By the time we reach *Wars I Have Seen,* there is practically nothing that separates Stein's vivid depiction of individual war experiences from Ernie Pyle's vivid depictions of individual soldiers' experiences. Practically nothing can finally distinguish modernist fiction from news. The privileged sphere of the "literary" is now everywhere and nowhere. The purview of the news is finally everything. Between Stein and Pyle, as I have argued, there is little besides the ability to end, arrest, or stand still that can distinguish them. But it may be that this is no small difference in the age of endless information.

CODA: MAKE IT NOW

HERE *Modernist Fiction and News* comes full circle back to the questions with which it began: where and how in the flood of information can experience be located and articulated? Where and how in the endless mass of "happenings" can something like Stein's "being existing" be represented, and what is the potential value of representing this form of experience? I have defined modernist fiction throughout as that set of texts that first faced with seriousness the new infinite potential of information recording, powerfully emblematized in the expansion and mass production of news narratives from which modernist fiction itself was inseparable. Modernist novels are thus self-conscious archives, both conservative and radical, revolutionary and reactionary in the exact same space, texts that at once authorize, sign, conserve, repress, and destroy information in peculiarly tense constellations that are or aspire to be productive of experience. In the preceding chapters, I have tried to read these constellations and their archival projects (and archive fevers) through the shock produced when they arrest and crystallize the stream of information and happenings into experiences of their own.

As Beatrice Hanssen explains, for Benjamin, "Once humans recognized language's unfathomed revolutionary potential, perhaps it might field a blow, issue a redemptive shock, undoing the numbing anaesthetic and aestheticized shock effects of modernity's culture of dispersal."[1] This was a faith in radical language acts that modernist novelists shared with Benjamin. Indeed, I have argued that the form most characteristic of the modernist strategy of nearness and shock is the anecdote as Benjamin conceives it. Over the course of this book it has frequently been possible to point to the anecdotal qualities of the texts examined, from the episodic nature of *Finnegans Wake* to the gossipy autobiographies of Gertrude Stein. In the broadest sense, the anecdotal perception of modernist fiction constitutes its form of engagement and negotiation with neighboring discourses within its media ecology. The anecdote is a narrative space that attempts to elude mediation and abstraction, and to communicate human-scaled experience with an arresting shock. If news, as Benjamin argues, leads readers to empathize with distant events, drawing Magritte's newspaper reader out of his kitchen or Woolf's sympathetic narrator to imaginatively peek over a widow's shoulder, then modernist fiction attempts again and again to bring distant events and experiences into the reader's kitchen, where abstract empathy might give way to unmediated and immediate pathos. The anecdote, as Benjamin argues, brings things into one's immediate space, without mediating contexts. It can allow concrete historical truth to emerge as a shock out of the distancing techniques of historicism. The anecdote is also perfectly poised to intervene in the early twentieth-century media ecology, with its reconfiguration of public and private spheres, because the anecdote itself occupies the liminal space between these spheres. The root of the anecdote, as we have seen, can paradoxically mean both "things unpublished" and "to give out, publish." The anecdote, then, is always in some sense private but in the process of becoming public, or public but retreating into the private. When modernist fiction is understood as primarily anecdotal it can be seen as always in the process of emerging into and retreating from the public media ecology. It is in the tense process of the private coming into public, and of experience emerging from the abstractions and empathies of historicism and news discourse, that we may be able to locate the historical character of modernist fiction and to recognize its complex forms of interaction and intervention.

Here I would like to step back a little in order to consider the value of this mode of reading the modernist novel and modernist fiction. When I talk to friends and acquaintances about this project, many are surprised by the extent to which the current trends and state of news discourse can be traced back to the New Journalism of the early twentieth century. It is common to hear that news discourse is in or is approaching a state of crisis. A simple Web search brings up many books about this contemporary crisis by journalists and scholars alike, with titles such as *Losing the News: The Future of the News That Feeds Democracy; What Is Happening to News: The Information Explosion and the Crisis in Journalism; Junk News: The Failure of the Media in the 21st Century; Bad News: The Decline of Reporting, the Business of News, and the Danger to Us All; Breaking the News: How the Media Undermine American Democracy; No Time to Think: The Menace of Media Speed and the 24-hour New Cycle; When the Press Fails: Political Power and the News Media from Iraq to Katrina.* The keywords in these representative titles tell a story and give a sense of the high stakes of the news crisis: democracy, information explosion, junk, failure, decline, business, danger, breaking, undermine, menace, speed, 24-hour, and power. It is common to hear concerns about the ways in which our culture's incredible (maybe even unthinkable) capacity for information storage threatens journalism, and thus the public sphere and democracy. It is common to hear complaints about the sensationalism of contemporary news discourse and its tendency to blur the lines between news, celebrity, and entertainment. Many accuse the press of dereliction of its public duty, or even complicity, in the rush to war in Iraq and Afghanistan. The fact that there are so many books on the subject also suggests that creative solutions and revisions are in high demand.

These concerns about the status quo of today's multinational corporate news and entertainment conglomerates feel urgent and timely, and yet the modernists considered in this book might not view the contemporary news environment as so very alien from their own, but perhaps rather as a magnification or intensification of what was already coming into place and becoming familiar, if not natural, to them. After all, they were among the first people in world history to live with and adapt to the capitalist organization of news. They were the first to see news content driven by circulation, demographics, and advertising revenues. They witnessed more extensive incursions into private life, personality, crime, and scandal than anybody had seen before. They saw news proprietors and barons bend all of the means of influence and manipulation at their disposal to make a case for going to war and for other press crusades. They saw increasing swaths of life become newsworthy to such an extent that it became a challenge to identify what was truly noteworthy. In short, they lived through a transition in which public life and the media ecology came to be dominated by the abstract, distant, fleeting, and alienating modes of experience that Benjamin calls *Erlebnis*. This transition not only threatened public life, narrative and storytelling, and the ability to select, conserve, and prioritize information, but also undermined the very status and grain of experience itself. By now this condition is arguably total, and to many the feeling of *Erlebnis* may feel entirely, if not always comfortably, naturalized.

Yet the modernists were also people who kept one foot outside of the transition and who thus had a chance to intervene seriously and creatively at a nascent and, therefore for us, perhaps illuminating moment in the development of recording technologies and the formation of the media ecology. Seeing the gradual but dramatic bleeding out of experience in public life as a media ecology dominated by *Erlebnis* emerged, modernist novelists began to establish a set of creative models for artistically evoking, recalling, and generating meaningful experiences and even a pathos of nearness that was increasingly scarce in modern life and narrative. In the context of the numbing and distancing rhythms of life experienced as *Erlebnis,* these textual experiments may be alternately experienced as shock and meaningful disruption. In a culture of news stories

that seem confidently to cover every avenue of life and every corner of
human experience, but which blur together in their profusion and seem to
push reported experiences ever more distant, modernist novels try to find
ways of arresting the flow, of asserting the intimate experience of an other,
and of demanding of the fictional audience a unique experience of reading. Whether it is Joyce asking readers to wrestle sense out of *Finnegans
Wake* until some intimate fragment of experience suddenly emerges, free
of any context but the reader's own space, or Dos Passos adopting the style
of news discourse but shooting it through with jarring shards of unsettling
experiential detail, or Stein's magnificent narrative and temporal contor-
tions in the service of articulating "being existing," modernist fiction asks
readers momentarily to arrest the condition of *Erlebnis* and "make it now."

This definition of the modernist novel leads to questions about the
methods for studying modernism. New modernist studies has often
contented itself with a purely historicist mode. While this undeniably
productive mode has led to powerful and necessary revisions of canonical modernism, increasing our comprehension of the complex interaction
between modernism and its first cultures, it may also be subject to the
shortcomings that Benjamin attributes to historicism if it cuts present
concerns off from the past, and fails to put history and modernist texts
in immediate relation to the present. It is possible to historicize a modernism so complexly rooted in the early twentieth century that it becomes
hermetically sealed from the only people capable of reading or benefiting
from modernism's creative models at any given time: those in the present.

As the centenaries of all the major modernist works loom just on our
horizon, modernism threatens to fall into historical abstraction as it never
quite has before. This threat is especially great for today's and tomorrow's
students, who very soon will have no firsthand memories of the twentieth
century at all. Alone, a thoroughly historicized modernism will not necessarily bring the modernist period any nearer nor make it more valuable
to such readers, nor will it necessarily rescue modernism from the abstractions that distances of the centennial kind bring. As we saw earlier, when
Benjamin wanted to redeem the stretch of abstracted time from Christ's
birth to the present, he invented a fictional anecdote that measured time
in the scale of concrete human lives. It may be something of a shock to
realize that a succession of 50-year-olds from the time of Christ's death
to Benjamin's present would have amounted to fewer than 40 generations. The purpose Benjamin attributed to this anecdotal fiction, recall,
was "to apply a standard to historical times that would be adequate and
comprehensible to human life. This pathos of nearness, the hatred of the
abstract configuration of human life in epochs, has animated the great
skeptics."[2] As I have argued in this book, modernist novelists employed

the same style of anecdotal shock in order to attempt to extract a pathos of nearness from the alienating rhythm of the world and its distant daily narratives. As Gertrude Stein said, and as other modernists knew, "Words are shocks."[3]

Modernist Fiction and News, then, proposes less a new modernist studies so much as a "now" modernist studies. This presentist approach studies modernism neither solely on its own historical or cultural terms nor for its own sake, but also because it presumes that modernism matters most right now, and always has. Critics who have recently studied modernism within mass media tend to recognize this. In *British Writers and the Media, 1930–1945,* Keith Williams argues that his study "may make the intellectual adaptation necessary for catching up with the dizzying economic and technological mutations of our current condition at least more conceivable by evaluating the promises and failures of this neglected transition in cultural history."[4] Similarly, in *Modernism on Fleet Street,* Patrick Collier makes explicit that "The modernists got to this roadblock before us; we continue the effort to think a way around it."[5] I am also very much in agreement with Mark Wollaeger, who argues eloquently for modernism's "valuable experience of difficulty" and believes that modernism "solicits the kind of rhetorical literacy appropriate to the discursive dilemmas that have evolved out of the media environment."[6] As Wollaeger says, "critical reading attentive to history and to nuances of language is a precondition for good citizenship."[7] His Joseph Conrad is thus a modernist novelist for the present moment, one who can be "an agent of critique, a writer whose oddly textured prose, disjointed narratives, and elusive tonal complexity demand the kind of rhetorical literacy necessary for navigating the deceptive terrain of public discourse."[8] Wollaeger matches a deep historicism with an urgent understanding that there is literally no time like the present.

While critical perception, attentiveness, and rhetorical literacy are much needed in the contemporary public sphere, reading modernism with one eye, or both, on the present might help to envision even more dramatic possibilities than the bourgeois public sphere can contain. For instance, Andreas Huyssen, as we have seen, looks with approval to Benjamin's affinities with the techniques of the Russian avant-garde that would produce a necessary disruption of lived experience, a disruption that could serve as "a prerequisite for any revolutionary reorganization of everyday life."[9] As Huyssen argues,

> it was especially Benjamin's emphatic notion of experience *(Erfahrung)* and profane illumination that separated him from Brecht's enlightened trust in ideology critique and pointed to a definite affinity between Benjamin

and the Russian avantgarde. Just at Tretyakov, in his futurist poetic strategy relied on shock to alter the psyche of the recipient of art, Benjamin, too, saw shock as a key to changing the mode of reception of art and to disrupting the dismal and catastrophic continuity of everyday life.[10]

Although Huyssen wants to align Benjamin with a European avant-garde antiseptically distinct from modernism, I hope *Modernist Fiction and News* adds to the dissenting view that this dichotomy is a false one, that modernist novelists, too, employed Benjaminian strategies of shock to disrupt "the dismal and catastrophic continuity of everyday life." Like Benjamin, modernist novelists cultivated strategies to represent experience within a media ecology in which more and more stories were being told, more and more information was being recorded and disseminated, and less and less of what was meaningful or noteworthy was being communicated or even, indeed, experienced.

This condition is one facet of the modernist period from which today's readers are not increasingly distant, but rather ever closer. Benjamin liked to talk about traces, for instance, the personal traces and impressions that the denizens of the nineteenth century left in the abundantly plush surfaces of their interiors. How many infinitely more traces does each of now us leave, as plush surfaces have given way to sophisticated recording devices that log every click, keystroke, and Internet search, track every digital page turned, and follow our global positions as we walk from the sofa to the refrigerator with phones in our pockets? In short, there is almost nothing that cannot now be recorded, stored, and reported, but among all of these packets of information, where does anything resembling meaningful experience reside? Moreover, the insistent stream of information itself, primarily through the media ecology, has transformed the rhythm and face of experience so much that our own experiences are perhaps reduced to the very quanta of information that we unendingly both produce and consume. The problems that the modernists first faced have thus become our own urgent problems. Increasingly, we find ourselves stuck in our own feedback loops of information. There may be no outside to this media ecology, but there are opportunities for meaningfully innovating with information and experience from within that modernist fiction open up for us, both as experiences of reading and as models for future critical creativity.

Contrary to views that see modernism as striving for autonomy or withdrawal from mass media, modernist novels attempt experimentally and with difficulty to articulate experience from within the media ecology. The concomitant act of reading modernist novels constitutes a second difficult experience that follows from the initial act of articulation.

Modernist fiction thus asks us and helps us to evaluate the place and types of experience in our lives and the lives of our contemporaries. The novels and narrative prose of Woolf, Joyce, Dos Passos, Stein, and others recall to us the qualities of nearness, mindfulness, and attentiveness that so easily slip from grasp. Modernism can then help to cultivate a habit of mindfulness that keeps one open to one's experiences and to the experiences of others. This kind of mindfulness is itself a form of *Erfahrung* that cuts through *Erlebnis*. What emerges in one's own intimate space in such an attentive condition can be a receptiveness to shock and pathos of a kind that temporarily opens possibilities that exist beyond our daily lives. There is no telling what may now be made new from such disruptions.

NOTES

INTRODUCTION

1. "Every morning brings us news from across the globe, yet we are poor in noteworthy stories" Walter Benjamin, "The Storyteller," in Howard Eiland and Michael W. Jennings, eds. *Selected Writings, Volume 3 1935–1938* (Cambridge: Harvard University Press, 2002), 147.
2. Walter Benjamin, "On Some Motifs in Baudelaire," in Howard Eiland and Michael W. Jennings, eds. *Selected Writings, Volume 4 1938–1940* (Cambridge: Harvard University Press, 2003), 316.
3. John McCole, *Walter Benjamin and the Antinomies of Tradition* (Ithaca and London: Cornell University Press, 1993), 272.
4. Quoted in Hamilton Fyfe, *Northcliffe: An Intimate Biography* (New York: Macmillan, 1930), 82. The passage is worth quoting in full:

   > You could search the Victorian newspapers in vain for any reference to changing fashions, for instance. You could not find in them anything that would help you to understand the personalities of public men. We cannot get from them a clear and complete picture of the times in which they were published, as one could from *The Daily Mail*. Before that was published, journalism dealt with only a few aspects of life. What we did was to extend its purview to life as a whole.

5. Matthew Arnold coined the term "new journalism" in 1887: "We have had opportunities of observing a new journalism which a clever and energetic man [William T. Stead of the *Pall Mall Gazette*] has lately invented. It has much to recommend it; it is full of ability, novelty, variety, sensation, sympathy, generous instincts; its one great fault is that it is *feather-brained*. It throws out assertions at a venture because it wishes them true; does not correct either them or itself, if they are false; and to get at the state of things as they truly are seems to feel no concern whatever. Well, the democracy, with abundance of life, movement, sympathy, good instincts, is disposed to be, like this journalism, feather-brained . . ." Quoted in Laurel Brake, "The Old Journalism and the New: Forms of Cultural Production in London in the 1880s," in *Papers for the Millions: The New Journalism in Britain, 1850s to 1914*, ed. Joel H. Wiener (New York, Westport, and London: Greenwood, 1988), 15.

6. "Thus, in the general expansion, and conditioned by the new kind of 'mass' advertising, the real 'Northcliffe Revolution' in the press occurred, taking the newspaper from its status as an independent private enterprise to its membership of a new kind of capitalist combine. The real basis of the twentieth-century popular press was thus effectively laid," Raymond Williams, *The Long Revolution* (London: Chatto and Windus, 1961), 229.

7. See Lennard Davis, *Factual Fictions: The Origins of the English Novel* (New York: Columbia University Press, 1983). Interestingly, as Davis notes, it is another technological shift that brings news and novel together in the sixteenth century. With the invention of the printing press, "narrative was given the ability to embody recentness, hence to record that which was novel—that is to be a 'novel.' " *Factual Fictions,* 48.

8. For histories and analyses of the New Journalism, see Alan J. Lee, *The Origins of the Popular Press in England, 1855–1914* (London: Croom Helm, 1976), and Joel H. Wiener ed., *Papers for the Millions: The New Journalism in Britain, 1850s to 1914* (New York, Westport, and London: Greenwood, 1988). For a consideration of Northcliffe's enduring legacy for mass news media into our period, see Peter Catterall, Colin Seymour-Ure, and Adrian Smith eds. *Northcliffe's Legacy: Aspects of the British Popular Press, 1896–1996* (New York: St. Martin's, 2000). Lucy Brown characterizes the New Journalism's differences from the Victorian press this way:

> At the beginning of the [nineteenth] century there was a popular press, stamped and unstamped, which enjoyed good sales, and which filled its columns with streams of criticism of tax-eaters, shopocrats, millocrats, and base lying Whigs. Such papers carried very little general news, and concentrated their attack on what had been said in Parliament. By the end of the century there were popular halfpenny papers, mostly in the evening, with summaries of the day's international and national news, and devoting much space to football news and romantic serials.

Lucy Brown, *Victorian News and Newspapers* (Oxford: Clarendon, 1985), 276.

9. Percy Bysshe Shelley, "A Defence of Poetry," in Donald H. Reiman and Neil Fraistat, eds. *Shelley's Poetry and Prose,* Second edn. (New York and London: W.W. Norton & Company, 2002), 535.

10. William Carlos Williams, *Asphodel: That Greeny Flower and Other Love Poems* (New York: New Directions, 1994) 18–19.

11. The words are William Stead's, owner of the *Pall Mall Gazette*: "We broke the old tradition and made journalism a living thing, palpitating with actuality, in touch with life at all points. We abolished with mystery of the editor, who, before our time, was a kind of invisible Grand Lama. We saw everybody, went everywhere, and did every mortal thing which seemed to us worth doing," William Thomas Stead, "Character Sketch: Mr. T.P. O'Connor, M.P," *Review of Reviews XXVI* (July–December 1902), 479.

12. Ezra Pound, *ABC of Reading* (New York: New Directions, 1934), 29.

13. As Mark Morrisson argues, "The publicity and mass publication techniques that made wealthy men of publishers like Harmsworth, Pearson,
and Newnes in England and Curtis, Hearst, Munsey, and McClure in
America were quickly adapted, in varying degrees, by suffragist, socialist,
and anarchist groups for their own purposes. These radical groups influenced modernist authors and editors to adapt commercial culture to the
needs of modernist literature, thus complicating the polarization of modernism to mass culture," Mark Morrisson, *The Public Face of Modernism:
Little Magazines, Audiences, and Reception, 1905–1920* (Madison: University of Wisconsin Press, 2001), 6. Similarly, Patrick Collier argues, "In a
sense, the narrative of anxiety about journalism has long been part of our
understanding of modernism, which was seen for years as a rejection of
mass culture in all its forms. More recently, in one of the most fertile
trends in modernist studies, scholars have shown, from multiple perspectives and with admirable detail, that modernists had multiple, conflicting,
often productive if always ambivalent relations with emergent mass culture," *Modernism on Fleet Street* (Aldershot and Burlington: Ashgate, 2006),
2. Morrisson and Collier, along with Keith Williams in *British Writers and
the Media, 1930–45* (Basingstoke: Macmillan, 1996) and others, have per-
ceptively increased critical awareness of modernism's multiple relationships
with the news. I have drawn much from these exemplary books, but I also
highlight some critical differences from them in my approach.

14. The discourse of the public sphere was initiated in Jürgen Habermas,
The Structural Transformation of the Public Sphere, trans. Thomas Berger
(Cambridge: MIT Press, 1989), and concerns the exercise of reason in civil
society over matters of public interest. Recent studies that ground their dis-
cussions of modernism and mass media in concern for the public sphere
include Collier, Morrisson, and Mark Wollaeger, *Modernism, Media, and
Propaganda: British Narrative from 1900 to 1945* (Princeton and Oxford:
Princeton University Press, 2006). For a fine overview of recent debates per-
taining to the concept of the public sphere among New Journalism scholars,
see Mark Hampton, "Representing the Public Sphere: The New Journalism and Its Historians," in Ann Ardis and Patrick Collier, eds. *Transatlantic Print Culture, 1880–1940: Emerging Media, Emerging Modernisms*
(Basingstoke and New York: Palgrave Macmillan, 2008), 15–29.

15. For the theoretical distinction Huyssen makes between modernism and the
historical avant-gardes, see Peter Bürger, *Theory of the Avant-Garde,* trans.
Michael Shaw (Minnesota: University of Minnesota Press, 1984).

16. Andreas Huyssen, *After the Great Divide: Modernism, Mass Culture,
Postmodernism* (Bloomington and Indianapolis: Indiana University Press,
1986), 14. Like many subsequent critics, I would question Huyssen's strict
division of modernism from the avant-garde, as well as his argument that
"Modernism constituted itself through a conscious strategy of exclusion,
an anxiety of contamination by its other; an increasingly consuming and
engulfing mass culture" (vii). Rather, I would stress, as Michael North
does, that Huyssen seems to accept unchallenged a "modernism [that] has

not been expanded or even changed very much [since its early academic canonization]; rather, it lives on, in a mummified state to provide a determinate negation for its successor," for example, in Huyssen's avant-gardes and postmodernism. Michael North, *Reading 1922* (New York and Oxford: Oxford University Press, 1999), 11. Thus, I would reclaim for modernism some of the revolutionary potential and commitment to cultural change that Huyssen reserves for the avant-garde, a distinction that collapses in many revised versions of modernism.

17. Raymond Williams, *The Politics of Modernism* (London and New York: Verso, 1989), 33.

18. Michael North, *Camera Works: Photography and the Twentieth-Century Word* (New York and Oxford: Oxford University Press, 2005), vi.

19. For example, in addition to those already mentioned, Todd Avery, *Radio Modernism: Literature, Ethics, and the BBC, 1922–1938* (Aldershot and Burlington: Ashgate, 2006); Timothy Campbell, *Wireless Writing in the Age of Marconi* (Minneapolis and London: University of Minnesota Press, 2006); Pamela Caughie ed., *Virginia Woolf in the Age of Mechanical Reproduction* (New York and London: Garland, 2000); Kevin Dettmar and Stephen Watt eds., *Marketing Modernism: Self-Promotion, Canonization, Rereading* (Ann Arbor: University of Michigan Press, 1996); Hugh Kenner, *The Mechanic Muse* (New York and Oxford: Oxford University Press, 1987); Jean Marie Lutes, *Front-Page Girls: Women Journalists in American Culture and Fiction, 1880–1930* (Ithaca and London: Cornell University Press, 2006); Thomas Strychacz, *Modernism, Mass Culture, and Professionalism* (Cambridge: Cambridge University Press, 1993); and Jennifer Wicke, *Advertising Fictions* (New York: Columbia University Press, 1988). Most of these studies conform to a major component of Douglas Mao and Rebecca L. Walkowitz's definition of the "new modernist studies," that is, attempts "to locate literary modernism in a rhetorical arena transformed by media's capacity to disseminate words and images in less time, across bigger distances, and to greater numbers of people than ever before," Douglas Mao and Rebecca L. Walkowitz, "The New Modernist Studies," *PMLA* 123.3 (May 2008), 743.

20. Friedrich A. Kittler, *Gramophone, Film, Typewriter,* trans. Geoffrey Winthrop-Young and Michael Wutz (Stanford: Stanford University Press, 1999), 7.

21. Ibid., 6.

22. Quoted in Ibid.

23. Ibid., 14.

24. Ibid., 10.

25. William Blake, *Blake's Poetry and Designs,* Second edn., eds. Mary Lynn Johnson and John E. Grant (New York: W.W. Norton & Co., 2008), 224.

26. Gerard Manley Hopkins, *Poems and Prose* (New York: Penguin, 1953), 54.

27. James Joyce, *Ulysses* (New York: Random House, 1986), 118. John S. Rickard glosses the Theosophist origins of Akasic memory: "Theosophists hold that the individual personality is composed, as Helena

Blavatsky writes, of two fundamental parts.... The Higher Self... survives the death of the body and goes on to continual rebirth in a succession of lives as it struggles to return to the Universal Soul that it and all other matter is part of. On the other hand, just as the body disintegrates after death, the Personal Self dissipates, yet the memories associated with the single life that it lived do not disappear, but are absorbed by the Universal Memory or imprinted on the Akasic Memory (a sort of film that surrounds the earth)," *Joyce's Book of Memory: The Mnemotechnic of 'Ulysses'* (Durham: Duke University Press, 1999), 105. Curiously, Rickard does not connect Stephen's meditation on memory to the setting of the "Aeolus" chapter in which it appears, a newspaper office, where Stephen is surrounded by machines that absorb and imprint their own collection of memories and traces.

28. Marcel Proust, *In the Shadow of Young Girls in Flower,* trans. James Grieve (New York: Viking, 2002), 50.

29. Marcel Proust, *Remembrance of Things Past, Volume One,* trans. C.K. Scott Moncrieff and Terence Kilmartin (New York: Random House, 1981), 515, emphasis added.

30. Although Derrida writes of actual archives, I believe that his analysis can be figuratively transferred to modernist texts with minimal permanent damage to either Derrida or the texts.

31. Marianne Moore, *Complete Poems* (New York: Penguin, 1981), 267.

32. The archon is the magistrate who founds and presides over the archive. For instance, Hugh Kenner characterizes Pound's work on the *Cantos* as representing "the freedom of a poem which he alone owned and operated," *The Pound Era* (Berkeley: University of California Press, 1971), 528.

33. Jacques Derrida, *Archive Fever: A Freudian Impression,* trans. Eric Prenowitz (Chicago: University of Chicago Press, 1996), 1–3.

34. For Derrida, the archive is not primarily concerned with the past, but rather points toward the future, a peculiar temporality defined as the "what will have been" of the archive (44–47). This resonates with recent criticism of modernism's programmatic cultural domination and self-fashioning, reminding us how conscious modernists were about shaping and excluding others from their legacies, or more specifically, from "what will have been" their legacies. See, for instance, Ann L. Ardis, *Modernism and Cultural Conflict 1880–1922* (Cambridge: Cambridge University Press, 2002), and Aaron Jaffe, *Modernism and the Culture of Celebrity* (Cambridge: Cambridge University Press, 2005).

35. Derrida, 19.

36. Ibid., 10–12.

37. This model has similarities with Fredric Jameson's concept of the political unconscious, which also posits an implicit dimension of political repression in texts. Thus, for Jameson, "The modernist project is more adequately understood as the intent, following Norman Holland's convenient expression, to 'manage' historical and social, deeply political impulses, that is to say, to defuse them, to prepare substitute gratifications for them, and the like," *The Political Unconscious: Narrative as a Socially Symbolic Act* (Ithaca:

Cornell University Press, 1981), 266. The benefit of the archive model is that to Jameson's "historical" and "social" it can add "technological," providing a renewed understanding of modernism as a set of strategies for managing the recording and storage technologies that share and help define its historical moment.

38. Derrida contests the idea that archivization contradicts repression: "As if one could not, precisely, recall and archive the very thing one represses, archive it while repressing it (because repression is an archivization), that is to say, to archive *otherwise,* to repress the archive while archiving the repression . . ." (64).

39. For example, Ann L. Ardis, *New Women, New Novels: Feminism and Early Modernism* (New Brunswick: Rutgers University Press, 1990), Rita Felski, *The Gender of Modernity* (Cambridge and London: Harvard University Press, 1995), Sandra Gilbert and Susan Gubar, *No Man's Land: The Place of the Woman Writer in the Twentieth Century, Volume I: War of the Words* (New Haven: Yale University Press, 1988), Lisa Rado ed., *Rereading Modernism: New Directions in Feminist Criticism* (New York and London: Garland, 1994), Bonnie Kime Scott, *Refiguring Modernism: The Women of 1928* (Bloomington and Indianapolis: Indiana University Press, 1995), and Susan Suleiman, *Subversive Intent: Gender, Politics, and the Avant-Garde* (Cambridge: Harvard University Press, 1990).

40. See *The Pound Era,* 3–5.

41. Shari Benstock, *Women of the Left Bank: Paris, 1900–1940* (Austin: University of Texas Press, 1986). Benstock's epigraph is from Kenner: "The young women strolled and talked; their talk is forgotten. After fifty years, though, one scrap of the master's survived."

42. For instance, one could write a history of modernist criticism based on Derrida's *trouble de l'archive*: because the archive does not speak for itself, but rather always poses a problem of translation, interpretation, repetition, and reproduction, then every revision of the archive, every attempt to reconfigure "what will have been" becomes part of the archive itself. However, there are finally distinct limitations to this figural model. Derrida ultimately connects archive fever to actual holocausts, and this obviously marks a limit to the use of the archive as a model for modernist texts.

43. Derrida, 19.

44. Ibid., 16.

45. Derrida omits discussion of film in the archive in *Archive Fever.*

46. Ibid., 19.

47. Williams, *Politics of Modernism,* 33.

48. Wollaeger, *Modernism, Media, and Propaganda,* xvi.

49. Ibid., 30, emphasis added. "Pseudo-environment" is a term Wollaeger adopts from Walter Lippmann's influential *Public Opinion* (New York: Harcourt, Brace, 1922), referring to "the increasingly mediated nature of existence with the circulation of stereotypes disseminated by film and photography and then re-evoked by newspapers" ibid., 25.

50. Benjamin, "The Storyteller," 144.

51. Benjamin, of course, does not use the term "media ecology," but he is acutely aware that forms of representation are historically in competition, and that in modernity information has threatened the ability to communicate experience through storytelling: "Historically, the various modes of communication have competed with one another. The replacement of the older relation by information, and of information by sensation, reflects the increasing atrophy of experience. In turn, there is a contrast between all these forms and the story, which is one of the oldest forms of communication. A story does not aim to convey an event per se, which is the purpose of information; rather, it embeds the event in the life of the storyteller in order to pass it on as experience to those listening," Walter Benjamin, "On Some Motifs in Baudelaire," 316.

52. Toni Morrison, "Foreword," *Beloved* (New York: Vintage, 2004), xvi.

53. Ibid., xvii, emphasis added.

54. See Middleton Harris ed., *The Black Book* (New York: Random House, 1974), 10.

55. Of course, Virginia Woolf famously asked, "Is life like this? Must novels be like this?" Virginia Woolf, "Modern Fiction," in *The Essays of Virginia Woolf, Volume IV, 1925–1928,* ed. Andrew McNeillie (London: The Hogarth Press, 1994), 160. Or, as David Trotter nicely encapsulates, modernist novelists felt "that the novel as traditionally conceived was no longer up to the job: that its imaginary worlds did not, in fact, correspond to the way one's fellows spent their entire lives," David Trotter, "The Modernist Novel," in *The Cambridge Companion to Modernism,* ed. Michael Levenson (Cambridge: Cambridge University Press, 1999), 70.

56. M.M. Bakhtin, "Discourse in the Novel," in *The Dialogic Imagination,* ed. Michael Holquist, trans. Caryl Emerson and Michael Holquist (Austin: University of Texas Press, 1981), 301.

57. Davis, *Factual Fictions,* 67.

58. David Lodge, *The Modes of Modern Writing; Metaphor, Metonymy, and the Typology of Modern Literature* (Ithaca: Cornell University Press, 1977), 25, emphasis in original. The extent to which Lodge's definition of realism relies upon its resemblance to journalism (as well as autobiography, travelogue, letters, diaries, and historiography) suggests that the relationship between the modernist and the realist novel is less of a literary nature and more of related discourses within an evolving media ecology.

59. "Why this transformation should be so important for the birth of the imagined community of the nation can best be seen if we consider the basic structure of two forms of imagining which first flowered in Europe in the eighteenth century: the novel and the newspaper. For these forms provided the technical means for 're-presenting' the *kind* of imagined community that is the nation," Benedict Anderson, *Imagined Communities: Reflections on the Origin and Spread of Nationalism,* Revised ed. (London and New York: Verso, 1991), 24–25. Anderson in part shares his perspective on news with Walter Benjamin. I discuss Anderson further in the next chapter.

60. See especially Georg Lukács, *Realism in Our Time,* trans. John Mander and Necke Mander (New York: Harper and Row, 1964).

61. What Lukács writes about journalism in *History and Class Consciousness* echoes his descriptions of modernism in *Realism In Our Time*: "Here it is precisely subjectivity itself, knowledge, temperament and powers of expression that are reduced to an abstract mechanism functioning autonomously and divorced both from the personality of their 'owner' and from the material and concrete nature of the subject matter in hand. The journalist's 'lack of convictions,' the prostitution of his experiences and beliefs is comprehensible only as the apogee of capitalist reification," Georg Lukács, *History and Class Consciousness: Studies in Marxist Dialectics,* trans. Rodney Livingstone (Cambridge: M.I.T. Press, 1972), 100.

62. As Beatrice Hanssen explains, for Benjamin language reflects the current impoverishment of language, but also contains revolutionary potential that would redeem experience: "For Benjamin, language, once released from the correspondence model of truth, might provide the path to another realm of possibilities, to the recognition of altogether different 'correspondences.' Set free from the nefarious effects of instrumental reason, language was to regain some of its lost aura. Once humans recognized language's unfathomed revolutionary potential, perhaps it might field a blow, issue a redemptive shock, undoing the numbing anaesthetic and aestheticized shock effects of modernity's culture of dispersal," Beatrice Hanssen, "Language and Mimesis in Walter Benjamin's Work," in David S. Ferris, ed. *The Cambridge Companion to Walter Benjamin* (Cambridge: Cambridge University Press, 2004), 55–56.

63. Thomas Strychacz shows that modernism is inseparable from the new professionalism in the early twentieth century, including the rise of professional journalism: "literary production in the twentieth century was to be shaped and legitimated by professional associations of writers, literary magazines, and by the rise of the university. Modernist writing, in particular, responded to a new discourse of professionalism," Thomas Strychacz, *Modernism, Mass Culture, and Professionalism* (Cambridge: Cambridge University Press, 1993), 5. Others have noted how many modernists were also practicing journalists, reviewers, or advertisers, so that in historical terms it is impossible to draw a line.

64. Quoted in Joel H. Wiener, "How New Was the New Journalism?" in *Papers for the Millions: The New Journalism in Britain, 1850s to 1914,* ed. Joel H. Wiener (New York, Westport, and London: Greenwood, 1988), 53.

65. For example, in *The Art of Scandal: Modernism, Libel Law, and the Roman à Clef* (New York and Oxford: Oxford University Press, 2009) Sean Latham provides an excellent illustration of how modernists exploited the same scandalous territory as the newspapers.

66. "Corresponding to the form of the new means of production, which in the beginning is still ruled by the form of the old (Marx), are images in the collective consciousness in which the new is permeated with the old. These images are wish images; in them the collective seeks both to overcome

and to transfigure the immaturity of the social product and the inadequacies in the social organization of production. At the same time, what emerges in these wish images is the resolute effort to distance oneself from all that is antiquated—which includes, however, the recent past. These tendencies deflect the imagination (which is given impetus by the new) back upon the primal past. In the dream in which each epoch entertains images of its successor, the latter appears wedded to elements of primal history [*Urgeschichte*]—that is, to elements of a classless society," Walter Benjamin, *The Arcades Project*, ed. Rolf Tiedemann, trans. Howard Eiland and Kevin McLaughlin (Cambridge: Harvard University Press, 1999), 4.

67. Richard Bridgman, *Gertrude Stein in Pieces* (New York: Oxford University Press, 1970), 259.

68. Gertrude Stein, "Narration, Lecture 3," in Catharine R. Stimpson and Harriet Chessman, eds. *Writings 1932–1946* (New York: Library of America, 1998), 345.

69. See the influential textbook on homosexuality by Havelock Ellis, *Studies in the Psychology of Sex: Sexual Inversion* (London: Wilson, 1897).

70. William Gass claims that when reading Stein, "We must set to work without reward or hope of any, and submit ourselves to the boredom of an etymological narrative." But Gass knows and shows that Stein's etymologies are seldom boring. William Gass, "Gertrude Stein and the Geography of the Sentence," in *The World Within the Word* (Boston: Godine, 1979), 90.

71. See, for example, Stein's "As a Wife Has a Cow A Love Story," in Catharine R. Stimpson and Harriet Chessman, eds. *Writings 1903–1932* (New York: Library of America, 1998), 501–503. For an account of the term "cow" in Stein's *oeuvre*, see Elizabeth Fifer, "Is Flesh Advisable? The Interior Theater of Gertrude Stein," *Signs* 4.3 (Spring 1979), 472–483.

72. As Harriet Scott Chessman notes, "Each of Stein's styles marks a new attempt to bring a bodily intimacy into language," Harriet Scott Chessman, *The Public Is Invited to Dance: Representation, the Body, and Dialogue in Gertrude Stein* (Stanford: Stanford University Press, 1989), 55. See especially "Part II: The Poetics of Intimacy" in Chessman's book.

73. Ulla Dydo, one of Stein's most expert and patient readers, has shown the ways in which Stein's compositional process involved "decontextuating" her texts' origins in her own experience. It is testament to the inseparability of the archive drive and the archive fever that Stein's decontextuated texts can "remain mere black and white until . . . reading makes the language rise from the page," Ulla Dydo with William Rice, *Gertrude Stein: The Language That Rises 1923–1934* (Evanston: Northwestern University Press, 2003), 43. That is to say, Stein's form of archivization is usually Derrida's "archiving otherwise," which forgets and erases, but can also yield to the patient analyst an extraordinary range of experience from Stein's texts.

74. As Derrida writes about actual (as well as virtual) archives, so Benjamin writes about actual collections of things. As I indicated earlier, I find these concepts useful enough as models for texts that the temporary loss of materiality that comes from abstracting them may be more or less pardonable.

At the same time, while Derrida's archive and Benjamin's collection are rooted in the material world, both are also concepts that express the larger abstract concerns of the respective thinkers, and even in their own work these terms take on the form of models.

75. Walter Benjamin, *The Arcades Project*, 204.

76. This, of course, does not mean that modernist authors and the institutions that supported them did not have calculated designs on the market, as critics such as Lawrence Rainey, Jennifer Wicke, Kevin Dettmar, and Stephen Watt remind us. It simply means that part of what was marketed were texts that enacted the withholding of experience from the market.

77. *Arcades Project*, 205.

78. "Collecting is a form of practical memory, and of all the profane manifestations of 'nearness' it is the most binding." *Arcades Project*, 205. Also, "It is rare for collectors to present themselves to the public. They hope to be regarded as scholars, connoisseurs, if needs be as owners too, but very rarely as that what they above all are: lovers," Walter Benjamin, *Walter Benjamin's Archive: Images, Texts, Signs*, eds. Ursula Marx, Gudrun Schwarz, Michael Schwarz, and Erdmut Wizisla, trans. Esther Leslie (London and New York: Verso, 2007), 25. One might even say that as lovers/collectors, Stein and Benjamin sometimes work similarly. Both archive private language, including pet names. Stein's work abounds with pet names that Toklas and Stein called one another, and Benjamin kept a list of all the pet names that he and Dora called their son. See ibid., 116–17.

79. Thus, Lawrence Rainey: "One omission of this study needs to be acknowledged. Some readers, especially those with literary critical training, will find far too little of the detailed examination of actual works that is sometimes held to be the only important or worthwhile critical activity," Lawrence Rainey, *Institutions of Modernism: Literary Elites and Public Culture* (New Haven and London: Yale University Press, 1998), 6. Following in this vein, for instance, Aaron Jaffe is committed to "more 'not-reading' than 'reading'" (*Modernism and the Culture of Celebrity*, 8). My sense is that the field faces the challenge of reconciling institutional history with close attention to primary texts. One almost senses that close attention to texts has come to seem synonymous with the kind of canonical high modernism that most scholars, myself included, seek to revise. Of course, there is good reason to be cautious about reproducing the ideologies of high modernism through its own canonical formalist techniques. Ann Ardis argues that the field must be "willing to more effectively de-naturalize both modernist protocols of literary analysis and the modernist mapping of turn-of-the-century British literary and cultural history" (*Modernism and Cultural Conflict*, 8). However, this should not rule out all intrinsic forms of criticism that would be alert to what responses modernist texts may give to the new questions we are learning to ask. A different, but related, challenge of studying modernism in relation to mass media is how to comprehend this relationship beyond its thematization in texts and their peripheral discourses. As Patrick Collier notes, "modernist writers' interventions in the cultural discussion of

journalism have remained scattered in bits of letters, diaries, essays, and passages in literary texts. And our historical memory of modernists' material interactions with the newspaper press—their writing of columns, advertising of their books and journals, interactions with journalists, reading of newspapers—have been similarly scattered in biographies and asides and footnotes of recent studies" (*Modernism on Fleet Street*, 2–3). As I hope *Modernist Fiction and News* demonstrates, not only were these seemingly scattered concerns vital to modernism, but they are in fact central and observable even in the most unexpected places as an organizing principle of many modernist texts.

80. In 1999, the same year that the Modernist Studies Association held its first annual conference, Michael North considered what it would mean to fully respond to Fredric Jameson's call for a sociology of modernism:

> The sociology of modernism that Jameson has demanded would consider institutions, modes of dissemination and production, such as publishers, galleries, and magazines. That there has been relatively little work in this area means that disagreements about modernism have been settled by reference to the intentions of its most visible perpetrators, with all the weaknesses and limitations that such analysis entails.
>
> (*Reading 1922*, 207)

In the decade since then scholars have written a great number of these valuable kinds of cultural histories. *Modernist Fiction and News* is indebted to such work, but it does not offer the kind of mass media history that Patrick Collier or Keith Williams do with respect to the news. Rather, it attempts to build on their work in order to position experience as a major term in scholarship that considers the relationship between modernism and news in the early twentieth-century media ecology.

81. Derrida, 62.

82. Ibid.

83. Celebrity and privacy are excellently treated in Jaffe and Collier, respectively.

84. Jean Chalaby, "Northcliffe: Proprietor as Journalist," in Peter Catterall, Colin Seymour-Ure, and Adrian Smith, eds. *Northcliffe's Legacy: Aspects of the British Popular Press, 1896–1996* (New York: St. Martin's, 2000), 32.

85. Harris, *The Black Book*, 10.

86. Morrison, *Beloved*, 176.

87. Quoted in Fyfe, 82.

88. Colin Seymour-Ure, "Northcliffe's Legacy," in Peter Catterall, Colin Seymour-Ure, and Adrian Smith, eds. *Northcliffe's Legacy: Aspects of the British Popular Press, 1896–1996* (New York: St. Martin's, 2000), 10.

89. Raymond Williams reports, for instance, that the total daily newspaper circulation was two million in 1910, and, due to "the demand for news in the war, the daily public [circulation] was above 5,000,000.... The full

expansion, to something like the full reading public, took place in the daily press during the Second War, reaching over 15,000,000 in 1947" (*The Long Revolution*, 198, 199).

90. That is, we might consider the extent to which Benjamin's own theory of history is contingent upon and a response to increased technological possibilities of the archive. What would the *Arcades Project* be without the technologically produced archive of the nineteenth century? And how would this project differ, if at all, if the archive of the nineteenth century included film, radio, television, e-mail, or Internet? The book that attended the exhibition of Benjamin's own archive evidences scraps, photographs of the Paris arcades, notebooks, newspaper clippings, lists, card indexes, the remnants of an extensive picture postcard collection and riddle collection, pictures of Benjamin's Russian dolls that have not themselves survived, and even a collection of words said by and anecdotes about his son, Stefan. Yet, as Erdmut Wizisla, notes, certain absences are conspicuous: "The one essential thing necessary for a reconstruction of Benjamin's radio work is missing: there is no recording of his voice," Erdmut Wizisla, "Preface" to *Walter Benjamin's Archive: Images, Texts, Signs*, eds. Ursula Marx, Gudrun Schwarz, Michael Schwarz, and Erdmut Wizisla, trans. Esther Leslie (London and New York: Verso, 2007), 4. Benjamin's work can also be considered modernist when one takes into account the considerable influence that the European avant-garde had on his thinking after 1924. See Michael Jennings, "Walter Benjamin and the European Avant-Garde," in David S. Ferris, ed. *The Cambridge Companion to Walter Benjamin* (Cambridge: Cambridge University Press, 2004), 18–34. Perhaps the most pronounced form in which the avant-garde entered Benjamin's materialist historiography is in his adoption of French Surrealism's technique of montage, which Benjamin would carry over into historiography. See Walter Benjamin, *The Arcades Project*, 461.

91. "Historicism rightly culminates in universal history. It may be that materialist historiography differs in method more clearly from universal history than from any other kind. Universal history has no theoretical armature. Its procedure is additive: it musters a mass of data to fill the homogeneous, empty time. Materialist historiography, on the other hand, is based on a constructive principle. Thinking involves not only the movement of thoughts, but their arrest as well. Where thinking suddenly comes to a stop in a constellation saturated with tensions, it gives that constellation a shock, by which thinking is crystallized as a monad. The historical materialist approaches a historical object only where it confronts him as a monad. In this structure he recognizes the sign of a messianic arrest of happening, or (to put it differently) a revolutionary chance in the fight for the oppressed past," Walter Benjamin, "On the Concept of History," in Howard Eiland and Michael W. Jennings, eds. *Selected Writings, Volume 4 1938–1940* (Cambridge: Harvard University Press, 2003), 396.

92. Michael Jennings, *Dialectical Images: Walter Benjamin's Theory of Literary Criticism* (Ithaca: Cornell University Press, 1987), 124. Jennings goes

on to remark that while Benjamin's literary theory and method thus resemble in many ways the various forms of Marxist analysis or even the arguments made about reading literature and experience in general, yet "Benjamin's analysis of the relationship between art and knowledge differentiates itself... in its greater specificity and especially in its untiring emphasis on the fragmentary and finally negative character of the experience contained in works of art," 125.

93. I adopt, in a sense, a version of Benjamin's own method. Rolf Tiedemann reminds us that Benjamin's method of illuminating history is inseparable from his "theory of mimetic ability, which is, at its core, *a theory of experience*" Rolf Tiedemann, "Dialectics at a Standstill: Approaches to the *Passagen-Werk*," in Gary Smith, ed. *On Walter Benjamin: Critical Essays and Recollections* (Cambridge and London: MIT Press, 1988), 269, emphasis added.

94. This important term shall be developed further in the next chapter. It comes from Walter Benjamin, *The Arcades Project*, 846.

95. For example, Jennings's *Dialectical Images* and Terry Eagleton, *Walter Benjamin, or Towards a Revolutionary Criticism* (London: Verso, 1981). In a different context, Andrew Benjamin argues that it is "impossible to remain strictly Benjaminian," Andrew Benjamin, "Introduction," in Andrew Benjamin, ed. *Walter Benjamin and Art* (London and New York: Continuum, 2005), 2. This is something Eagleton seems to acknowledge when he claims to "manhandle [Benjamin's texts] for my own purposes, blast them out of the continuum of history, in ways I think he would have approved" (*Walter Benjamin*, i). So Jennings explains, "When we use Benjamin to a particular end or in the service of a particular cause, then, we are always proceeding in a Benjaminian way, not so much in that we use his ideas to construct our own critical constellations but in that we 'mortify' Benjamin's own words, we rip them from their context and so expose Walter Benjamin's own pretensions to higher knowledge" (*Dialectical Images*, 213).

96. As we have seen, Benjamin is usually associated with French and Soviet avant-gardes, which have sometimes in turn been defined against Anglo-American modernism in critical and theoretical accounts such as Bürger's and Huyssen's.

97. As a thought exercise, imagine that all of Joyce's work had only really come to the attention of American critics in the 1970s-1990s, as was the case for Benjamin. This is, of course, impossible to imagine for many reasons, not least of which is Joyce's influence on the very thinkers who would conceive of the poststructuralism that emerged at this time to reshape the intellectual sphere. And, in any event, Joyce survived the critical transition to poststructuralism particularly well. How different would our notions of other modernists be if they had come into Anglo-American criticism as late as Benjamin did?

98. An excellent example of such an application of Benjamin's thought to Virginia Woolf is Pamela Caughie ed., *Virginia Woolf in the Age of Mechanical Reproduction* (New York and London: Garland, 2000).

99. I am thinking of the controversy that surrounds the Institute for Social Research's role in reshaping, to some extent, the artwork essay. For a balanced discussion of this controversy, see Martin Jay, *The Dialectical Imagination: A History of the Frankfurt School and the Institute of Social Research, 1923–1950* (Boston and Toronto: Little, Brown, 1973), 205–6. In any event, Benjamin's later work would demonstrate a desire, perhaps unanticipated in the artwork essay, to reclaim aura.

100. Benjamin, *The Arcades Project*, 462.

101. David S. Ferris, "Introduction: Reading Benjamin," in David S. Ferris, ed. *The Cambridge Companion to Walter Benjamin* (Cambridge: Cambridge University Press, 2004), 13–14.

102. Under the influence of Benjamin, Jameson has more recently written of the "need to combine a Poundian mission to identify Utopian tendencies with a Benjaminian geography of their sources and a gauging of their pressure at what are now multiple sea levels. Ontologies of the present demand archeologies of the future, not forecasts of the past," Fredric Jameson, *A Singular Modernity: Essay on the Ontology of the Present* (London and New York: Verso, 2002), 215.

103. For Benjamin, history needs to be productively arrested. As Werner Hamacher explains, "The movement of a work, of an era and of the course of history are arrested not in order to present them as a dead thing to sad contemplation, but in order to expose time and make it intrinsically productive," Werner Hamacher, " 'Now': Walter Benjamin and Historical Time," in Andrew Benjamin, ed. *Walter Benjamin and History* (New York: Continuum, 2005), 55.

CHAPTER 1

1. Walter Benjamin, "The Storyteller," in Howard Eiland and Michael W. Jennings, eds. *Selected Writings, Volume 3 1935–1938* (Cambridge: Harvard University Press, 2002), 147.

2. Walter Benjamin, *The Arcades Project*, ed. Rolf Tiedemann, trans. Howard Eiland and Kevin McLaughlin (Cambridge: Harvard University Press, 1999), 846.

3. Walter Benjamin, "Eduard Fuchs, Collector and Historian," in Howard Eiland and Michael W. Jennings, eds. *Selected Writings, Volume 3 1935–1938* (Cambridge: Harvard University Press, 2002), 262.

4. Beatrice Hanssen, "Language and Mimesis in Walter Benjamin's Work," in David S. Ferris, ed. *The Cambridge Companion to Walter Benjamin* (Cambridge: Cambridge University Press, 2004), 55.

5. Margaret Cohen usefully elucidates the way Benjamin draws from Surrealism, Marx, and Freud in his conception of phantasmagoria: "Benjamin proposed to differentiate himself from Surrealism, in particular, by remedying its lack of rigorous theorization concerning how collective and individual psychic processes interpenetrated. Benjamin's point of departure was the rhetorical affinity between the dream vocabulary Marx sometimes used to

describe the mystifications of capitalism, and the importance of dream in a Freudian schema. Perhaps the supernatural dimensions to modern life, Benjamin speculated, were manifestations of a dream sleep that came over Europe with the invention of modern capitalism; what was then needed was a way to promote awakening from the dreams of the nineteenth century. Benjamin found the notion of a dreaming collective all the more appealing because the psychoanalytic notion of dreams as the fulfillment of wishes meshed with his interest in the unrealized hopes and desires contained in the garbage of history," Margaret Cohen, "Benjamin's Phantasmagoria: The *Arcades Project*," in David S. Ferris, ed. *The Cambridge Companion to Walter Benjamin* (Cambridge: Cambridge University Press, 2004), 205.

6. Susan Buck-Morss, *The Dialectics of Seeing: Walter Benjamin and the Arcades Project* (Cambridge and London: MIT Press, 1989), 253.

7. Walter Benjamin, "On Some Motifs in Baudelaire," in Howard Eiland and Michael W. Jennings, eds. *Selected Writings, Volume 4 1938–1940* (Cambridge: Harvard University Press, 2003), 315–16.

8. Benjamin, "The Storyteller," 147.

9. Benjamin echoes these concerns in a short piece called "The Newspaper." However, there, in a characteristically dialectical turn, he also sees the newspaper as a site of potential for readers to become authors: "The fact that nothing binds the reader more tightly to his paper than his all-consuming impatience [to see his interests expressed], his longing for daily nourishment, has long been exploited by publishers, who are constantly inaugurating new columns to address the reader's questions, opinions, and protests. Hand in hand, therefore, with the indiscriminate assimilation of facts goes the equally indiscriminate assimilation of readers, who are instantly elevated to collaborators. Here, however, a dialectical moment lies concealed: the decline of writing in this press turns out to be the formula for its restoration in a different one... The reader is at all times ready to become a writer—that is, a describer or even a prescriber," Walter Benjamin, "The Newspaper," in Howard Eiland and Michael W. Jennings, eds. *Selected Writings, Volume 2 1927–1934* (Cambridge: Harvard University Press, 1999), 741. One need only think of Internet discourse communities such as news blogs to find evidence of this dialectical turn in our moment.

10. Benedict Anderson, *Imagined Communities: Reflections on the Origin and Spread of Nationalism,* Revised ed. (London and New York: Verso, 1991), 33.

11. Ibid., 33.

12. Werner Hamacher, "'Now': Walter Benjamin and Historical Time," in Andrew Benjamin, ed. *Walter Benjamin and History* (New York: Continuum, 2005), 47.

13. Anderson, 34–35.

14. Max Pensky, "Method and Time: Benjamin's Dialectical Images," in David S. Ferris, ed. *The Cambridge Companion to Walter Benjamin* (Cambridge: Cambridge University Press, 2004), 187.

15. Benjamin, *The Arcades Project,* 64.

16. John McCole, *Walter Benjamin and the Antinomies of Tradition* (Ithaca: Cornell University Press, 1993), 276.

17. I would include even the quasi-circular mythic time of *Finnegans Wake*, which invites readers to "rearrive" at its first page from its last, in this formulation when compared to the newspaper's endless projection of homogenous, empty time into the indefinite future. If *Finnegans Wake* is endless, it is so in a formally significant manner.

18. There is of course never a morning when one unfolds the paper only to find it blank, the news having ended yesterday with no new news to replace it today.

19. As McCole puts it, "To shy away from the face of death, as bourgeois society was doing, is to defraud oneself of the moment of experience in which its authority is grounded," 277.

20. Benjamin later dispersed most of the material in the following passage into separate convolutes, but it is the particular constellation of these ideas in the first draft that interests me here.

21. *The Arcades Project*, 846. Benjamin names Anatole France as an example of such a skeptic. However, in anticipation of the connections I go on to make between Benjamin's anecdotal form and modernist fiction, consider Joyce's characterization of *Ulysses* and its relationship to Irish nationalism: "It is the work of a sceptic, but I don't want it to appear the work of a cynic," See Frank Budgen, *James Joyce and the Making of 'Ulysses'* (New York: Harrison Smith and Robert Haas, 1934), 152.

22. Toni Morrison, *Beloved* (New York: Vintage, 2004), xvii.

23. Ibid., 846, emphasis in original.

24. Here Benjamin is likely influenced by Brecht, whose new drama was opposed to empathy *(Mitleid)*.

25. Irving Wohlfarth, "Et Cetera? The Historian as Chiffonnier," *New German Critique* 39 (Fall 1986), reprinted in Beatrice Hanssen, ed. *Walter Benjamin and the Arcades Project* (London and New York: Continuum, 2006), 19.

26. Benjamin, "On Some Motifs in Baudelaire," 315.

27. Virginia Woolf, "Sympathy," in *The Complete Shorter Fiction of Virginia Woolf*, ed. Susan Dick (San Diego: Harcourt, 1989), 108. Subsequent references will be given parenthetically within the text. Compare to "A Death in the Newspaper," also in *Complete Shorter Fiction*, 315.

28. Magritte copied the image in the upper left quadrant from a medical book, F.E. Bilz's (1899) *La Nouvelle Médication Naturelle (The Natural Method of Healing)*.

29. A.M. Hammacher, *René Magritte*, trans. James Brockway (New York: Harry N. Abrams, 1985, 1995), 82.

30. *The Arcades Project*, 846.

31. "The Copernican revolution in historical perception is as follows. Formerly it was thought that a fixed point had been found in 'what has been,' and one saw the present engaged in tentatively concentrating the forces of knowledge on this ground. Now this relation is to be overturned, and what has been

is to become the dialectical reversal—the flash of awakened consciousness. Politics attains primacy over history. The facts become something that just now first happened to us, first struck us; to establish them is the affair of memory," *The Arcades Project*, 389.

32. As Tiedemann writes, "Past history would be grounded in the present, analogous to Kant's epistemological grounding of objectivity in the depths of the subject," Rolf Tiedemann, "Dialectics at a Standstill: Approaches to the *Passagen-Werk*," in Gary Smith, ed. *On Walter Benjamin: Critical Essays and Recollections* (Cambridge and London: MIT Press, 1988), 282.

33. Buck-Morss, x.

34. As Bernd Witte puts it, "The historical manifestations of human society are conceived by him as dream images whose displacements it is the historian's task to decode. Like the Messiah at the end of time, the historian must rearrange the 'demented' images and thereby endow the world with its true meaning," Bernd Witte, *Walter Benjamin: An Intellectual Biography*, trans. James Rolleston (Detroit: Wayne State University Press, 1991), 110.

35. Thus, Elissa Marder: "The gesture of 'actualization' that Benjamin identifies in Proust becomes the germ of his own conception of the 'dialectical image' of history in the *Passagen-Werk*. The dialectical image is not a representation of history, but it presents to us the history of a past time that happened without our knowing it, and which comes looking for us, momentarily, at the moment of awakening," Elissa Marder, "Walter Benjamin's Dream of 'Happiness,' " in Beatrice Hanssen, ed. *Walter Benjamin and the Arcades Project* (New York: Continuum, 2006), 192.

36. *The Arcades Project*, 846.

37. As Robert Gibbs explains, "Anecdotes make characters come into our world. And so the great monuments must be entered in our world, and not seen as a time-machine that takes us back to theirs. They retain their life when we go and seem them," Robert Gibbs, "Messianic Epistemology: Thesis XV," in Andrew Benjamin, ed. *Walter Benjamin and History* (New York: Continuum, 2005), 209.

38. It should be noted that the anecdote has not been without its partisans in recent decades, particularly among the new historicists. See, for example, Joel Fineman, "The History of the Anecdote: Fiction and Fiction," in H. Aram Veeser, ed. *The New Historicism* (New York: Routledge, 1989) and Catherine Gallagher and Stephen Greenblatt, "Counterhistory and the Anecdote," in *Practicing New Historicism* (Chicago: University of Chicago Press, 2000). For a different approach, see also Jane Gallop, *Anecdotal Theory* (Durham and London: Duke University Press, 2002).

39. Harry D. Harootunian, "The Benjamin Effect: Modernism, Repetition, and the Path to Different Cultural Imaginaries," in Michael P. Steinberg, ed. *Walter Benjamin and the Demands of History* (Ithaca and London: Cornell University Press, 1996), 75.

40. Buck-Morss, 253.

41. Julia Briggs, *Virginia Woolf: An Inner Life* (Orlando: Harcourt, 2005), 62.

42. Virginia Woolf, *The Diary of Virginia Woolf, Volume Two, 1920–1924,* ed. Anne Olivier Bell (New York: Harcourt Brace & Company, 1978), 14.

43. Any full answer to this question would also have to consider Leonard and Virginia Woolf's ownership of the means of production as a condition for Woolf's new literary experimentalism. As Michael Whitworth puts it, "Owning the Hogarth Press liberated Woolf's experimentalism. Its first publication, 'The Mark on the Wall,' was her first sustained experiment in literary form," Michael Whitworth, "Virginia Woolf and Modernism," in Sue Roe and Susan Sellers, eds. *The Cambridge Companion to Virginia Woolf* (Cambridge: Cambridge University Press, 2000), 150.

44. Virginia Woolf, "The Mark on the Wall," in Susan Dick, ed. *The Complete Shorter Fiction of Virginia Woolf* (San Diego: Harcourt, 1989), 83. Subsequent references are given in parenthesis within the text.

45. If we knew for certain that the second speaker in "The Mark on the Wall" were a man, Woolf's story could just as easily be titled "Man with a Newspaper."

46. Although Woolf leaves the gender of the second speaker unspecified, some critics have assumed that this speaker is a man, and thus that the news and war with which this speaker is aligned can be contrasted to the feminine thought experience represented by the narrator. For example, Laura Marcus claims, "The mark is identified by the male speaker who enters the room at the end of the story as a snail," Laura Marcus, *Virginia Woolf* (London: Northcote House, 1997), 19. Whether or not this is a sound assumption, this division of gender would seem to coincide with the gendered characterizations of the narrator's own reverie. For instance, Marcus also argues that the story, "explores the difference between the 'masculine' point of view—fact-bound, hierarchical, constraining—and a free-associative thinking which revels in the multiple imaginings opened up by freedom from the desire to find out what things 'really' are" (19). While this dichotomy surely structures much of the story, it may make for a more complex, or at least a more nuanced, reading if we image the second speaker to be a second woman. In the end, however, it may be more important to reflect on how readers respond to Woolf's purposeful ambiguity in this matter, and to think through how this indeterminacy may work to challenge binaries established elsewhere in the story.

47. To borrow Roland Barthes's terms: "Let us designate as *hermeneutic code* (HER) all the units whose function it is to articulate in various ways a question, its response, and the variety of chance events which can either formulate the question or delay its answer; or even, constitute an enigma and lead to its solution," Roland Barthes, *S/Z*, trans. Richard Miller (New York: Hill and Wang, 1974), 17.

48. Woolf also holds our sense of narrative time in suspension. At many points it is difficult to tell whether the present tense of the narrator's thoughts represents the active retelling of past thoughts, closer to the time she first noticed the mark, or whether the tense indicates the time of the story's telling. For a close examination of the story's temporality, see Marc D. Cyr, "A Conflict

of Closure in Virginia Woolf's 'The Mark on the Wall,'" *Studies in Short Fiction* 33 (1996), 197–205.

49. Marcus, 18.

50. Rebecca L. Walkowitz, *Cosmopolitan Style: Modernism Beyond the Nation* (New York: Columbia University Press, 2006), 88.

51. It is important to maintain a sense of just how audacious this thought experiment is. As Vincent Sherry puts it, "To dedicate lengthy and even recondite attentions to the microscopic spot on the wall entails a sort of archly matter-of-fact outrageousness. A strange reason-seemingness provides the performative pretense of the piece," Vincent Sherry, *The Great War and the Language of Modernism* (New York and Oxford: Oxford University Press, 2004), 260.

52. Here I again draw upon Jacques Derrida's *Archive Fever* to envision modernism as simultaneously driven by a conservation or archive drive and a repressive, suppressive, and destructive impulse, or an archive fever.

53. Sherry, 256.

54. For considerations of Woolf as a war novelist, see Mark Hussey ed., *Virginia Woolf and War: Fiction, Reality, and Myth* (Syracuse: Syracuse University Press, 1991).

55. For a perspective on the influence of news media during World War I on Woolf, see Karen L. Levenback, "Virginia Woolf's 'War in the Village' and 'The War from the Street': An Illusion of Immunity," in Mark Hussey, ed. *Virginia Woolf and War: Fiction, Reality, and Myth* (Syracuse: Syracuse University Press, 1991).

56. Sherry, 258.

CHAPTER 2

1. Joel H. Wiener, "How New Was the New Journalism?," in *Papers for the Millions: The New Journalism in Britain, 1850s to 1914,* ed. Joel H. Wiener (New York, Westport, and London: Greenwood, 1988), 54.

2. Sean Latham, *The Art of Scandal: Modernism, Libel Law, and the Roman à Clef* (New York and Oxford: Oxford University Press, 2009).

3. James Lull and Stephen Hinerman, "The Search for Scandal," in *Media Scandals: Morality and Desire in the Popular Culture Marketplace,* eds. James Lull and Stephen Hinerman (New York: Columbia University Press, 1997), 3.

4. James Joyce, *Finnegans Wake* (New York: Viking, 1939), 489.35.

5. The clipping is not cataloged in Robert Scholes, *The Cornell Joyce Collection: A Catalogue* (Ithaca: Cornell University Press, 1961). See David Rando and Katherine Reagan, "Guide to the James Joyce Collection" at *Division of Rare and Manuscript Collections, Cornell University Library,* 2003. Web.

6. Quoted in Richard Ellmann, *James Joyce,* Revised ed. (New York: Oxford University Press, 1982), 637.

7. Patrick Collier, *Modernism on Fleet Street* (Aldershot and Burlington: Ashgate, 2006), 107.

8. See letters to Nora of 6 and 7 August 1909 in James Joyce, *Selected Letters,* ed. Richard Ellmann (London: Faber and Faber, 1975), 157–59.

9. James Joyce, *Ulysses,* ed. Hans Walter Gabler et al. (New York: Random House, 1986), 16.1236–1238. Subsequent references are given parenthetically in the text, in the form of chapter and line numbers.

10. Leo Bersani, "Against *Ulysses,*" in *James Joyce's Ulysses: A Casebook,* ed. Derek Attridge (New York and Oxford: Oxford University Press, 2004), 204.

11. Quoted in Frank Budgen, *James Joyce and the Making of* Ulysses (New York: Harrison Smith and Robert Haas, 1934), 16.

12. Mark Wollaeger, "Reading *Ulysses*: Agency, Ideology, and the Novel," in *James Joyce's Ulysses: A Casebook,* ed. Derek Attridge (New York and Oxford: Oxford University Press, 2004), 134.

13. *Finnegans Wake,* 135.34–35. In the following pages, I cite extensively from *Finnegans Wake* in order to suggest the density of references to and engagement with questions of journalism and experience in the book. I have also tried to incorporate passages from the *Wake* into my own sentences whenever possible in order to suggest readings of passages without having to resort to pale paraphrases that would reduce the multivalences of Joyce's work. When I do gloss passages, I emphasize news overtones at the expense of other content. These glosses should thus be understood as partial and tentative interpretations with emphases that help to trace the particular route through *Finnegans Wake* that I have set before myself, and not as an attempt to paraphrase what *Finnegans Wake* appears to say. Indeed, part of the argument as it will unfold in this chapter is that the *Wake*'s resistance to paraphrase is itself a critique of the presumption that in the book there exists a literal level of experience that can be objectively reported. Subsequent references to *Finnegans Wake* are given parenthetically in the text, in the form of page and line numbers.

14. See letter to Maria and Aldous Huxley dated August 15, 1928 in D.H. Lawrence, *The Selected Letters of D.H. Lawrence* (Cambridge: Cambridge University Press, 1997), 405.

15. Eugene Jolas, "The Revolution of Language and James Joyce," in *James Joyce's Finnegans Wake: A Symposium* (New York: New Directions, 1972), 79.

16. John Bishop, *Joyce's Book of the Dark: Finnegans Wake* (Madison: University of Wisconsin Press, 1986), 27.

17. Ibid., 395n2.

18. Ibid., 395n2.

19. Eric Partridge, *A Dictionary of Slang and Unconventional English,* 8th ed., ed. Paul Beale (New York: Routledge, 2002).

20. Bishop, 395n2.

21. Quoted in Ellmann, 546.

22. See the chapter, "Reading the Evening World," in Bishop, *Joyce's Book of the Dark: Finnegans Wake,* 26–41. While Bishop makes a powerful case for *Finnegans Wake* as a book of the night and dreaming, Derek Attridge poses a compelling challenge to these assumptions in "Finnegans Awake, or the

Dream of Interpretation," in *Joyce Effects: On Language, Theory, and History* (Cambridge: Cambridge University Press, 2000), 133–55.

23. Hugh Kenner, *Dublin's Joyce* (Bloomington: Indiana University Press, 1956), 313.

24. See the chapter, " 'Tell a Graphic Lie': *Ulysses,* Reform, and Repression," in Collier, *Modernism on Fleet Street,* 107–136.

25. Margot Norris, *The Decentered Universe of Finnegans Wake: A Structuralist Analysis* (Baltimore: Johns Hopkins University Press, 1976), 75.

26. For a thorough consideration of the place of communication technologies in Joyce's writing, see Donald F. Theall, *James Joyce's Techno-Poetics* (Toronto, Buffalo, and London: University of Toronto Press, 1997). For an examination of the impact of wireless technology on modernism, see Timothy C. Campbell, *Wireless Writing in the Age of Marconi* (Minneapolis and London: University of Minnesota Press, 2006).

27. Arthur Power, *Conversations with Joyce* (New York: Harper & Row, 1974), 61.

28. Ibid., 64.

29. For a thorough account, as well as a complete survey of Joyce's notes on the Bywaters case in his working notebooks and their subsequent incorporation in *Finnegans Wake,* see Vincent Deane, "Bywaters and the Original Crime," in *Finnegans Wake: Teems of Times,* ed. Andrew Treip (Amsterdam: Rodopi, 1994), 165–204.

30. See the entry for Bywaters in Adaline Glasheen, *Third Census of 'Finnegans Wake': An Index of the Characters and Their Roles* (Berkeley: University of California Press, 1977), 47. As Clive Hart writes, "Joyce's intense interest in the notorious Bywaters and Thompson case of 1922 provides hints for the possibility of further meanings in parts of *Finnegans Wake*." See Hart's "Foreword," in Arthur Power, *Conversations with Joyce,* 7.

31. Deane, 171.

32. See James Joyce, *The Finnegans Wake Notebooks at Buffalo Vi.B.10,* ed. Vincent Deane, Daniel Ferrer, and Geert Lernout (Turnhout, Belgium: Brepols, 2001), 9–10.

33. James S. Atherton, *The Books at the Wake: A Study of Literary Allusions in James Joyce's Finnegans Wake,* Expanded and Corrected ed. (Mamaroneck: Appel, 1974), 27.

34. Luca Crispi, Sam Slote, and Dirk Van Hulle, "Introduction," in *How Joyce Wrote Finnegans Wake: A Chapter-by-Chapter Genetic Guide,* ed. Luca Crispi and Sam Slote (Madison: University of Wisconsin Press, 2007), 6.

35. Deane, 178.

36. Bill Cadbury, "Development, in the Plebiscite, of and Away from the Bywaters Case," *Genetic Joyce Studies* 1 (2001), Web. See also Bill Cadbury, " 'The March of a Maker': Chapters I.2–4," in *How Joyce Wrote Finnegans Wake: A Chapter-by-Chapter Genetic Guide,* ed. Luca Crispi and Sam Slote (Madison: University of Wisconsin Press, 2007), 66–97.

37. Cadbury, Web.

38. The newspaper page is reproduced in James Joyce, *The Finnegans Wake Notebooks at Buffalo Vi.B.10,* ed. Vincent Deane, Daniel Ferrer, and Geert Lernout (Turnhout, Belgium: Brepols, 2001), 10. A full transcription of the *Sketch* article appears on pages 86–88 of that volume.
39. Joyce, *The Finnegans Wake Notebooks at Buffalo Vi.B.10,* 86–87.
40. Ibid., 88, 87.
41. Ibid., 87.
42. Ibid., 88.
43. Deane, 168.
44. Joyce, *The Finnegans Wake Notebooks at Buffalo Vi.B.10,* 87.
45. Cadbury, Web.
46. Joyce, *The Finnegans Wake Notebooks at Buffalo Vi.B.10,* 87.
47. See James Joyce, *The Finnegans Wake Notebooks at Buffalo Vi.B.33,* ed. Vincent Deane, Daniel Ferrer, and Geert Lernout (Turnhout, Belgium: Brepols, 2003).
48. Ibid., 8.
49. For specific references to Dante's *Inferno* in this passage and for an excellent discussion of Joyce's use of Paolo and Francesca in his work and his imaginative relationship with Dante in general, see Mary Reynolds, *Joyce and Dante: The Shaping Imagination* (Princeton: Princeton University Press, 1981). For specific consideration of Dante in *Finnegans Wake,* see Lucia Boldrini, *Joyce, Dante, and the Poetics of Literary Relations: Language and Meaning in Finnegans Wake* (Cambridge: Cambridge University Press, 2001).
50. Charles Singleton, *Inferno: Italian Text and Translation* (Princeton: Princeton University Press, 1989), Canto V, line 106, p. 53.
51. Ibid., Canto V, line 142, p. 57.
52. Alessandro Francini Bruni, "Recollections of Joyce," in *Portraits of the Artist in Exile: Recollections of James Joyce by Europeans,* ed. Willard Potts (San Diego: Harcourt Brace Jovanovich, 1979), 45.

CHAPTER 3

1. See Virginia Woolf, "Mr Bennett and Mrs Brown," in *The Essays of Virginia Woolf, Volume III, 1919–1924,* ed. Andrew McNeillie (San Diego: Harcourt Brace Jovanovich, 1988), 384–389.
2. Ibid., 384.
3. Ibid., 387.
4. Ibid., 385.
5. Gertrude Stein, *Everybody's Autobiography* (Cambridge: Exact Change, 1993), 71.
6. John Chamberlain, "John Dos Passos's Experiment with the 'News' Novel," *New York Times,* March 13, 1932, Book Review, 2.
7. Ibid., 2.
8. E.L. Doctorow, "Foreword" to John Dos Passos, *The 42nd Parallel* (New York: Houghton Mifflin, 2000), ix.

9. Benedict Anderson, *Imagined Communities: Reflections on the Origin and Spread of Nationalism,* Revised ed. (London and New York: Verso, 1991), 33.

10. Melvin Landsberg, *Dos Passos' Path to U.S.A.: A Political Biography 1912–1936* (Boulder: The Colorado Associated University Press, 1972), 1.

11. Landsberg himself treats the Newsreels first in his analysis of *U.S.A.*, lending them a kind of thematic priority despite his overt claims. In contrast, Donald Pizer treats the Camera Eye sections first in his discussion of the trilogy's "modes," and his reading emphasizes authorial matters accordingly. See Donald Pizer, *Dos Passos' U.S.A.: A Critical Study* (Charlottesville: University Press of Virginia, 1988).

12. David Seed, "Media and Newsreels in Dos Passos' *U.S.A.*," *Journal of Narrative Technique* 14.3 (1984), 186.

13. Ibid., 191.

14. Pizer, 54.

15. Jean-Paul Sartre, "John Dos Passos and 1919," in *Literary and Philosophical Essays,* trans. Annette Michelson (New York: Collier Books, 1962), 103.

16. Ibid., 98. Sartre's talk of destiny would seem to contradict the views of Doctorow, Chamberlain, Seed and others who associate Dos Passos's method of plot with historical contingency, but in fact they all agree on this point. Sartre argues, "Dos Passos' time is his own creation; it is neither fictional nor narrative. It is rather, if you like, historical time" (95). Sartre differs only in that he views the historical contingencies that overpower the characters as effects of the dehumanizing conditions of capitalism which narrow the possibilities of human life into what amounts to inevitable destiny.

17. Ibid., 99–100.

18. Ibid., 94.

19. Sartre asks us to think about with what repugnance we would see our own experiences pressed into Dos Passos's style: "Yesterday you saw your friend and expressed to him your passionate hatred of war. Now try to relate this conversation to yourself in the style of Dos Passos. 'And they ordered two beers and said that war was hateful. Paul declared he would rather do anything than fight and John said he agreed with him and both got excited and said they were glad they agreed. On his way home, Paul decided to see John more often.' You will start hating yourself immediately. It will not take you long, however, to decide that you *cannot* use this tone in talking about yourself" (102). It is likely that the flattening effect that Sartre imitates would be devastating to the ways in which we normally think about ourselves. The little scene he paints, one of flat declaration, levels all depth of feeling in the passage, from feeling that war is hateful to feeling excited to have found a likeminded person. Not only are these feelings flattened, but our attitude toward these characters is affected as well. They seem pitiable or pathetic, like ants that meet and circle each other excitedly, about to get crushed by an unwitting boot.

20. Ibid., 94.

21. Ibid., 98.

22. Brian McHale, "Talking U.S.A.: Interpreting Free Indirect Discourse in Dos Passos's *U.S.A.* Trilogy, Part Two," *Degrés* 17 (1979), d8. See also Brian McHale, "Talking U.S.A.: Interpreting Free Indirect Discourse in Dos Passos's *U.S.A.* Trilogy, Part One," *Degrés* 16 (1978), c–c7.

23. McHale, "Talking U.S.A.: Interpreting Free Indirect Discourse in Dos Passos's *U.S.A.* Trilogy, Part Two," d8–9.

24. John Dos Passos, *U.S.A.* eds. Daniel Aaron and Townsend Ludington (New York: Library of America, 1996), 143. Subsequent pages references are given parenthetically within the text.

25. Robert Browning, "Two in the Campagna," in *The Poems of Browning, Volume III 1847–1861,* eds. John Woolford, Daniel Karlin, and Joseph Phelan (Harlow: Pearson Longman, 2007), 601–607.

26. Landsberg, 194–95. This identification perhaps stresses all the more the extent to which the preceding scene can be characterized as paradisiacal.

27. Matthew Arnold, "Dover Beach," in *The Poems of Matthew Arnold,* ed. Kenneth Allott (London: Longmans, Green and Company, 1965), 239–243.

28. Juan A. Suárez, *Pop Modernism: Noise and the Reinvention of the Everyday* (Urbana and Chicago: University of Illinois Press, 2007), 81, 84.

29. Michael North, *Camera Works: Photography and the Twentieth-Century Word* (New York and Oxford: Oxford University Press, 2005), 142.

30. Quoted in Townsend Ludington, *John Dos Passos: A Twentieth Century Odyssey* (New York: E.P. Dutton, 1980), 261.

31. The financial motivations of World War I are a major theme of *U.S.A.* There are numerous passages throughout the trilogy that point to the Morgan loans of the Allies as the crucial factor that involved America in World War I: "They went over with the A.E.F to save the Morgan Loans, to save Wilsonian Democracy..." (89); "we clapped and yelled for the revolution and hissed for Morgan and the capitalist war" (302); "We're in this war to defend the Morgan loans" (353–54); "at the Harvard Club they're all in the Intelligence Service making the world safe for the Morgan-Baker-Stillman combination of banks" (374); "*Safeguard the Morgan Loans*" (449); "The Morgans had to fight or go bankrupt" (471); "I'm a good American, but dot don't mean dot I vill foight for Banker Morgan, not vonce" (505); "MORGAN ON WINDOWLEDGE/KICKS HEELS AS HE SHOWERS/CROWD WITH TICKERTAPE" (562); "First it was *neutrality in thought and deed,* then *too proud to fight* when the *Lusitania* sinking and the danger to the Morgan loans and the stories of the British and French propagandists set all the financial centers in the East bawling for war" (567); "By 1917 the Allies had borrowed one billion, ninehundred million dollars through the House of Morgan: we went overseas for democracy and the flag" (647); "he opposed loans to the Allies, seconded Bryan in his lonely fight to keep the interests of the United States as a whole paramount over the interests of the Morgan banks and the anglophile businessmen of the East" (1167).

Harper and Brothers, who published *The 42nd Parallel* and had a retired loan from Morgan, refused to publish 1919 with the satirical "House of Morgan" biography intact. As a result of the disagreement, Dos Passos published 1919 and *The Big Money* with Harcourt, Brace and Company instead. Donald Pizer explores the interesting changes Dos Passos subsequently made to *The 42nd Parallel* when preparing the first single-volume edition of *U.S.A.* in 1938, initially in the interest of resetting it to conform to the two later novels (See Pizer, 32–35). After Dos Passos moved to Harcourt, Brace, Thomas Wells, president of Harper at the time of the debate, wrote to Eugene Saxton, who had been Dos Passos's editor: "I think it's damn sound business to keep on terms of easy friendship with the world's strongest private banking house whose influence extends far more widely than any other among the banks of New York. . . . Never in a single instance did Morgan try to control or influence us" (quoted in Ludington, 296). It is striking that the manner in which the lives in Dos Passos's book are indirectly shaped by the House of Morgan becomes mirrored or repeated in the history and physical shape of his own trilogy.

32. Pizer, 36.

CHAPTER 4

1. Gertrude Stein, "What are Master-Pieces and Why Are There So Few of Them," in *Writings 1932–1946*, eds. Catharine R. Stimpson and Harriet Chessman (New York: Library of America, 1998), 360.

2. Bob Perelman, *The Trouble With Genius: Reading Pound, Joyce, Stein, and Zukofsky* (Berkeley: University of California Press, 1994), 154.

3. Gertrude Stein, "Narration, Lecture 3," in *Writings 1932–1946*, eds. Catharine R. Stimpson and Harriet Chessman (New York: Library of America, 1998), 346.

4. Ibid., 344.

5. Gertrude Stein, *The Autobiography of Alice B. Toklas*, in *Writings, 1903–1932*, eds. Catharine R. Stimpson and Harriet Chessman (New York: Library of America, 1998), 732. Subsequent references are given parenthetically within the text.

6. Janet Malcolm, *Two Lives: Gertrude and Alice* (New Haven and London: Yale University Press, 2007), 13.

7. Catharine R. Stimpson, "Gertrude Stein and the Lesbian Lie," in *American Women's Autobiography: Fea(s)ts of Memory*, ed. Margo Culley (Madison: University of Wisconsin Press, 1992), 153.

8. Gertrude Stein, "Lifting Belly," in *Writings, 1903–1932*, eds. Catharine R. Stimpson and Harriet Chessman (New York: Library of America, 1998), 424.

9. Jacques Derrida, *Archive Fever: A Freudian Impression*, trans. Eric Prenowitz (Chicago and London: Chicago University Press, 1996), 64.

10. Ibid., 44.

11. Dydo tracks the composition, form, and publication history of Stein's texts in meticulous detail, from their origins in small *carnets* to more formal *cahiers*, and from typescript to publication. Dydo shows the ways in which Stein would begin works with erotic notes, poems, or dedications to Alice

Toklas, often answered by Alice herself, compositional residues that are removed, reordered, or hollowed out in the drafting process. See Ulla Dydo with William Rice, *Gertrude Stein: The Language That Rises 1923–1934* (Evanston: Northwestern University Press, 2003), 49.

12. Kirk Curnutt places Stein's mid-1930s writing about identity in the context of the then-current "celebrity identity crisis," the anxiety among celebrities that their external images did not accurately reflect their authentic inner selves. See Kirk Curnutt, "Inside and Outside: Gertrude Stein on Identity, Celebrity, and Authenticity," *Journal of Modern Literature* 23.2 (Winter 1999–2000), 291–308.

13. Gertrude Stein, "Narration, Lecture 3," 345.

14. Gertrude Stein, *Everybody's Autobiography* (Cambridge: Exact Change, 1993), 312. Subsequent page references are given parenthetically within the text.

15. As Stein notes, "In The Making of Americans I was making a continuous present a continuous beginning again and again, the way they do in making automobiles or anything. . . . Now I am writing about what is which is being existing." *Everybody's Autobiography,* 258.

16. Gertrude Stein, "Narration, Lecture 3," 350.

17. For other views of Stein's crisis of identity and autobiography in the 1930s, see Nancy Blake, "Everybody's Autobiography: Identity and Absence," *Recherches Anglaises et Américaines* 15 (1982): 135–145; Lynn Z. Bloom, "Gertrude Is Alice Is Everybody: Innovation and Point of View in Gertrude Stein's Autobiographies," *Twentieth Century Literature* 24.1 (1978): 81–93; Laurel Bollinger, "'One as One Not Mistaken but Interrupted': Gertrude Stein's Exploration of Identity in the 1930s," *Centennial Review* 43.2 (1999): 227–258; Timothy W. Galow, "Gertrude Stein's *Everybody's Autobiography* and the Art of Contradictions," *Journal of Modern Literature* 32.1 (Fall 2008): 111–128; Brian Reed, "Now Not Now: Gertrude Stein Speaks," *English Studies in Canada* 33.4 (December 2007): 103–113; Lisi Schoenbach, "'Peaceful and Exciting': Habit, Shock, and Gertrude Stein's Pragmatic Modernism," *Modernism/Modernity* 11.2 (April 2004): 239–259; Donald Sutherland, *Gertrude Stein: A Biography of Her Work* (New Haven: Yale University Press, 1951); and Barbara Will, *Gertrude Stein, Modernism, and the Problem of "Genius"* (Edinburgh: Edinburgh University Press, 2000).

18. Gertrude Stein, "Narration, Lecture 3," 346.

19. Ibid., 347.

20. Tzvetan Todorov, "The Typology of Detective Fiction," in *The Poetics of Prose* (Ithaca: Cornell University Press, 1977), 46.

21. This is true at least in the classical detective story. Thrillers, however, often represent crimes in progress, as exciting developments in primarily suspenseful narratives. The detection in thrillers may serve little more than to foreground mystery and suspense while readers await the next exciting crime in this structural variation.

22. Harriet Scott Chessman, *The Public Is Invited to Dance: Representation, the Body, and Dialogue in Gertrude Stein* (Stanford: Stanford University Press, 1989), 139.

23. Ibid.

24. Richard Bridgman, *Gertrude Stein in Pieces* (New York: Oxford University Press, 1970), 271.

25. Ibid.

26. Shirley C. Neuman, *Gertrude Stein: Autobiography and the Problem of Narration* (Victoria, B.C.: University of Victoria Press, 1979), 48, 49.

27. This is evident in titles of texts such as *The Making of Americans* and *The Geographical History of America*.

28. Gertrude Stein, "What are Master-Pieces and Why Are There So Few of Them," 360.

CHAPTER 5

1. Gertrude Stein, "Narration, Lecture 3," in *Writings 1932–1946*, eds. Catharine R. Stimpson and Harriet Chessman (New York: Library of America, 1998), 350.

2. Ibid., 346.

3. Harriet Scott Chessman, *The Public Is Invited to Dance: Representation, the Body, and Dialogue in Gertrude Stein* (Stanford: Stanford University Press, 1989), 100. See also David M. Owens who argues, "It is a story of lovers existing in a time and place of war. The poem reflects how the war affects their lives and how they cope with the anxiety of it." David M. Owens, "Gertrude Stein's 'Lifting Belly' and the Great War," *Modern Fiction Studies* 44.3 (Fall 1998), 608.

4. Gertrude Stein, "Lifting Belly," in *Writings, 1903–1932*, eds. Catharine R. Stimpson and Harriet Chessman (New York: Library of America, 1998), 415.

5. Gertrude Stein, *The Autobiography of Alice B. Toklas*, in *Writings, 1903–1932*, eds. Catharine R. Stimpson and Harriet Chessman (New York: Library of America, 1998), 815.

6. Ibid., 671.

7. See Edward Burns and Ulla E. Dydo with William Rice eds., *The Letters of Gertrude Stein and Thornton Wilder* (New Haven and London: Yale University Press, 1996) and Janet Malcolm, *Two Lives: Gertrude and Alice* (New Haven and London: Yale University Press, 2007). Other articles that have given attention to Stein's wartime life since 1996 include Phoebe Stein Davis, " 'Even Cake Gets to Have Another Meaning': History, Narrative, and 'Daily Living' in Gertrude Stein's World War II Writings," *Modern Fiction Studies* 44.3 (1998), 568–607; Zofia Lesinska, "Gertrude Stein's War Autobiographies: Reception, History, and Dialogue," *Literature Interpretation Theory* 9.4 (April 1999), 313–342; Liesl M. Olson, "Gertrude Stein, William James, and Habit in the Shadow of War," *Twentieth Century Literature* 49.3 (Fall 2003), 328–359; and Jill Purett, "Gertrude Stein's 'Emotional Autobiography': A Body in Occupied France," in *New Essays on Life Writing and the Body*, ed. Christopher Stuart and Stephanie Todd (Newcastle upon Tyne: Cambridge Scholars, 2009), 58–69.

8. Malcolm, 6.

9. Malcolm finally argues that there are limits to what the biographer can know: stories change, and people lie, misunderstand, forget, suppress, or repress. The biographer is limited in the final analysis by the "instability of human knowledge" (185). This is surely to some extent true, but there are also ways in which it conflicts with Malcolm's own masterful demonstration how much we actually *can* know about Stein through her evasive texts, by reading them as "submerged autobiography" (38) and by recognizing that Stein's most hermetic material may also be her most startlingly confessional. As we saw in the previous chapter, Stein's autobiographical experiments challenge the implicit archivization versus suppression structure, but Malcolm seems alternately and unpredictably to reject and embrace it at different moments in her text.

10. Ibid., 26–27. Compare to Gertrude Stein, *Wars I Have Seen* (New York: Random House, 1945), 50. There are several negligible misquotations in Malcolm's version.

11. Malcolm, 28. The line appears in *Wars I Have Seen,* 3.

12. Ibid., 28.

13. *Wars I Have Seen,* 50. Subsequent page references are given parenthetically within the text.

14. At a later point in *Two Lives,* Malcolm, no stranger to psychoanalysis, recounts cutting Stein's imposing tome *The Making of Americans* down to size: "I finally solved the problem of the book's weight and bulk by taking a kitchen knife and cutting it into six sections" (114). This parody of displaced castration seems playful, even if it evidences some anxiety about an uncastrated Stein that runs back from Malcolm to Stein's earliest critics, also intent to cut her down to size.

15. Davis, 572.

16. Gertrude Stein, dustcover of *Wars I Have Seen* (New York: Random House, 1945).

17. Ibid.

18. Even this imperative to conserve the experience of war is oddly mirrored in the physical form of the book, which announces its own wartime conservation of materials in the opening pages: "THIS IS A RANDOM HOUSE WARTIME BOOK: IT IS MANUFACTURED UNDER EMERGENCY CONDITIONS AND COMPLIES WITH THE GOVERNMENT'S REQUEST TO CONSERVE ESSENTIAL MATERIALS IN EVERY POSSIBLE WAY."

19. Joseph J. Mathews, *Reporting the Wars* (Minneapolis: University of Minnesota Press, 1957), 193–194.

20. Ernie Pyle, "Battle and Breakout in Normandy," in *Reporting World War Two, Part Two: American Journalism 1944–1946,* eds. Samuel Hynes, Anne Matthews, Nancy Caldwell Sorel, and Roger J. Spiller (New York: Library of America, 1995), 194.

21. Ibid., 199.

22. Ibid., 201.

23. Ibid., 207.

24. Ibid., 210.
25. Ibid., 216.
26. Ibid., 217.
27. Mathews, 194–195.
28. Gertrude Stein, "Narration, Lecture 3," 344–5.
29. As such, this small fiction might be compared to Benjamin's fiction of the 40 men who would have lived since the birth of Christ if each one lived to be 50 and died on the day his son was born. Just as Benjamin uses his fictional anecdote to represent a length of time that threatens to become abstract in intimate human terms, Stein's fictional anecdote about the woman giving birth to a litter of dogs may capture the dislocations and violence done to daily life by the war in concrete, human terms. Both rely on a mechanism of unanticipated recognition and the shock of nearness. Both are haunted by birth and death.
30. Pyle, 213.
31. Northcliffe, quoted in Fyfe, *Northcliffe*, 82.
32. Walter Benjamin, "On the Concept of History," in Howard Eiland and Michael W. Jennings, eds. *Selected Writings, Volume 4 1938–1940* (Cambridge: Harvard University Press, 2003), 396.
33. Ibid.
34. Ibid.

CODA

1. Beatrice Hanssen, "Language and Mimesis in Walter Benjamin's Work," in David S. Ferris, ed. *The Cambridge Companion to Walter Benjamin* (Cambridge: Cambridge University Press, 2004), 56.
2. Walter Benjamin, *The Arcades Project,* ed. Rolf Tiedemann, trans. Howard Eiland and Kevin McLaughlin (Cambridge: Harvard University Press, 1999), 846.
3. Gertrude Stein, *Useful Knowledge* (Barrytown: Station Hill Press, 1988), 111.
4. Keith Williams, *British Writers and the Media, 1930–45* (Basingstoke: Macmillan, 1996), 19.
5. Patrick Collier, *Modernism on Fleet Street* (Aldershot and Burlington: Ashgate, 2006), 205.
6. Mark Wollaeger, *Modernism, Media, and Propaganda: British Narrative from 1900 to 1945* (Princeton and Oxford: Princeton University Press, 2006), 265.
7. Ibid.
8. Ibid., 267.
9. Andreas Huyssen, *After the Great Divide: Modernism, Mass Culture, Postmodernism* (Bloomington and Indianapolis: Indiana University Press, 1986), 14.
10. Ibid.

BIBLIOGRAPHY

Anderson, Benedict. *Imagined Communities: Reflections on the Origin and Spread of Nationalism*. Revised ed. London and New York: Verso, 1991.

Ardis, Ann L. *Modernism and Cultural Conflict 1880–1922*. Cambridge: Cambridge University Press, 2002.

——. *New Women, New Novels: Feminism and Early Modernism*. New Brunswick: Rutgers University Press, 1990.

Arnold, Matthew. *The Poems of Matthew Arnold*. Ed. Kenneth Allott. London: Longmans, Green and Company, 1965.

Atherton, James S. *The Books at the Wake: A Study of Literary Allusions in James Joyce's Finnegans Wake*. Expanded and Corrected ed. Mamaroneck: Appel, 1974.

Attridge, Derek. "Finnegans Awake, or the Dream of Interpretation." *Joyce Effects: On Language, Theory, and History*. Cambridge: Cambridge University Press, 2000. 133–155.

Avery, Todd. *Radio Modernism: Literature, Ethics, and the BBC, 1922–1938*. Aldershot and Burlington: Ashgate, 2006.

Bakhtin, M. M. "Discourse in the Novel." *The Dialogic Imagination*. Ed. Michael Holquist. Trans. Caryl Emerson and Michael Holquist. Austin: University of Texas Press, 1981. 259–422.

Barthes, Roland. *S/Z*. Trans. Richard Miller. New York: Hill and Wang, 1974.

Benjamin, Andrew. "Introduction." *Walter Benjamin and Art*. Ed. Andrew Benjamin. London and New York: Continuum, 2005. 1–2.

Benjamin, Walter. *The Arcades Project*. Ed. Rolf Tiedemann. Trans. Howard Eiland and Kevin McLaughlin. Cambridge: Harvard University Press, 1999.

——. "Eduard Fuchs, Collector and Historian." *Selected Writings, Volume 3 1935–1938*. Eds. Howard Eiland and Michael W. Jennings. Cambridge: Harvard University Press, 2002. 260–302.

——. "The Newspaper." *Selected Writings, Volume 2 1927–1934*. Eds. Howard Eiland and Michael W. Jennings. Cambridge: Harvard University Press, 1999. 741–742.

——. "On Some Motifs in Baudelaire." *Selected Writings, Volume 4 1938–1940*. Eds. Howard Eiland and Michael W. Jennings. Cambridge: Harvard University Press, 2003. 313–355.

——. "On the Concept of History." *Selected Writings, Volume 4 1938–1940*. Eds. Howard Eiland and Michael W. Jennings. Cambridge: Harvard University Press, 2003. 389–400.

——. "The Storyteller." *Selected Writings, Volume 3 1935–1938*. Eds. Howard Eiland and Michael W. Jennings. Cambridge: Harvard University Press, 2002. 143–166.

——. *Walter Benjamin's Archive: Images, Texts, Signs*. Eds. Ursula Marx, Gudrun Schwarz, Michael Schwarz, and Erdmut Wizisla. Trans. Esther Leslie. London and New York: Verso, 2007.

Benstock, Shari. *Women of the Left Bank: Paris, 1900–1940*. Austin: University of Texas Press, 1986.

Bersani, Leo. "Against *Ulysses*." *James Joyce's Ulysses: A Casebook*. Ed. Derek Attridge. New York and Oxford: Oxford University Press, 2004. 201–229.

Bishop, John. *Joyce's Book of the Dark: Finnegans Wake*. Madison: University of Wisconsin Press, 1986.

Blake, Nancy. "Everybody's Autobiography: Identity and Absence." *Recherches Anglaises et Américaines* 15 (1982): 135–145.

Blake, William. *Blake's Poetry and Designs,* Second ed. Eds. Mary Lynn Johnson and John E. Grant. New York: W. W. Norton & Co, 2008.

Bloom, Lynn Z. "Gertrude Is Alice Is Everybody: Innovation and Point of View in Gertrude Stein's Autobiographies." *Twentieth Century Literature* 24.1 (1978): 81–93.

Boldrini, Lucia. *Joyce, Dante, and the Poetics of Literary Relations: Language and Meaning in Finnegans Wake*. Cambridge: Cambridge University Press, 2001.

Bollinger, Laurel. " 'One as One Not Mistaken but Interrupted': Gertrude Stein's Exploration of Identity in the 1930s." *Centennial Review* 43.2 (1999): 227–258.

Brake, Laurel. "The Old Journalism and the New: Forms of Cultural Production in London in the 1880s." *Papers for the Millions: The New Journalism in Britain, 1850s to 1914*. Ed. Joel H. Wiener. New York, Westport, and London: Greenwood, 1988. 1–24.

Bridgman, Richard. *Gertrude Stein in Pieces*. New York: Oxford University Press, 1970.

Briggs, Julia. *Virginia Woolf: An Inner Life*. Orlando: Harcourt, 2005.

Brown, Lucy. *Victorian News and Newspapers*. Oxford: Clarendon, 1985.

Browning, Robert. *The Poems of Browning, Volume III 1847–1861*. Eds. John Woolford, Daniel Karlin, and Joseph Phelan. Harlow: Pearson Longman, 2007.

Bruni, Alessandro Francini. "Recollections of Joyce." *Portraits of the Artist in Exile: Recollections of James Joyce by Europeans*. Ed. Willard Potts. San Diego: Harcourt Brace Jovanovich, 1979. 39–46.

Buck-Morss, Susan. *The Dialectics of Seeing: Walter Benjamin and the Arcades Project*. Cambridge and London: MIT Press, 1989.

Budgen, Frank. *James Joyce and the Making of Ulysses*. New York: Harrison Smith and Robert Haas, 1934.

Bürger, Peter. *Theory of the Avant-Garde.* Trans. Michael Shaw. Minnesota: University of Minnesota Press, 1984.

Burns, Edward and Ulla E. Dydo with William Rice, eds. *The Letters of Gertrude Stein and Thornton Wilder.* New Haven and London: Yale University Press, 1996.

Cadbury, Bill. "'The March of a Maker': Chapters I. 2–4." *How Joyce Wrote Finnegans Wake: A Chapter-by-Chapter Genetic Guide.* Ed. Luca Crispi and Sam Slote. Madison: University of Wisconsin Press, 2007. 66–97.

——. "Development, in the Plebiscite, of and Away from the Bywaters Case." *Genetic Joyce Studies* 1 (2001). Web.

Campbell, Timothy C. *Wireless Writing in the Age of Marconi.* Minneapolis and London: University of Minnesota Press, 2006.

Caughie, Pamela, ed. *Virginia Woolf in the Age of Mechanical Reproduction.* New York and London: Garland, 2000.

Chalaby, Jean. "Northcliffe: Proprietor as Journalist." *Northcliffe's Legacy: Aspects of the British Popular Press, 1896–1996.* Eds. Peter Catterall, Colin Seymour-Ure, and Adrian Smith. New York: St. Martin's, 2000. 27–44.

Chamberlain, John. "John Dos Passos's Experiment with the 'News' Novel." *New York Times,* March 13, 1932: Book Review, 2.

Chessman, Harriet Scott. *The Public Is Invited to Dance: Representation, the Body, and Dialogue in Gertrude Stein.* Stanford: Stanford University Press, 1989.

Cohen, Margaret. "Benjamin's Phantasmagoria: The *Arcades Project.*" *The Cambridge Companion to Walter Benjamin.* Ed. David S. Ferris. Cambridge: Cambridge University Press, 2004. 199–220.

Collier, Patrick. *Modernism on Fleet Street.* Aldershot and Burlington: Ashgate, 2006.

Crispi, Luca, Sam Slote, and Dirk Van Hulle. "Introduction." *How Joyce Wrote Finnegans Wake: A Chapter-by-Chapter Genetic Guide.* Eds. Luca Crispi and Sam Slote. Madison: University of Wisconsin Press, 2007.

Curnutt, Kirk. "Inside and Outside: Gertrude Stein on Identity, Celebrity, and Authenticity." *Journal of Modern Literature* 23.2 (Winter 1999–2000): 291–308.

Cyr, Marc D. "A Conflict of Closure in Virginia Woolf's 'The Mark on the Wall.'" *Studies in Short Fiction* 33 (1996): 197–205.

Davis, Lennard. *Factual Fictions: The Origins of the English Novel.* New York: Columbia University Press, 1983.

Davis, Phoebe Stein. "'Even Cake Gets to Have Another Meaning': History, Narrative, and 'Daily Living' in Gertrude Stein's World War II Writings." *Modern Fiction Studies* 44.3 (1998): 568–607.

Deane, Vincent. "Bywaters and the Original Crime." *Finnegans Wake: Teems of Times.* Ed. Andrew Treip. Amsterdam: Rodopi, 1994. 165–204.

Derrida, Jacques. *Archive Fever: A Freudian Impression.* Trans. Eric Prenowitz. Chicago: University of Chicago Press, 1996.

Dettmar, Kevin J. H. and Stephen Watt, eds. *Marketing Modernism: Self-Promotion, Canonization, Rereading.* Ann Arbor: University of Michigan Press, 1996.

Doctorow, E. L. Foreword. *The 42nd Parallel.* 1930. By John Dos Passos. New York: Houghton Mifflin, 2000. vii–xi.

Dos Passos, John. *U.S.A.* Eds. Daniel Aaron and Townsend Ludington. New York: Library of America, 1996.

Dydo, Ulla with William Rice. *Gertrude Stein: The Language That Rises 1923–1934.* Evanston: Northwestern University Press, 2003.

Eagleton, Terry. *Walter Benjamin, or Towards a Revolutionary Criticism.* London: Verso, 1981.

Ellis, Havelock. *Studies in the Psychology of Sex: Sexual Inversion.* London: Wilson, 1897.

Ellmann, Richard. *James Joyce.* Revised ed. New York: Oxford University Press, 1982.

Felski, Rita. *The Gender of Modernity.* Cambridge and London: Harvard University Press, 1995.

Ferris, David S. "Introduction: Reading Benjamin." *The Cambridge Companion to Walter Benjamin.* Ed. David S. Ferris. Cambridge: Cambridge University Press, 2004. 1–17.

Fifer, Elizabeth. "Is Flesh Advisable? The Interior Theater of Gertrude Stein." *Signs* 4.3 (Spring 1979): 472–483.

Fineman, Joel. "The History of the Anecdote: Fiction and Fiction." *The New Historicism.* Ed. H. Aram Veeser. New York: Routledge, 1989. 49–76.

Fyfe, Hamilton. *Northcliffe: An Intimate Biography.* New York: Macmillan, 1930.

Gallagher, Catherine and Stephen Greenblatt, *Practicing New Historicism.* Chicago: University of Chicago Press, 2000.

Gallop, Jane. *Anecdotal Theory.* Durham and London: Duke University Press, 2002.

Galow, Timothy W. "Gertrude Stein's *Everybody's Autobiography* and the Art of Contradictions." *Journal of Modern Literature* 32.1 (Fall 2008): 111–128.

Gass, William. "Gertrude Stein and the Geography of the Sentence." *The World within the Word.* Boston: Godine, 1979. 63–123.

Gibbs, Robert. "Messianic Epistemology: Thesis XV." *Walter Benjamin and History.* Ed. Andrew Benjamin. New York: Continuum, 2005. 197–214.

Gilbert, Sandra and Susan Gubar. *No Man's Land: The Place of the Woman Writer in the Twentieth Century, Volume I: War of the Words.* New Haven: Yale University Press, 1988.

Glasheen, Adaline. *Third Census of "Finnegans Wake": An Index of the Characters and Their Roles.* Berkeley: University of California Press, 1977.

Habermas, Jürgen. *The Structural Transformation of the Public Sphere.* Trans. Thomas Berger. Cambridge: MIT Press, 1989.

Hamacher, Werner. "'Now': Walter Benjamin and Historical Time." *Walter Benjamin and History.* Ed. Andrew Benjamin. New York: Continuum, 2005. 38–68.

Hammacher, A. M. *René Magritte.* Trans. James Brockway. New York: Harry N. Abrams, 1995.

Hampton, Mark. "Representing the Public Sphere: The New Journalism and Its Historians." *Transatlantic Print Culture, 1880–1940: Emerging Media,*

Emerging Modernisms. Eds. Ann Ardis and Patrick Collier. Basingstoke and New York: Palgrave Macmillan, 2008. 15–29.

Hanssen, Beatrice. "Language and Mimesis in Walter Benjamin's Work." *The Cambridge Companion to Walter Benjamin*. Ed. David S. Ferris. Cambridge: Cambridge University Press, 2004. 54–72.

Harootunian, Harry D. "The Benjamin Effect: Modernism, Repetition, and the Path to Different Cultural Imaginaries." *Walter Benjamin and the Demands of History*. Ed. Michael P. Steinberg. Ithaca and London: Cornell University Press, 1996. 62–87.

Harris, Middleton, ed. *The Black Book*. New York: Random House, 1974.

Hart, Clive. Foreword. *Conversations with Joyce*. By Arthur Power. New York: Harper & Row, 1974. 5–7.

Hopkins, Gerard Manley. *Poems and Prose*. New York: Penguin, 1953.

Hussey, Mark, ed. *Virginia Woolf and War: Fiction, Reality, and Myth*. Syracuse: Syracuse University Press, 1991.

Huyssen, Andreas. *After the Great Divide: Modernism, Mass Culture, Postmodernism*. Bloomington and Indianapolis: Indiana University Press, 1986.

Jaffe, Aaron. *Modernism and the Culture of Celebrity*. Cambridge: Cambridge University Press, 2005.

Jameson, Fredric. *The Political Unconscious: Narrative as a Socially Symbolic Act*. Ithaca: Cornell University Press, 1981.

———. *A Singular Modernity: Essay on the Ontology of the Present*. London and New York: Verso, 2002.

Jay, Martin. *The Dialectical Imagination: A History of the Frankfurt School and the Institute of Social Research, 1923–1950*. Boston and Toronto: Little, Brown, 1973.

Jennings, Michael. *Dialectical Images: Walter Benjamin's Theory of Literary Criticism*. Ithaca: Cornell University Press, 1987.

———. "Walter Benjamin and the European Avant-Garde." *The Cambridge Companion to Walter Benjamin*. Ed. David S. Ferris. Cambridge: Cambridge University Press, 2004. 18–34.

Jolas, Eugene. "The Revolution of Language and James Joyce." *James Joyce's Finnegans Wake: A Symposium*. By Samuel Beckett et al. New York: New Directions, 1972. 77–92.

Joyce, James. *Finnegans Wake*. New York: Viking, 1939.

———. *The Finnegans Wake Notebooks at Buffalo Vi.B.10*. Eds. Vincent Deane, Daniel Ferrer, and Geert Lernout. Turnhout, Belgium: Brepols, 2001.

———. *The Finnegans Wake Notebooks at Buffalo Vi.B.33*. Eds. Vincent Deane, Daniel Ferrer, and Geert Lernout. Turnhout, Belgium: Brepols, 2003.

———. *Selected Letters*. Ed. Richard Ellmann. London: Faber and Faber, 1975.

———. *Ulysses*. Ed. Hans Walter Gabler et al. New York: Random House, 1986.

Kenner, Hugh. *Dublin's Joyce*. Bloomington: Indiana University Press, 1956.

———. *The Mechanic Muse*. New York and Oxford: Oxford University Press, 1987.

———. *The Pound Era*. Berkeley: University of California Press, 1971.

Kittler, Friedrich A. *Gramophone, Film, Typewriter*. Trans. Geoffrey Winthrop-Young and Michael Wutz. Stanford: Stanford University Press, 1999.

Landsberg, Melvin. *Dos Passos' Path to U.S.A.: A Political Biography 1912–1936*. Boulder: The Colorado Associated University Press, 1972.

Latham, Sean. *The Art of Scandal: Modernism, Libel Law, and the Roman à Clef*. New York and Oxford: Oxford University Press, 2009.

Lawrence, D. H. *The Selected Letters of D. H. Lawrence*. Cambridge: Cambridge University Press, 1997.

Lee, Alan J. *The Origins of the Popular Press in England, 1855–1914*. London: Croom Helm, 1976.

Lesinska, Zofia. "Gertrude Stein's War Autobiographies: Reception, History, and Dialogue." *Literature Interpretation Theory* 9.4 (April 1999): 313–342.

Levenback, Karen L. "Virginia Woolf's 'War in the Village' and 'The War from the Street': An Illusion of Immunity." *Virginia Woolf and War: Fiction, Reality, and Myth*. Ed. Mark Hussey. Syracuse: Syracuse University Press, 1991. 40–57.

Lippmann, Walter. *Public Opinion*. New York: Harcourt, Brace, 1922.

Lodge, David. *The Modes of Modern Writing; Metaphor, Metonymy, and the Typology of Modern Literature*. Ithaca: Cornell University Press, 1977.

Ludington, Townsend. *John Dos Passos: A Twentieth Century Odyssey*. New York: E. P. Dutton, 1980.

Lukács, Georg. *History and Class Consciousness: Studies in Marxist Dialectics*. Trans. Rodney Livingstone. Cambridge: M.I.T. Press, 1972.

——. *Realism in Our Time*. Trans. John Mander and Necke Mander. New York: Harper and Row, 1964.

Lull, James and Stephen Hinerman. "The Search for Scandal." *Media Scandals: Morality and Desire in the Popular Culture Marketplace*. Eds. James Lull and Stephen Hinerman. New York: Columbia University Press, 1997. 1–33.

Lutes, Jean Marie. *Front-Page Girls: Women Journalists in American Culture and Fiction, 1880–1930*. Ithaca and London: Cornell University Press, 2006.

Malcolm, Janet. *Two Lives: Gertrude and Alice*. New Haven and London: Yale University Press, 2007.

Mao, Douglas and Rebecca L. Walkowitz. "The New Modernist Studies." *PMLA* 123.3 (May 2008): 737–748.

Marcus, Laura. *Virginia Woolf*. London: Northcote House, 1997.

Marder, Elissa. "Walter Benjamin's Dream of 'Happiness.'" *Walter Benjamin and the Arcades Project*. Ed. Beatrice Hanssen. New York: Continuum, 2006. 184–200.

Mathews, Joseph J. *Reporting the Wars*. Minneapolis: University of Minnesota Press, 1957.

McCole, John. *Walter Benjamin and the Antinomies of Tradition*. Ithaca and London: Cornell University Press, 1993.

McHale, Brian. "Talking U.S.A.: Interpreting Free Indirect Discourse in Dos Passos's *U.S.A.* Trilogy, Part One." *Degrés* 16 (1978): c–c7.

——. "Talking U.S.A.: Interpreting Free Indirect Discourse in Dos Passos's *U.S.A.* Trilogy, Part Two." *Degrés* 17 (1979): d–d20.

Moore, Marianne. *Complete Poems*. New York: Penguin, 1981.

Morrison, Toni. *Beloved*. New York: Vintage, 2004.

Morrisson, Mark. *The Public Face of Modernism: Little Magazines, Audiences, and Reception, 1905–1920*. Madison: University of Wisconsin Press, 2001.

Neuman, Shirley C. *Gertrude Stein: Autobiography and the Problem of Narration*. Victoria: University of Victoria Press, 1979.

Norris, Margot. *The Decentered Universe of Finnegans Wake: A Structuralist Analysis*. Baltimore: Johns Hopkins University Press, 1976.

North, Michael. *Camera Works: Photography and the Twentieth-Century Word*. New York and Oxford: Oxford University Press, 2005.

———. *Reading 1922*. New York and Oxford: Oxford University Press, 1999.

Olson, Liesl M. "Gertrude Stein, William James, and Habit in the Shadow of War." *Twentieth Century Literature* 49.3 (Fall 2003): 328–359.

Owens, David M. "Gertrude Stein's 'Lifting Belly' and the Great War." *Modern Fiction Studies* 44.3 (Fall 1998): 608–618.

Partridge, Eric. *A Dictionary of Slang and Unconventional English*. Eighth ed. Ed. Paul Beale. New York: Routledge, 2002.

Pensky, Max. "Method and Time: Benjamin's Dialectical Images." *The Cambridge Companion to Walter Benjamin*. Ed. David S. Ferris. Cambridge: Cambridge University Press, 2004. 177–198.

Perelman, Bob. *The Trouble with Genius: Reading Pound, Joyce, Stein, and Zukofsky*. Berkeley: University of California Press, 1994.

Pizer, Donald. *Dos Passos' U.S.A.: A Critical Study*. Charlottesville: University Press of Virginia, 1988.

Pound, Ezra. *ABC of Reading*. New York: New Directions, 1934.

Power, Arthur. *Conversations with Joyce*. New York: Harper & Row, 1974.

Proust, Marcel. *In the Shadow of Young Girls in Flower*. Trans. James Grieve. New York: Viking, 2002.

———. *Remembrance of Things Past, Volume One*. Trans. C. K. Scott Moncrieff and Terence Kilmartin. New York: Random House, 1981.

Purett, Jill. "Gertrude Stein's 'Emotional Autobiography': A Body in Occupied France." *New Essays on Life Writing and the Body*. Eds. Christopher Stuart and Stephanie Todd. Newcastle upon Tyne: Cambridge Scholars, 2009. 58–69.

Pyle, Ernie. "Battle and Breakout in Normandy." *Reporting World War Two, Part Two: American Journalism 1944–1946*. Eds. Samuel Hynes, Anne Matthews, Nancy Caldwell Sorel, and Roger J. Spiller. New York: Library of America, 1995. 194–220.

Rado, Lisa, ed. *Rereading Modernism: New Directions in Feminist Criticism*. New York and London: Garland, 1994.

Rainey, Lawrence. *Institutions of Modernism: Literary Elites and Public Culture*. New Haven and London: Yale University Press, 1998.

Rando, David and Katherine Reagan. "Guide to the James Joyce Collection." *Division of Rare and Manuscript Collections, Cornell University Library*, 2003. Web.

Reed, Brian. "Now Not Now: Gertrude Stein Speaks." *English Studies in Canada* 33.4 (December 2007): 103–113.

Reynolds, Mary. *Joyce and Dante: The Shaping Imagination.* Princeton: Princeton University Press, 1981.

Rickard, John S. *Joyce's Book of Memory: The Mnemotechnic of 'Ulysses.'* Durham: Duke University Press, 1999.

Sartre, Jean-Paul. "John Dos Passos and 1919." *Literary and Philosophical Essays.* Trans. Annette Michelson. New York: Collier Books, 1962. 94–103.

Schoenbach, Lisi. " 'Peaceful and Exciting': Habit, Shock, and Gertrude Stein's Pragmatic Modernism." *Modernism/Modernity* 11.2 (April 2004): 239–259.

Scott, Bonnie Kime. *Refiguring Modernism: The Women of 1928.* Bloomington and Indianapolis: Indiana University Press, 1995.

Seed, David. "Media and Newsreels in Dos Passos' *U.S.A.*" *Journal of Narrative Technique* 14.3 (1984): 182–192.

Seymour-Ure, Colin. "Northcliffe's Legacy." *Northcliffe's Legacy: Aspects of the British Popular Press, 1896–1996.* Eds. Peter Catterall, Colin Seymour-Ure, and Adrian Smith. New York: St. Martin's, 2000. 9–25.

Shelley, Percy Bysshe. *Shelley's Poetry and Prose.* Second ed. Eds. Donald H. Reiman and Neil Fraistat. New York and London: W. W. Norton & Company, 2002.

Sherry, Vincent. *The Great War and the Language of Modernism.* New York and Oxford: Oxford University Press, 2004.

Singleton, Charles. *Inferno: Italian Text and Translation.* Princeton: Princeton University Press, 1989.

Stead, William Thomas. "Character Sketch: Mr. T. P. O'Connor, M. P." *Review of Reviews* XXVI (July–December 1902): 473–479.

Stein, Gertrude. "As a Wife Has a Cow A Love Story." *Writings 1903–1932.* Eds. Catharine R. Stimpson and Harriet Chessman. New York: Library of America, 1998. 501–503.

——. *The Autobiography of Alice B. Toklas. Writings, 1903–1932.* Eds. Catharine R. Stimpson and Harriet Chessman. New York: Library of America, 1998. 653–913.

——. *Everybody's Autobiography.* Cambridge: Exact Change, 1993.

——. "Lifting Belly." *Writings, 1903–1932.* Eds. Catharine R. Stimpson and Harriet Chessman. New York: Library of America, 1998. 410–458.

——. "Narration, Lecture 3." *Writings 1932–1946.* Eds. Catharine R. Stimpson and Harriet Chessman. New York: Library of America, 1998. 337–351.

——. *Useful Knowledge.* Barrytown: Station Hill Press, 1988.

——. "What are Master-Pieces and Why Are There So Few of Them." *Writings 1932–1946.* Eds. Catharine R. Stimpson and Harriet Chessman. New York: Library of America, 1998. 353–363.

——. *Wars I Have Seen.* New York: Random House, 1945.

Stimpson, Catharine R. "Gertrude Stein and the Lesbian Lie." *American Women's Autobiography: Fea(s)ts of Memory.* Ed. Margo Culley. Madison: University of Wisconsin Press, 1992. 152–166.

Strychacz, Thomas. *Modernism, Mass Culture, and Professionalism.* Cambridge: Cambridge University Press, 1993.

Suárez, Juan A. *Pop Modernism: Noise and the Reinvention of the Everyday.* Urbana and Chicago: University of Illinois Press, 2007.

Suleiman, Susan. *Subversive Intent: Gender, Politics, and the Avant-Garde.* Cambridge: Harvard University Press, 1990.

Sutherland, Donald. *Gertrude Stein: A Biography of Her Work.* New Haven: Yale University Press, 1951.

Theall, Donald F. *James Joyce's Techno-Poetics.* Toronto, Buffalo, and London: University of Toronto Press, 1997.

Tiedemann, Rolf. "Dialectics at a Standstill: Approaches to the *Passagen-Werk.*" *On Walter Benjamin: Critical Essays and Recollections.* Ed. Gary Smith. Cambridge and London: MIT Press, 1988. 260–291.

Trotter, David. "The Modernist Novel." *The Cambridge Companion to Modernism.* Ed. Michael Levenson. Cambridge: Cambridge University Press, 1999. 70–99.

Todorov, Tzvetan. "The Typology of Detective Fiction." *The Poetics of Prose.* Ithaca: Cornell University Press, 1977. 44–52.

Walkowitz, Rebecca L. *Cosmopolitan Style: Modernism beyond the Nation.* New York: Columbia University Press, 2006.

Whitworth, Michael. "Virginia Woolf and Modernism." *The Cambridge Companion to Virginia Woolf.* Eds. Sue Roe and Susan Sellers. Cambridge: Cambridge University Press, 2000. 146–163.

Wicke, Jennifer. *Advertising Fictions.* New York: Columbia University Press, 1988.

Wiener, Joel H. "How New Was the New Journalism?" *Papers for the Millions: The New Journalism in Britain, 1850s to 1914.* Ed. Joel H. Wiener. New York, Westport, and London: Greenwood, 1988. 47–71.

Will, Barbara. *Gertrude Stein, Modernism, and the Problem of "Genius."* Edinburgh: Edinburgh University Press, 2000.

Williams, Keith. *British Writers and the Media, 1930–45.* Basingstoke: Macmillan, 1996.

Williams, Raymond. *The Long Revolution.* London: Chatto and Windus, 1961.

——. *The Politics of Modernism.* London and New York: Verso, 1989.

Williams, William Carlos. *Asphodel: That Greeny Flower and Other Love Poems.* New York: New Directions, 1994.

Witte, Bernd. *Walter Benjamin: An Intellectual Biography.* Trans. James Rolleston. Detroit: Wayne State University Press, 1991.

Wizisla, Erdmut. Preface. *Walter Benjamin's Archive: Images, Texts, Signs.* Eds. Ursula Marx, Gudrun Schwarz, Michael Schwarz, and Erdmut Wizisla. Trans. Esther Leslie. London and New York: Verso, 2007. 1–6.

Wohlfarth, Irving. "Et Cetera? The Historian as Chiffonnier." *Walter Benjamin and the Arcades Project.* Ed. Beatrice Hanssen. London and New York: Continuum, 2006. 12–32.

Wollaeger, Mark. *Modernism, Media, and Propaganda: British Narrative from 1900 to 1945.* Princeton and Oxford: Princeton University Press, 2006.

——. "Reading *Ulysses*: Agency, Ideology, and the Novel." *James Joyce's Ulysses: A Casebook*. Ed. Derek Attridge. New York and Oxford: Oxford University Press, 2004. 129–154.

Woolf, Virginia. "A Death in the Newspaper." *The Complete Shorter Fiction of Virginia Woolf*. Ed. Susan Dick. San Diego: Harcourt, 1989. 315.

——. *The Diary of Virginia Woolf, Volume Two, 1920–1924*. Ed. Anne Olivier Bell. New York: Harcourt Brace & Company, 1978.

——. "The Mark on the Wall." *The Complete Shorter Fiction of Virginia Woolf*. Ed. Susan Dick. San Diego: Harcourt, 1989. 83–89.

——. "Modern Fiction." *The Essays of Virginia Woolf, Volume IV, 1925–1928*. Ed. Andrew McNeillie. London: The Hogarth Press, 1994. 157–165.

——. "Mr Bennett and Mrs Brown." *The Essays of Virginia Woolf, Volume III, 1919–1924*. Ed. Andrew McNeillie. San Diego: Harcourt Brace Jovanovich, 1988. 384–389.

——. "Sympathy." *The Complete Shorter Fiction of Virginia Woolf*. Ed. Susan Dick. San Diego: Harcourt, 1989. 108–111.

INDEX

Note: The letter 'n' following the locators refers to notes cited in the text.